# OCR
# ICT
## for AS

## Paul Long • Glen Millbery • Sonia Stuart •

DYNAMIC
LEARNING
Innovate • Motivate • Personalise

HODDER
EDUCATION
AN HACHETTE UK COMPANY

The Publishers would like to thank the following for permission to reproduce copyright material:

**Photo credits: p.8** © vario images GmbH & Co.KG/Alamy; **p.13** MGM/The Kobal Collection; **p.33** © Helene Rogers/Alamy; **p.34** Alex Sharpe www.std8.com; **p.35** *l* © AGphotographer - Fotolia.com, *r* © Marianna Day Massey/ZUMA/Corbis; **p.38** © Steven May/Alamy; **p.46** *tl* © pieter goossens/ iStockphoto.com, *tr* www.PurestockX.com, *b* Jerry Bergman/Rex Features; **p.48** *l* Steve Connolly, *c* © Beaconstox/Alamy, *r* © David R. Frazier Photolibrary, Inc./Alamy; **p.51** *l* © Helene Rogers/Alamy, *r* ©iStockphoto.co/Mike McCune; **p.55** *l* © Picture Contact/Alamy, *r* Realistic Reflections/Getty Images; **p.82** *t* © Joe Tree/Alamy, *c* © geogphotos/Alamy, *b* Hodder Education; **p.91** Rex Features; **p.205** Digital Vision/Punchstock; **p.226** © Alex Maloney/zefa/Corbis; **p.231** © photodisc/Getty Images; **p.233** © Helen King/Corbis; **p.235** *t* © Gianni Muratore/Alamy, *b* © David R. Frazier Photolibrary, Inc./Alamy; **p.277** Elizabeth Young/Stone/Getty Images; **p.293** © Janine Wiedel Photolibrary/Alamy.

**Acknowledgements: p.15** BBC.co.uk; **p.29** Young Person's Railcard.

Every effort has been made to trace all copyright holders, but if any have been inadvertently overlooked the Publishers will be pleased to make the necessary arrangements at the first opportunity.

*t* = top, *b* = bottom, *l* = left, *r* = right, *c* = centre

Although every effort has been made to ensure that website addresses are correct at time of going to press, Hodder Education cannot be held responsible for the content of any website mentioned in this book. It is sometimes possible to find a relocated web page by typing in the address of the home page for a website in the URL window of your browser.

Hachette's policy is to use papers that are natural, renewable and recyclable products and made from wood grown in sustainable forests. The logging and manufacturing processes are expected to conform to the environmental regulations of the country of origin.

Orders: please contact Bookpoint Ltd, 130 Milton Park, Abingdon, Oxon OX14 4SB. Telephone: (44) 01235 827720. Fax: (44) 01235 400454. Lines are open 9.00 – 5.00, Monday to Saturday, with a 24-hour message answering service. Visit our website at www.hoddereducation.co.uk

© Paul Long, Glen Millbery and Sonia Stuart 2008

First published in 2008 by
Hodder Education,
an Hachette UK Company
338 Euston Road
London NW1 3BH

Impression number     5  4

Year                2012 2011 2010  2009

Cover photo Image 100 Ltd.

Illustrations by Barking Dog Art, Tony Jones Art Construction and DC Graphic Design Ltd.

Typeset in Stone Sans 11pt by DC Graphic Design Limited, Swanley Village, Kent

Printed in Italy

A catalogue record for this title is available from the British Library

ISBN: 978 0340 958 285

# Contents

# Data, information, knowledge and processing

## Introduction

This chapter covers the fundamental knowledge required to support all the other chapters in this book. You will need to make sure you know the concepts and definitions covered here so that you can understand future chapters.

This chapter covers:

- **Data, information and knowledge**
- **Representation methods**
- **Data types**
- **Sources of data**
- **Static and dynamic data**
- **Quality of information**
- **Encoding data**
- **Validation and verification**
- **Back-up and archive**
- **Cost of information**
- **Input–Process–Output feedback loop**

## Describe the term data, using an example, clearly identifying the fact that the term has no meaning

Data is a big part of our lives – anything that is written or spoken is made up of data. If you break any words down you eventually, at the bottom of the pile, find data.

The official definition is:

**Data is the raw facts and figures before they have been processed.**

"Raw facts and figures" means without meaning. It should not be possible to understand what the letters and figures stand for. For example:

**BAT45&&7**
**478GH89"**

These are examples of data. There is no way to tell what they mean – at this time they are just a random series of numbers and letters.

The key facts you need to know are that:

- data can be alphanumeric characters (letters and numbers), sound or graphics
- data is raw facts before it has been processed
- data has no meaning.

If you have to give an example of data, make sure that it is just a set of random numbers and letters and there is no meaning to it.

**QUESTIONS**

1 Using an example, describe the term data.
2 Identify **two** characteristics of data.
3 What is meant by an alphanumeric character?

# Describe what is meant by the term information

Information is made by taking the data and processing it.

Processing is performing some action on the data. This might be sorting, searching or editing. The act of processing gives the data meaning. It is not possible to search the data unless you have some idea of what you are looking for.

There is a formula that you need to know that shows how data can become information:

**Information = Data + [Structure] + [Context] + Meaning**

In some cases, the data (raw facts and figures) does not need to have a structure and a context in order to become information. However, it is always better to know the complete formula.

 **Keywords**

| | |
|---|---|
| Data | the raw facts and figures |
| Structure | how the data is presented. Are the numbers actually numbers or should they be read as text? Should the data be organised in any way (e.g. grouped by numbers of characters)? What, if any, encoding system has been used? |
| Context | an environment where our prior knowledge and understanding can make sense of the data. |
| Meaning | data in the correct structure and placed within the context. |
| Knowledge | the application of information to a situation. |

## Examples of converting data into information

| Data | Structure | Context | Meaning |
|---|---|---|---|
| 12102005 | 12/10/2005 | UK date | Date of hotel room booking |
| 31 32 34 32 31 | Numbers | Celsius | Temperature over 5 days in Venice |
| SKBL10 | First 2 letters – type of garment<br>Second 2 letters – colour<br>Last 2 numbers – size | A shop stock code | A black skirt, size 10 |
| 1 | Selected from a scale of 1–4 | How enjoyable was the film? 1 being good, 4 being bad | The film was good |

**< Activity >**

Fill in the following table, showing how data can be turned into information. Use the context given at the top of the table.

| | Context | | |
|---|---|---|---|
| | Fish shop | Holiday website | TV programme listings magazine |
| Data | | | |
| Structure | | | |
| Context | | | |
| Meaning | | | |

**< Tip >**

You will need to be able to give an example of information. The example you give must be relevant to the context of the question being asked in the examination. If the question is about hotels, give an example to do with hotels.

**QUESTIONS**

1 Give a definition of information.
2 Within the definition of information, what is meant by structure?
3 Within the definition of information, what is meant by context?
4 Within the definition of information, what is meant by meaning?
5 Within the context of a car sales garage, show how data can become information.

# Representation methods to convey meaning

For people to be able to use information they must be able to recognise, extract and pass it on. If information is only known by one person and is not passed on to anyone else then its value is limited.

Ideally, information should be available in many different formats. However, there are restrictions. Some information needs to be kept secure and if it became known then it could cause problems, for example:

- secret service intelligence
- business information.

< Activity >

Give examples of information that should be kept secure. Explain who should have access to this information and the implications of other people finding it out.

Another restriction is the language barrier. If information is presented in one particular language then someone who does not understand that language might have difficulty acquiring the information.

People who are disabled are likely to be restricted in acquiring information. This will depend on their disability, for example people who have visual (seeing) or aural (hearing) problems may have problems acquiring information if it is in the wrong format.

It is not possible to give all information in all formats. Some decision has to be made which format to use within each situation.

It can be difficult to select and justify different methods (known as representation methods) of conveying information for different situations. The main representation methods are:

- text (including writing)
- graphics (including pictures)
- sound (including voice)
- moving pictures (animation or video)
- light-emitting diode (LED).

Each method has its advantages and disadvantages. However, the user (i.e. the individual who needs to acquire the information) and the location where the information is being given must be considered when selecting a representation method.

General examples of the advantages and disadvantages of each of the representation methods are given in the next table.

| Representation | Advantages | Disadvantages |
|---|---|---|
| Text | ■ Clear to understand<br>■ Lots of detail | ■ Need to be able to read<br>■ Need to understand the language<br>■ Can be confusing – level of language<br>■ Lots of text cannot be read quickly – road signs |
| Graphics | ■ Multilingual – do not need language to understand an image – e.g. male and female<br><br>■ Can match what you see – physical shapes | ■ Can be confusing if you do not know the symbols – does everyone know the road signs?<br><br>■ Some symbols do not mean the same thing in different countries |
| Sound | ■ No fixed position<br>■ No line of sight required<br>■ Good for visually impaired people | ■ No good in large areas – distortion of sound<br>■ Usually language based<br>■ May not know the sound – e.g. different alarms have different sounds<br>■ Need to be able to hear |
| Moving pictures | ■ Lots of information conveyed<br>■ Not language dependent<br>■ Can exemplify text | ■ Linear – if you do not see the beginning you may not understand<br>■ Problems if sound |
| LED | ■ Can allow data to be kept secure<br>■ Can be used in noisy places<br>■ Similar to graphics | ■ Need to be able to see the lights<br>■ Combinations of lights may need to be known to be understood |

---

### < Activity >

Make a copy of the table below. Look around the room that you are in and fill in your table. Add as many rows as required. Identify the type of representation (text, sound, pictures, moving pictures, light (LED); a description of the representation; how it is used; and the intended audience. The first one has been done for you.

| Type of representation | Description | Use | Audience |
|---|---|---|---|
| Light | LED on the keyboard | To show when the Caps Lock key has been pressed | All users of the keyboard who can see |
| | | | |
| | | | |

The context in which the information is being acquired needs to be considered:

- User manuals are often provided as text and graphics, not sound.
- Fire alarms are sound rather than text based.
- Electronic tills are text and sound based.
- Early-learning toys are sound, picture and text based.

These are only examples. User manuals might be computerised and include sound. Fire alarm systems can include LED arrows pointing to an exit.

## QUESTIONS

1 Identify **three** different representation methods.
2 What are the advantages of using graphics instead of sound in a software user manual?
3 Give **three** situations where the use of sound to convey information would be appropriate.
4 Give **three** situations where the use of text to convey information would be appropriate.
5 Explain, using examples, why it might be advantageous for an electronic till to use graphics as well as sound and text.
6 Why are road signs symbols and not text?

# Describe what is meant by the term knowledge and distinguish between information and knowledge

Data on its own is meaningless. When we add context, structure and meaning to data we get information. Knowledge is the application of that information to a situation – in other words, putting the information to use.

For example:

**Data:**              46, 54
**Information:** Scores for team 1 and team 2, respectively, in a pub quiz.
**Knowledge:** Team 2 won.

It is easiest to think of knowledge as being the action that you need to take or a general rule you can determine from the information.

For example:

> "I know what I need to get to win the quiz."
> "How do you know?"
> "Because the quiz master just told me that team 1 got 46."

This is taking information and applying it to acquire knowledge.

| Data | Information | Knowledge |
|------|-------------|-----------|
| 2 and 4 | Ice cream shop in Lynton, Devon.<br><br>2 kg of ice cream sold in January, 4 kg of ice cream sold in July. | More ice cream is sold in July – the hotter the temperature the more ice cream is sold.<br>More ice cream is sold in July because there are more tourists around. |
| 101 | BBC1 channel number | Sky number to input to get BBC1. |

Information is based on certainties. There is a formula that allows us to determine where the information has come from and how it is derived. It has a context, a structure and raw data. If we take all of these we can associate a meaning to the data, then it becomes information.

Certainties are things that will occur the same way every single time, or mean the same thing every single time. They do not change or alter for that event.

Knowledge can change. It does not mean that every time it will or does, but it can change. More information can be added to our knowledge and as we add more information we revise our knowledge.

**Figure 1.1** Using information

Imagine you are driving towards a junction for the first time and you see some traffic lights turn from green to amber.

| Data | Information | Knowledge |
|------|-------------|-----------|
| The amber light is the data. | The information is that you will need to stop. | The knowledge is how to stop the vehicle you are driving and when you need to start braking to stop the vehicle where you need it to. |

As you approach the traffic lights you will need to be aware of conditions that determine your knowledge of the situation. For example:

- the proximity of traffic behind you
- the road conditions
- tyre grip
- the weather

All these will affect your knowledge of the situation. Individual pieces of information will affect the knowledge that we have of the current situation and affect the action that we take (in this example, when to brake and with how much force, whether to be aware of possible aquaplaning or skidding, etc.).

---

**QUESTIONS**

1 What is the difference between information and knowledge?
2 Using an example, show how data can be turned into knowledge.
3 What is meant by the term knowledge?
4 Within the context of mobile phone call charges, show how knowledge can be adapted by the user being given additional information.

---

# Describe different data types (Boolean, real, integer, string, date/time), selecting an appropriate data type for a given situation

The fundamental building blocks, the facts and figures, are made up of alphanumeric characters. An alphanumeric character is any character that can be displayed on a computer screen. It could be a letter, number or symbol.

Alphanumeric characters can be grouped into different data types.

A data type is the sort of alphanumeric character that can be allocated. There are five data types that you need to be aware of:

- Boolean
- Real
- Integer
- Text/String
- Date/Time

## Boolean

The Boolean data type is one which can contain one of only two values – true and false. These two values can be used to represent anything containing two states, for example:

- Male/Female
- Yes/No
- L6th/U6th

It is used to hold data where the response can only be one of two values. It is often phrased as a question, for example:

- Is the motorway open yet?
- Does the property have a garden?
- Are you male?

## Real

This data type contains numbers which will have decimal places, for example:

- 45.78
- 123.0323
- 12.00

It is used to hold numbers where precision is important, for example:

- measurements in a house/building (2.7 m wide)
- prices of goods (£1.75)
- height of people (1.82 m)

## Integer

The integer data type contains whole numbers with NO decimal places, for example:

- 45
- 125
- 1250

It is used where the accuracy may not be of vital importance or the value allocated is specifically a whole number, for example:

- TV channels
- large amounts of money – house prices
- coding responses – 1–4

Currency may be a real or an integer. If it is a small amount of currency then it will be real (£16.99), however if the amount is large, then it is an integer (house prices: £175 000). In general the units used may influence whether a number is represented as a real or an integer – a price in pence may be an integer (75p), but the same price in pounds is real (£0.75).

< Tip >

When storing numbers and prices, if there is a leading or trailing identifier (a currency symbol (e.g. £) or a measurement (e.g, cm)), the data type does not change. The identifier is not included as part of the data type. Do NOT then think than £2.99 or 32 cm should be stored as text because of the pound sign or unit – they are not. They would still be stored as real or integer as appropriate.

## Text/String

This is any alphanumeric character. This includes numbers, text and symbols, for example:

- 12345
- Examination
- 123GD56
- 10 Downing Street
- ✌☝☺✈✄

Text is used to convey basic information, for example on labels:

- Forename of a person (Darren)
- Postcode (B17 4BH)
- Telephone number (01234 567890)

As the examples show, text/string is used to hold telephone numbers. In a computer, telephone numbers are stored as text. This is because the telephone number contains a leading 0, spaces and, most importantly, no mathematical calculations are performed on telephone numbers, so there is no need to store it as a number.

## Date/Time

This contains numbers and letters, which, depending on the format used, displays the date or the time to different degrees of accuracy, for example:

- 12:45:45
- 1995
- 7th September 2007

In reality, the computer works out a date fom a number. A predetermined date, 1st January 1900 is given a value -1. Every date is then calculated numerically, so 1st January 2000 is stored as 36526 – the number of days that has passed since day 1.

|  | Boolean | Real | Integer | String | Date/Time |
|---|---|---|---|---|---|
| Definition | One of only two values | Numbers with decimals | Whole numbers | Alphanumeric characters | Numbers and letters |
| Example | True | 123.32 | 87 | Hello | 03/05/1988 |

**< Activity >**

Within the context, give an example of how each of the data types could be used.

|  | Context | | |
|---|---|---|---|
|  | Estate agency | Removal company | School |
| Boolean |  |  |  |
| Real |  |  |  |
| Integer |  |  |  |
| String |  |  |  |
| Date/Time |  |  |  |

## ▪ Why is it important to allocate the correct data type to the data?

Various processes are carried out on data, including sorting, searching and mathematical processes (addition, subtraction, etc.).

Some of these processes can only be carried out on some data types. For example:

- Text can only be added together to form a longer string such as "hello" + "there" = "hellothere". This is called concatenation.
- Boolean could not store the results of a survey with many choices.
- Multiplication cannot be carried out on text.

**QUESTIONS**

1 Using an example, describe the Boolean data type.
2 Give **three** examples where the use of an integer data type would be more appropriate than a real data type.
3 Give **two** reasons why a telephone number is stored as text.

# Give examples of different sources from which data can be derived and explain the advantages and disadvantages of using each source

Data has to come from somewhere – it does not just appear. If you need some data, you must consider where to get it from.

If you have been given the task of creating a leaflet for a local cinema, you will need to find some data to go into the leaflet.

Where this data comes from is known as the source.

**Figure 1.2** Source of data

## Direct and indirect data

Direct (primary) data is data collected from an original source. It is often easiest to think of direct data as data that has been physically collected by you.

Indirect (secondary) data has two interpretations:

- Data that has been used for a purpose different to that for which it was originally collected. For example, collecting data on how many tickets have been sold for a film to make sure it is not oversold, and then using the data to find the most popular film.
- The people/companies involved in collecting the data are different to those using the data. Typically this might be organisations that conduct market surveys and then sell the results to other companies who use it in advertising.

**< Activity >**

Using the context given, identify four direct sources of information and four indirect sources of information for producing leaflets.

| | Context | |
|---|---|---|
| | Estate Agency | Removal company |
| Direct | | |
| Indirect | | |

## QUESTIONS

1 What is the difference between direct and indirect sources of data?
2 Give **two** examples of archives that would need to be accessed to find data.
3 Information on the number of girls who play football in a town is required. Describe **one** direct and **one** indirect method of collecting this data that will provide this information.

## Advantages and disadvantages of collecting data from different sources

The choice of the data collection method is often taken out of the hands of the individual, for example it is not possible to collect historical data from an original source. The advantages and disadvantages will depend on the situation.

| | Advantages | Disadvantages |
|---|---|---|
| Direct | ■ The source and collection method is known and verified.<br>■ The exact data required can be collected.<br>■ Can change the data being collected in response to answers. | ■ May not get a large range of data.<br>■ Data may not be available – location/time. |
| Indirect | ■ Large range of data available that could not have been collected directly.<br>■ Data can be available from different locations and time periods.<br>■ Analysis might already have been completed on some of the data. | ■ Do not know if any bias was placed on the collection.<br>■ Cannot be certain of accuracy of the recording of data.<br>■ May not have all the information about how, when and where it was collected to make a valued opinion on its usefulness.<br>■ If the information was not originally collected, may not be able to get hold of it. |

## QUESTIONS

1 Describe **two** advantages of using an original source to collect information on how good different MP3 players are.
2 Give **two** situations where using indirect data is a better option than direct. For each situation, give a different reason why.
3 Describe **one** situation where there is an advantage to using both direct and indirect methods of collecting data.

# Compare the use of static information sources with dynamic sources

An information source is a repository of data that can be accessed when required. There are two main types of information source: static and dynamic.

A static information source is one where the data, once created, does not change. A dynamic information source is one where the data can change and be updated.

Static information sources include books and CDs. Dynamic sources include pages on the World Wide Web and CD-RW.

With static information sources, the data contained within it does not change. This means that it can be found when it is needed. For example, if a teacher had created a worksheet based on the source they would know that the student could find the information.

If the teacher used a book as the source they can be confident that the content has not changed since they last looked. If they used a web page as the source, there is no guarantee that it will be the same – in fact it could even change halfway through the lesson.

**Figure 1.3** Changing content

The data stored on a CD-ROM is static. Once the data is burned on to the CD-ROM it cannot be changed. A common use of a CD-ROM for storing static data is an encyclopedia. Companies may also promote their products by producing a catalogue or brochure on a CD-ROM and sending it to all their customers or clients.

It is likely that static information sources have gone through some editing process. If it is a book or a CD there is a rigorous system for checking the data. The end result is content which can be relied on to be accurate.

< Activity >

Some CD-ROMs, especially those for encyclopedias, can appear to update their content. Investigate how this is possible. Is this really dynamic content?

Dynamic information is information that changes or can be changed. A dynamic web page contains content that a user can interact with, such as information that is tied to a database. The user can request information, such as ticket availability or product information, for retrieval from a database. The information retrieved will be up to date but not necessarily accurate.

Anyone with a computer and a telephone line can create a website. They can put whatever they want on the website and it can be viewed worldwide. Just because something is on the Web does not make it correct. Any information found on the Web needs to be treated with caution until it is verified by a separate source.

A book or a CD (static) has limited accessibility. Only one person can see a single copy of a book and a CD requires a CD drive to view its contents. Information on the Web is accessible by thousands of people simultaneously.

### QUESTIONS

1 What is the difference between static and dynamic data?
2 Describe, with examples, **two** reasons why websites are classified as dynamic sources of data.
3 Describe **two** situations where the use of static data is preferable. Give reasons for your choices.
4 Describe **two** problems of using dynamic data.

## Comparison of CD-ROMS and websites

There are advantages and disadvantages to data being held in a static form, on a CD-ROM, and in a dynamic form on websites.

| CD-ROM | Websites |
|---|---|
| There is a limited amount of information available. | The WWW provides a large volume of information. |
| Does not require Internet access. | Only people with Internet access can access the information. |
| More reliable source of information. | The information is not always reliable. |
| Does require a suitable computer with CD-ROM drive. | You do not need a CD-ROM drive or a computer – can access using a mobile phone. |
| Data cannot be updated very quickly. | Data can be updated very quickly. |
| The CD can be scratched/broken or lost/stolen. | Internet access might not be working. Difficulty accessing the pages. |

| CD-ROM | Websites |
|---|---|
| Software to search the data on the CD can be included with the CD along with any additional necessary software. | The user may not have the correct browser software. |
| If there are errors, correction notices would have to be sent out to people. | The WWW provides many different opinions. |
| There is a cost involved in making and sending the CD-ROMs. | Can potentially reach everybody. |
| A required CD-ROM can take time to arrive. | People come to a website rather than the CD-ROM being sent to a person. |
| Several CD-ROMs may need to be looked at to find the required information. | Hyperlinks can lead the individual to related sites. |
| The CD-ROM is in a single location – have to possess it to look at it. | The same WWW resource can be accessed from anywhere as long as the address is known. |

## QUESTIONS

1 What are the advantages for a toy company of producing its catalogue on CD-ROM instead of a website?
2 What are the advantages for an electronic gadget import company of producing its catalogue on a website instead of CD-ROM?
3 What are the advantages of using the websites instead of a CD-ROM to search for information?

# Describe how the following can affect the quality of the information produced: accuracy, relevance, age, completeness, presentation, level of detail

Garbage In Garbage Out (GIGO) is a well-known concept in ICT. It means that if the data that is input into the system is not very good, then you will not be able to translate it into information that is useful.

Or, put another way, if you put incorrect data into a system you will get incorrect information out of it.

There are six factors that determine how good the data is. Different factors are applicable to different scenarios.

- Accuracy
- Relevance
- Age
- Completeness
- Presentation
- Level of detail

These six factors are explained below and an estate agency is used as the context.

## Accuracy

The data needs to be accurate. If it is not accurate you cannot rely on the information it provides.

If you ask for the price of a house and you are given an incorrect figure, the information is worthless.

## Relevance

The information must be relevant. If you have some information but it does not relate to the topic it is worthless.

Having information that is not relevant can be a disadvantage. It increases the volume of data and this could mean a longer time is required to look at it.

If you ask for the distance of a property from different places within town, to be told how far it is from a bus stop on the other side of town or how far it is to the mayor's house is irrelevant.

## Age

The information might be too old. Information can change over time. If you know the information is from the past it may not be relevant now.

If you ask for the price of a house, to be given a figure that is five years old is of no value to you.

## Completeness

If you only have part of the information then it is worthless. Think back to the formula for information – data requires a context, structure, and meaning for it to have value and be useful.

If you want to view a house and you are only given the house number but no road name, or the date of the viewing but not the time, then the information is not worth anything.

## Presentation

If the information is not presented in such a way that you can understand or find what you want it loses value. The presentation might be improved by sorting or using a different method of representation, for example a picture or graph instead of text.

Pictures of a property make house brochures easier to digest. Also, house brochures are presented in an organised way (as if you were walking through the house). This consistent presentation makes it easier to compare properties.

## Level of detail

You can be given too much or too little information. The volume of data determines whether you have enough to make a decision or too much. If you have too much it can be difficult to find what you require.

If you are buying a house, having every minor alteration and samples of different colour schemes used in the house is too much information.

On the other hand, being told how many bedrooms there are but no details, for example the length and width, is too little.

There is a balance between too much and too little and it can be difficult to get it correct.

**Figure 1.4** Quality of information

< Activity >

# HOUSE FOR SALE

Price: between £200,000 and £290,000

In Grove Street

The garden is 102.12 m long. It is a delightful area with a post-modern design. The grass used has been imported from China from a small grass grower who supplies the grass seeds to many different countries, including Hawaii.

The house has 4 bedrooms, a few reception rooms and some toilets. When the house was built in the 1800s the walls were a lovely crimson colour.

If you are interested in viewing this house, give us a ring.

Using the above leaflet, go through each of the six factors affecting the quality of information and analyse how well the leaflet addresess them.

Redesign the leaflet to take into account the factors.

The six factors are not usually present just on their own. For example, level of detail is linked to completeness, presentation can be linked to age.

< Activity >

Within the contexts given, give examples of how the six factors can affect the quality of information produced.

|  | Context | |
| --- | --- | --- |
|  | Removal company | Exam results |
| Accuracy |  |  |
| Relevancy |  |  |
| Age |  |  |
| Completeness |  |  |
| Presentation |  |  |
| Level of detail |  |  |

**QUESTIONS**

1 Describe each of the six factors affecting the quality of information.
2 For each factor, give an example of how it affects the quality of information produced.
3 Demonstrate, using examples, how one factor can have a knock-on effect and influence other factors.

# Describe the advantages and disadvantages of encoding data

We collect data for a purpose. If the data that has been collected cannot be organised in such a way that it can be used for the original purpose then it is worthless.

There needs to be some method of standardising the information so that it is fulfils its purpose and is organised. One method is known as encoding data (putting data into code or shorthand data). This has nothing to do with secret messages (ciphers, which are often called codes).

Encoding data is taking the original data and storing it in a different representation. What is stored is not the actual data but a representation of it. An everyday example is using a postcode to represent an address or part of an address.

The following are examples of representations of data. It is easy to work out what the codes stand for.

| Mon | Tue | Wed | Thu |
|-----|-----|-----|-----|
| Jan | Feb | Mar | Apr |

Other codes are not as easy to understand.

BLTR36
RDSK16

It is not possible to interpret the data unless you have the key

BL = Blue, RD = Red
TR = Trouser, SK = Skirt
Last two digits = size

< Activity >

Create **three** different sets of codes. Hand them to another student and get them to try and understand what the codes represent and how they work.

## ◼ Disadvantages and problems of encoding data

The precision of the data entered is coarsened. This means that the data entered into the computer is not as accurate as the data originally given.

Imagine you are doing a survey of hair colour and the options that you give people are:

- black
- red
- blonde
- grey
- brown.

This may cover most of the major colours, but most people do not categorise their hair in these precise terms. They may think of themselves as chestnut or strawberry blonde.

This will mean that the actual data entered into the computer is inaccurate. If the data is seen to be inaccurate then the integrity of the system will be questioned – how can the results be believed if the data is not correct?

If you were to ask a question, the response that you are given is unlikely to fit exactly into any encoding system you try to come up with. This is why many surveys ask you to give marks on a scale instead of allowing you to comment freely.

However, if you are trying to encode free comments you will need to make some value judgements. Value judgements are where an absolute value is placed on some vague text. Different people will apply different value judgements to the same text.

You are doing a survey outside a cinema about the film that has just finished. You ask the people coming out of the cinema: 'Did you enjoy the film?'

The responses might include:

> 'Yes, it was great.'
> 'It was OK.'
> 'Most of it was excellent, but some bits were rubbish.'
> 'Complete rubbish, except for the end.'

If you have a scale of 1–4 (1 being excellent, 4 being rubbish) how do you code these statements? Different people will give the same statement a different mark on the scale.

It would be difficult to set up and analyse a database where all possible values were allowed, therefore we need to try to organise the data. However a balance needs to be achieved between having enough categories to get most of the responses, thereby making the data usable, and not having enough and so having to coarsen the data or make too much of a value judgement.

There are some other disadvantages to encoding data. If the user does not know how the codes are being used, they will not be able to encode any new data or be able to interpret the data that is currently held on computer.

It is possible that if some encoding system was devised that uses a system of numbers and letters to identify objects, for example:

**BL36TR          meaning Black Trousers 36" waist**

then eventually the number of codes will be used up and a new encoding system will need to be developed. This will of course mean re-encoding all of the existing data.

Once a survey has been done and all the information encoded and entered into the computer it is unlikely that the computer operator will have access to the original survey forms. This means that they have to accept what is on the computer. If there are any errors, value judgements that are incorrect or codes that have been input incorrectly they would not know. This means that any information that is extracted will be taken as being correct.

< Activity >

Create an encoding system to encode people's facial features: hair colour, eye colour, skin tone, etc.

Try out the encoding system. What are the advantages and disadvantages of the system you have created?

Is it easy to understand and use?

Investigate the Dewey Decimal system of encoding for libraries. Is it easy to follow? Could it be improved?

## Advantages of encoding

Encoding data is not all doom and gloom. There are some advantages as well.

The computer memory requirements are a lot less when information is encoded. Instead of storing **Black Trousers 36" waist**, you would only need to store **BL36TR**. This may not seem a lot, but when you are storing thousands of records, the space saving is considerable. This means you do not need as large a hard drive and back-up capability and this in turn costs less money.

It can be quicker to enter a code into the computer than to type in all the details. Of course, with new users, there is a delay as they work out the codes. The code is also more suitable to bar code tagging which allows the code to be scanned (probably automatically) into the database.

Hopefully, there will be fewer errors. As the codes follow a set pattern, it is possible to apply validation to the different parts of the code. In the example:

**BL36TR**

- the first two letters must match a colour code in the database,
- the second two numbers must be between two values,
- the final two letters must match an item code in the database.

This cannot ensure that the data is correct, but it does ensure that it matches the codes. Fewer errors will occur than with free text data entry.

The data takes on a very precise structure when encoded. It is easier to sort and search the data because it is organised. It is also possible to analyse and graph data if it is tightly structured.

## ▩ Summary of encoding

| Advantages | Disadvantages |
|---|---|
| **Less memory requirement**<br>Storing less information therefore less memory is required. | **Precision of data coarsened**<br>For example, Light Blue encoded as Blue. |
| **Security**<br>If the codes are not apparent then it is difficult to know and understand the meaning of the codes. | **Encoding of value judgements**<br>For example, "Was the film good?" to be encoded as a judgement of 1–4. This will be encoded differently by different people and makes comparisons difficult. |
| **Speed of input**<br>The codes take less time to enter therefore it is quicker to input large amount of data. | **The user needs to know the codes used**<br>If the user does not know the codes they cannot use them. |
| **Data validation**<br>Since the codes follow a strict set of numbers and letters they are easy to validate. | **Limited number of codes**<br>If codes are made up of a range of letters and numbers the options will be limited. |
| **Organisation of data**<br>If the data is in a standardised format then it can be compared and organised. | **Difficult to track errors**<br>Validation will ensure the code is entered correctly but the nature of the code will make it difficult to see if the code is actually correct. |

---

### QUESTIONS

1 What is meant by encoding data?
2 Describe **three** advantages of encoding data.
3 Describe **three** disadvantages of encoding data.
4 Explain, using an example, how data can be encoded.
5 Give **two** situations where the encoding of data is appropriate.
  For each situation, explain why data needs to be encoded.

---

# Describe and give examples of a range of validation methods and their purpose

In order for it to be useful within a computer system, the data first has to be entered into the system. Errors can occur at the point of entry of data into the system.

Validation is a check that is performed by the computer as the data is being entered. It tries to prevent entry of any data that does not conform to pre-set rules.

There are many different rules that can be created, however they will not stop incorrect data being entered, they will just ensure that the data that is entered is:

■ sensible
■ reasonable
■ within acceptable boundaries
■ complete.

The checks that can be applied fall into several categories:

- Range
- Type
- Presence
- Length
- Lookup
- Picture
- Check digit

## Range checks

A range check sets an upper and a lower boundary for the data. The data entered must lie between these two values.

For example, in a secondary school a student can be in Years 7–13. A lower boundary of 7 and an upper boundary of 13 can be set.

## Type checks

This makes sure that the data entered is of the correct type. Types of data include: Numeric, String, Boolean and Date/Time.

Type checks will not allow you to enter the wrong data type, for example if you try to enter text into a numeric field it will be rejected.

## Presence checks

These are also called existence checks. Not every field or question will need to be answered. However, there will be some that must have an answer and be filled in.

By applying a presence check, the computer will insist that a value is entered for that field.

For example, if you are storing details about a student, you need to know their name, address and phone number. These are vital pieces of information. You may not need to store an email address as not every student has one.

## Length checks

When any data is entered into a computer it has a length. A single character has a length of 1, 'Hello' has a length of 5.

A length check ensures that the data cannot be more than a set number of characters.

## Lookup checks

A lookup check takes the value entered and compares it against a list of values in a separate table. It can return confirmation of the value entered or a second list based on that value. An example would be entering in the postcode and the system looking up the postcode and returning a list of possible addresses.

## Picture checks

This is also known as a format check or an input mask. Some data entries might be a combination of numbers and letters, therefore you cannot apply a type check. However the location of the numbers and letters within the data might be in the same place every time.

For example, some item codes might look like:

**RT678H**
**FD634K**
**FG789E**

■ The first two entries are letters.
■ The next three entries are numbers.
■ The last entry is a letter.

This would allow a format check to be applied to the field, for example:

**LLNNNL**

where L is letter and N is number.

This makes sure that only letters can be entered for the first two and last value and numbers for the middle three.

## Check digit

A check digit is calculated using a set of numbers and then added to the end of them.

When the code is created, the check digit is created and added to the code. Before the code is then processed, the check digit is recalculated and compared with the one in the code. If they are the same, processing continues. If they are not, an error has occurred and the code value needs to be re-entered.

Check digits are commonly used when the data is transmitted. Corruption can occur during transmission of data and the check digit is used to ensure that the data received is the same as that sent.

The International Standard Book Number (ISBN), the number that uniquely identifies a book, has a check digit. A 10-digit ISBN is calculated using Modulus 11.

The following example shows how to use Modulus 11 to calculate a check digit. An ISBN is 0-7487-9116-7

1 Remove the last digit from the ISBN: 0-7487-9116
2 Write out the remaining numbers. Starting from the right-hand number, put a 2 under it. Put a 3 under the next one and so on.

| Number | 0 | 7 | 4 | 8 | 7 | 9 | 1 | 1 | 6 |
|--------|----|---|---|---|---|---|---|---|---|
| Code | 10 | 9 | 8 | 7 | 6 | 5 | 4 | 3 | 2 |

**3** Multiply the number by the code.

| Number | 0 | 7 | 4 | 8 | 7 | 9 | 1 | 1 | 6 |
|--------|----|----|----|----|----|----|---|---|----|
| Code | 10 | 9 | 8 | 7 | 6 | 5 | 4 | 3 | 2 |
| Result | 0 | 63 | 32 | 56 | 42 | 45 | 4 | 3 | 12 |

**4** Add the results together.
$0 + 63 + 32 + 56 + 42 + 4 + 45 + 3 + 12 = 257$

**5** Divide the total by 11. You need to write down the remainder.
$257 \div 11 = 23$ remainder 4

**6** Take the remainder away from 11. The value that is left is the check digit.
$11 - 4 = 7$
The check digit is 7.
This is compared with the original check digit. If they are the same then the data has been transmitted correctly.
If the remainder is 0, then the check digit is 0.
If the remainder is 1, then the check digit is X.
A check digit calculation is very good for finding transposition errors. If two numbers were swapped around then they would have different weightings and the check digit would be different.

## < Activity >

1 Configure a spreadsheet for a user to confirm whether or not an ISBN check digit is correct.

2 Use the Modulus 11 calculation to confirm the check digit of the following ISBNs. For any that are incorrect, give the correct check digit.

  a) 1-854-87918-9

  b) 0-552-77109-X

  c) 0-330-28414-3

  d) 0-330-34742-X

  e) 0-330-35183-3

3 Examine the form on the next page and identify all the different validation methods that could be applied to it. Give a reason for each method of validation used.

**Application for Climbing Course**

Surname _____  Forename(s) _____

Address _____

_____

Postcode _____  Tel No. _____

Date of birth ___/___/___  Age _____  Male ☐  Female ☐

Previous experience:  Experienced ☐  Moderate ☐  Beginner ☐

Signature of applicant _____  date ___/___/___

---

**Consent of parent or guardian** (for young people under 18 years of age)

I agree to my son/daughter/ward participating in the Climbing Course

Signature of Parent/Guardian _____

Name _____

---

**For office use only:**

**Applicant accepted:  Yes/No**  **Date of course:** ___/___/___

**Figure 1.5** Example of a form

---

**QUESTIONS**

1  Describe **three** different validation methods.
2  When is it appropriate to use range validation? Give examples of its use.
3  Why is validation used?
4  Describe how validation methods can be used when collecting details from a prospective house purchaser in an estate agency.
5  Give **three** examples of data that could be entered into a form that are incorrect but would pass three different validation rules.

# Describe and give examples of a range of verification methods and their purpose

If you have collected some information on paper, at some point it will need to be entered into the computer.

Once you have entered it into the computer you will have two copies: the paper-based original and that stored in the computer.

The paper-based copy is known as the source document.

The copy on the computer is known as the object document.

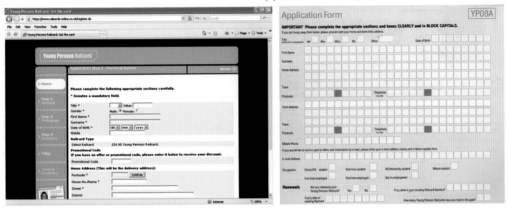

**Figure 1.6** Electronic and paper document

Verification is making sure that the information on the source document is the same as the information on the object document.

Put simply, it is making sure that the same information that is on the paper has been entered and not changed in any way. It does not ensure that the information is correct.

There are two main methods of verification:

- Double entry
- Manual verification

## Double entry

This is essentially entering the data twice. The computer then compares the two sets of data and if it finds any differences it informs the user who can then make appropriate changes.

Passwords are one method of double entry that you will have come across. Often you are asked to enter a password twice so correct entry can be verified.

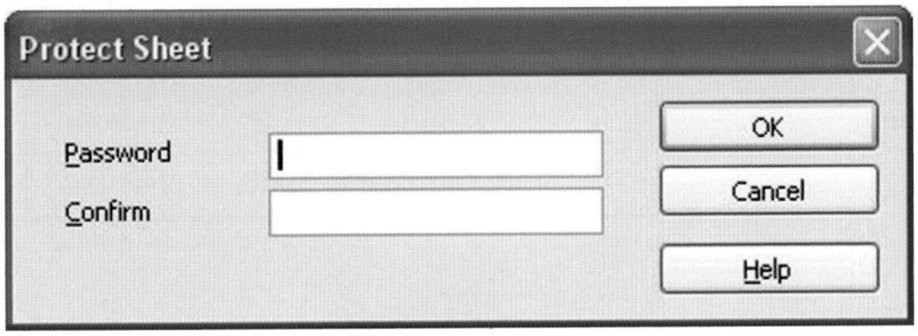

**Figure 1.7** Confirming a password

Double entry could be by the same person or different people.

The main problem with double entry is that if the same error is made both times then the computer will not find a difference.

## ■ Manual verification

Manual verification is essentially proofreading the data.

This involves visually comparing the source data with the entry typed into the computer. It relies on a person being able to follow two sets of data and find any differences. Unfortunately, this is not a very reliable method. It is very difficult to transfer attention between paper and screen. It is also difficult to keep track of where you are on the paper and where you are looking on the screen.

---

### QUESTIONS

1 Describe **two** methods of verification.
2 Give **two** disadvantages of double entry verification.
3 Give **one** advantage of manual verification.
4 Explain why verification cannot ensure that the data is accurate.

---

## ■ Common errors

The two most common errors caused when entering data into a computer are transcription errors and transposition errors.

Transcription errors are where you have made a mistake copying the data. For example, it may be by striking the wrong key on the keyboard or hitting two keys at once.

Examples of transcription errors include:

|  | Wrong | Correct |
|---|---|---|
| Postcode | TN**18** 7TH | TN28 7TH |
| Surname | Stua**et** | Stuart |
| Date | **25**th March 2004 | 26th March 2004 |

Transposition errors are where you have reversed two numbers or letters.

|  | Wrong | Correct |
|---|---|---|
| Postcode | TN**82** 7TH | TN28 7TH |
| Surname | St**au**rt | Stuart |
| Date | 26th March 20**40** | 26th March 2004 |

## No degree of accuracy

Neither validation nor verification can ensure that the data that has been entered is accurate.

Validation, as stated earlier, can make sure the data is:

■ sensible
■ reasonable
■ within acceptable boundaries
■ complete.

However, it is still possible to enter data that meets the validation rules but is wrong. In the table, all the data examples entered would pass the validation rule but in every case it is incorrect.

| Rule | Data entered | Data intended to be entered |
| --- | --- | --- |
| Presence | 24 Apple Court | 23 Apple Court |
| Range: between 0 and 5 | 4 | 2 |
| Type: Numeric | 244 | 245 |
| Length: 4 characters | Help | Held |

Similarly, verification methods also cannot make sure that the data entered is correct. They can make sure that it is the same as what was written down but can give no certainty of accuracy.

For example, imagine that on a data capture form the individual has written down that their birthday was 26th February 1965. If their birthday was actually the 16th February 1965, then verification methods would not pick up the error.

# Explain the difference between backing up and archiving of data and give reasons why they are necessary

Back-up is keeping a copy of the current data. If there is a failure of the computer system (e.g. a power failure leading to corruption, a virus, files accidentally deleted, etc.), then the back-up can be used to restore the data.

Back-up is important so that data is not lost. Data is valuable and needs to be protected. It is suggested that the data held on the computer system is one of the most important assets of a business.

There are many different back-up devices and strategies such as:

■ external memory: floppy disk, memory card, etc.
■ external hard drive
■ tape
■ making a second copy on a different disk, possibly storing it off site.

The back-up needs to be organised and it must be possible to locate the files that you need. If you have several copies of the file, it is important to know which one is the latest back-up. There are many different programs that will automate back-ups and restore data for you.

Archiving is for long-term storage of data that is not required immediately. In fact, archived data is often not required at all. It is taken off the system and stored in case it is required for an investigation in the future. When archiving, data is written to a large capacity storage device at long intervals, unlike back-ups, which should be written at short intervals.

Files should be archived when they are no longer needed immediately, but should be readily available if needed so they cannot be permanently deleted. Examples of these types of files are:

- last year's financial or sales records
- completed projects
- other materials not required on a day-to-day basis.

In a school, leavers' records are not required on a day-to-day basis but might be required in the future (for up to seven years after leaving) to write a reference for a student. The leavers' data would be archived.

The general procedure that should be used for archiving files is:

1  Copy the file onto the archival media (disk or tape).
2  Verify the copied files (make sure that the two copies are exactly the same and the copy has worked).
3  Delete the original files.

When you archive old files, you eliminate the waste of time and media that results from backing up unused files, free up hard drive space, and improve the performance of the system.

**QUESTIONS**

1  Using an example, define what is meant by the term 'back-up'.
2  Using an example, define what is meant by the term 'archive'.
3  Why is it important to back up data?
4  What is the difference between archiving and back-up of data?
5  What storage medium should be used for archiving?

< Tip >

Archiving data does not make a copy of the data. It is removing the data from the current system.

Back-up is making a copy of the data.

# Describe the costs of producing information

Information needs to be produced. It does not just appear. Information is not free – it costs money to produce it. It takes time to collect the data, input it, process it and produce an output that meets the required purpose.

There are four main areas where costs are incurred in the production of information:

- Hardware
- Software
- Consumables
- Personnel

## Hardware

**Figure 1.8** Hardware

Hardware can be used to collect the information, process it and output it. It can also be used to store data for use at a later date. It may be necessary for the organisation to purchase items of hardware.

The initial costs of the hardware are expensive but these can be offset by the length of time the hardware is kept. Also, once it has been acquired, it can be used for other tasks, again spreading the costs.

Ongoing hardware costs include repair and maintenance costs as well as upgrade costs. It is necessary to keep the hardware in good working order and the organisation could have a maintenance contract or have the equipment repaired when required.

As time progresses, the storage requirements of the organisation will increase. If, for example, they are producing a newsletter, they will want to keep all back issues on the computer. This will have an implication on disk space and they may need to increase the capacity of the hard drive. This has a knock-on effect on back-up, which will therefore also require greater capacity.

< Activity >

Fill in the following table, giving examples of what the hardware could be used for, the cost of the hardware and its estimated life.

| Device | Use | Cost | Life |
|---|---|---|---|
| Scanner | | | |
| Printer | | | |
| 2 GB memory key | | | |
| Digital camera | | | |
| Digital tablet | | | |
| LCD monitor | | | |

## Software

**Figure 1.9** Software

Software licences need to be purchased. This will include the operating system and utilities, as well as that used to produce the information. The licences can be purchased as a one-off cost or re-licensed year to year.

The software might also require a technical support agreement so if there are difficulties, support is available to solve the problems. Support might be bought from the software manufacturer or from a third-party: both are likely to cost money.

There may be training costs associated with the software, such as courses that the users will need to go on. They may also require reference manuals.

Over time, the software may need to be upgraded. If the software is upgraded, there are more puchasing costs, though it may be possible to acquire the new version licence at a lower cost. There are also potential costs associated with upgrading software, not only for installation time, but possibly to purchase new hardware to make the system work efficiently.

**< Activity >**

Investigate the cost of training courses for a piece of software such as QuarkXPress or Adobe Photoshop.

## Consumables

**Figure 1.10** Paper and ink cartridges

Consumables are items that get used. Paper and printer ink/toner are the two main consumables.

## Personnel

Personnel costs are the costs related to people working in the organisation. Employees' salaries need to be paid or people may need to be hired to produce the information. This is a long-term cost. They may be required to collect, collate, enter, process and output the information.

When staff first begin to work on a project, it is likely that they will take longer than staff who have been doing the work for some time. They will need some time to get used to the system and software. Over a few months, as they get used to procedures and software, the time will reduce until they eventually meet the deadlines. This 'bedding in' time needs to be built into the costs.

When the people using the software go on training courses there may be costs associated with covering their job while they are away, as well as the training costs.

Depending on the information that is being produced, there may be additional costs that involve checking the accuracy of the data.

Personnel costs are likely to be the most expensive costs incurred in producing information.

< Activity >

Imagine that you are producing a leaflet for a new vegetable delivery service.

Using the four costs discussed, list all the expenditure associated with producing a leaflet and give a cost to each item.

**QUESTIONS**

1 Describe the hardware items required to collect and input data required for a fashion magazine.
2 Explain why an organisation might need to upgrade the software it uses to produce information.
3 Explain the personnel costs incurred by an organisation that produces a leaflet completely from scratch.

# Describe clearly the terms input, processing, output, storage and feedback, drawing a diagram to illustrate how they are related

Any ICT system can be broken down into:

■ input
■ processing
■ storage
■ output
■ feedback.

This can be represented as a diagram. Some of the elements may be manual.

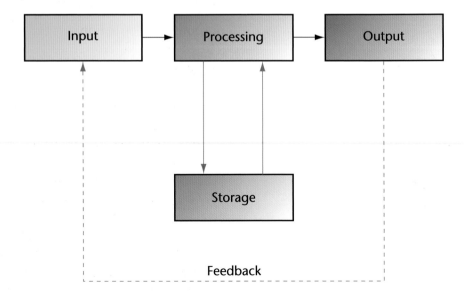

**Figure 1.11** ICT system block diagram

### Input

This is taking information that is external to the system and entering it into the system. This may be manual input (e.g. keyboard) or automated input (e.g. OMR). It may also be input by electronic means (e.g. via a network or CD/disk).

### Processing

This is an action performed on the data. Processing can include sorting, searching or performing calculations on the data.

### Storage

This is where data is held. It may be the data that has been input, data required during processing or the results of processing. This is data that is still within the system.

### Output

This is taking information that was in the system and outputting it. The method used may result in printed output, output on screen, electronic output (e.g. disk/CD).

There is always a problem when looking at input, storage and output. Where do CDs and disks fit in? In themselves, they are storage devices. However, if the data stored on them is being entered into the system via the storage device then they are input media and if the data on them is being taken outside of the system they are output media. If they are storing data within the system then they are storage devices as well!

### Feedback

This is where the output from the system forms part of the input to the system. Feedback is usually applied to real-time situations. If the response to the feedback is automatic then the process is a closed loop. If there is an operator involved then the process is an open loop.

A feedback example is taking the register at school using a computer.

1 The teacher takes the register for their class. This is input into the computer.
2 The data is processed. The student is found on the system and the correct response marked by their name: present, absent, etc. This data is stored in the system.
3 The system can then generate an absence list for the session. This is the output.
4 The teacher can look at the absence list at a later time, question the offending student and find out why they were absent. The teacher then updates the list with the reason. This is feedback.

< Activity >

Using the following scenario, describe the terms input, processing, storage, output and feedback.

A school trip to The Lake District is being organised. Letters are sent each week to all parents whose children are going, with how much they need to pay. If they send money in during the week, the records are altered. Once they have paid the full amount no more letters are sent to the parents.

## ■ Turnaround documents

In some systems a turnaround document is used. This is a document that has gone through the system and is output. It is printed by the computer. Additional data is recorded on the document and this is then input into the system at a later date.

Turnaround documents are used by utility companies to allow the home owner to record meter readings. The document has the name, address and account number of the home owner already on it. The home owner adds the meter reading and sends it back.

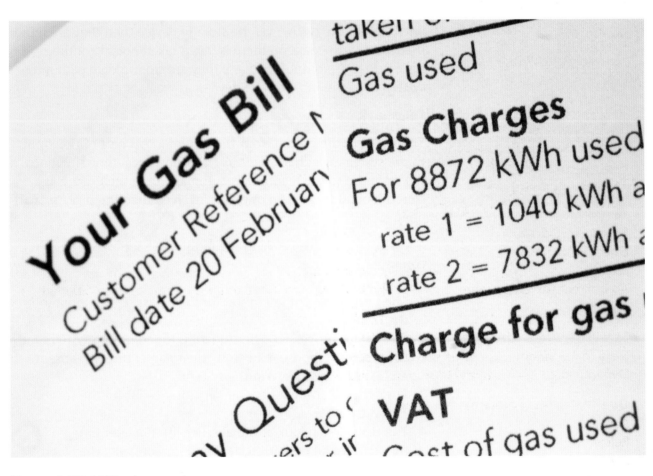

**Figure 1.12** Utility documents

At the bottom of page 37 is an example of feedback. The document is output from the system and forms part of the input at a later date.

---

**QUESTIONS**

1 Describe these terms: input, storage, processing, output and feedback.
2 Draw a diagram to show the input, storage, processing, output and feedback for a vehicle cruise control system.
3 What is the difference between closed-loop and open-loop feedback?
4 What are the advantages of using a turnaround document?

---

# Summary

**Data, information and knowledge**
Data is made up of alphanumeric characters.
information = data + structure + context + meaning
Knowledge is the application and use of the information.

**Representation methods**
Text (including writing)
Graphics (including pictures)
Sound (including voice)
Moving pictures (animation or video)
LED (sequence of lights)

**Data types**
Boolean: true or false
Real: numbers with decimals
Integer: whole numbers
Text/String: alphanumeric characters
Date/Time

**Sources of data**
Direct and indirect
A direct source is where you have collected the data.
An indirect source is where someone else has collected it, either for the same or for a different purpose.

**Static and dynamic data**
Static data cannot be changed (e.g. CD-ROM).
Dynamic data can be updated (e.g. web pages).

**Quality of information**
Accuracy
Relevance
Age
Completeness
Presentation
Level of detail

## Encoding data

Validation and verification
　Neither can ensure the accuracy of the entered data.

Validation
　Ensures that entered data is reasonable, complete, sensible and within acceptable boundaries.
　This is achieved by:
　　Range check
　　Type check
　　Presence check
　　Length check
　　Picture check

Verification
　Ensures the source and object data are the same. This is achieved by:
　　Proofreading
　　Computer verification

## Back-up and archive

Back-up is making a copy of the data.
Archive is removing the data from direct access.

## Cost of information

Hardware: specialist equipment, such as scanner, camera, graphics tablet, etc.
Software: desktop publishing or graphics software, etc.
Personnel: new employees and the training of individuals
Consumables: electricity, ink and paper

## Generic ICT system

Input: external data placed into the system
Process: manipulating the data
Storage: holding the data for later use
Output: data being passed outside of the system
Feedback: output influencing the input

## Test 1

Answer the following questions in the context of a rugby supporters' club that needs to keep data on its members.

| | | |
|---|---|---|
| 1 | Describe the term data and give an example of data. | [2] |
| 2 | Show how data can become information. | [3] |
| 3 | The club is producing a leaflet for its members. Identify **two** different methods of representing information they could use and give an advantage of each method. | [4] |
| 4 | Describe **three** different costs the club would incur if they decided to produce the leaflet in house. | [6] |
| 5 | The club is setting up a database to hold details of its members. The data needs to be encoded before it is entered into the database. Describe **three** advantages of encoding data. | [6] |

6  Describe and give examples of **three** different methods of validation the database could use. Identify an appropriate field for each type of validation. [9]

7  Data is inputted into the system, processed, stored and outputted from the system. Draw a diagram to show how the terms: input, process, storage and output are related. [4]

## Test 2

Answer the following questions in the context of a small company that writes online user manuals for different application software.

1  The manuals contain text, graphics and sound. Describe the advantages of each type of representation method and give an example of its use in the manual. [9]

2  The manuals are designed to give the reader information that they can turn into knowledge. Describe the difference between information and knowledge. [4]

3  The content of the manual could come from a direct or an indirect source. Describe what is meant by a direct and an indirect source of data. Give an example of each that could be used to get information for the manual. [6]

4  The manuals will only sell if the quality of the information contained within them is high. Identify **three** factors that affect the quality of information and, for each, use an example to describe how it could affect the information in the manual. [6]

5  The information in the manual has value. Explain under what circumstances the manual may lose its value. [2]

6  The manual can contain static and dynamic data. Describe the difference between static and dynamic data and give an example of each that could be used in the manual. [4]

7  Describe what feedback the company could receive on its manuals and how it could use the feedback to improve future manuals. [4]

# Software and hardware components of an information system

## Introduction

This chapter covers the hardware and software that make up a computer system. You will need to make sure that you understand the type of question and the answers required as the hardware devices will change and improve.

This chapter covers:

- The difference between hardware and software
- Standardisation and its impact
- Input, output and storage devices
- Specialist hardware devices
- Specialist software
- Different types of software
- Characteristics of different user interfaces

## Describe the difference between hardware and software, giving examples of each to illustrate the description

Hardware is things you can touch. It is the physical components that make up the computer. Examples include the mouse, keyboard, processor, monitor, printer, etc.

Software is the programming code that makes the computer work. There are two main types of software: system software (operating systems), which controls the workings of the computer; and applications, such as word-processing programs, spreadsheets and databases.

Any examples you give must be in general terms. You must not give proprietary (makers') names. For example, 'Word' is not acceptable, but 'word processor' is.

The following table gives the correct terms.

| Allowed | NOT allowed (examples of) |
| --- | --- |
| Word processor | Word |
| | WordPerfect |
| Spreadsheet | Excel |
| | Quattro Pro |
| Database | Access |
| | Paradox |
| | FileMaker |
| Presentation | PowerPoint |
| Email / PIM | Outlook |
| | Lotus Notes |
| Operating system | Windows |
| | Linux |
| | Mac OS |

**QUESTIONS**

**1** Using an example, define what is meant by the term hardware.
**2** Using an example, define what is meant by the term software.
**3** What is the difference between software and hardware?

# Explain the lack of standardisation affecting both hardware and software

Standardisation is the imposition, by a third party, or with agreement, of a set of standards on manufacturers.

There is a set of standards (rules and benchmarks) that both software and hardware must adhere to if it is to be recognised by certain bodies.

There are different standards in other parts of business, such as standards for food preparation, voltage and measurements, etc. In ICT there are several organisations that monitor and develop standards:

- W3C: the World Wide Web Consortium develops standards for the Internet.
- ISO: the International Standards Organisation currently has over 14 000 standards.

In a perfect world, everything would meet the same standard. This means that everything is built and works to the same level of quality. A standard will ensure that items of a similar type, but from completely different manufacturers, perhaps on different sides of the world, will work together using the same protocols.

Unfortunately there is a lack of standardisation in ICT. This is not to say that it is missing altogether. There are standards for hardware and software, but there are many different standards and they are not always compatible with each other.

A lack of standardisation among hardware has the following disadvantages.

| | |
|---|---|
| Cost | If you purchase a computer that is not part of a global standard then all the subsequent upgrades and parts you buy will have to come from specific sources and are likely to be very expensive.<br>If you do not buy items that are compatible with your computer, then they might not work correctly, or at all. |
| Availability | If there is limited availability for a piece of hardware then the supply itself may be limited. Limited supply has a knock-on adverse effect on cost. |
| Technical support | If availability is limited, then the support for it is also likely to be limited and expensive. |

The standardisation of hardware is not just about different types of computers. It may be about computers of the same type but of different ages. Computers purchased three or four years ago will probably not be able to use new processors, RAM or graphics cards because the standard itself has moved on. This is seen in the rapid development in wireless network devices.

Software standards are a little different. Although there is a set of standards released by the operating system manufacturers (so that application programs can be written to work with the OS and be accredited) there is limited compatibility between the standards.

Think about word processors. In an ideal world, every document written in any word processor would be able to be viewed in any other word processor.

### < Activity >

1 Launch your word processor and look at the different files that can be imported.

2 Do some research to see if there are any word-processor types missing.

Software standards are not just linked to operating systems. Web pages are written for different computers, running different operating systems and different browsers, and standards mean that the pages can be viewed on many different platforms. However, there are elements of web pages that cannot be viewed correctly in different browsers (e.g. colours and alignment).

A lack of standardisation among web browsers means that you might not see the page exactly as the designer intended it. In many cases this might not matter, but it could mean that the corporate colours of a company are displayed slightly differently, that some text does not appear where it should, or that some code may not work properly thereby limiting the functionality of the website.

From a manufacturer's point of view, lack of standardisation is not necessarily a bad thing. It means they can continually release new hardware, resulting in built-in obsolescence in the devices and they can make more money because of it.

## Takeovers

When one company takes over another there is likely to be incompatibilities with the computer systems used. The two companies might have standardised within themselves, but a lack of global standards might mean that systems do not function with one another. This can have the following negative impacts:

- no communication between systems
- miscommunication between systems leading to incorrect data being shared
- new equipment having to be purchased
- staff need to be trained to use the new systems
- lack of technical support on the new system.

---

**QUESTIONS**

1  What are standards?
2  Describe **two** effects on a user of having different hardware standards.
3  What are the problems of having different standards?
4  How does standardisation affect how web pages are displayed?
5  What are the advantages of a lack of standardisation to a company?

---

# Identify an appropriate input device for a given situation and justify the choice made

An input device is a piece of hardware that gets data from outside the computer system into the computer system.

Any manual input device increases the risk of inaccurate data being entered.

There are many different input devices and it is not possible to list them all. Different input devices are suitable for different uses, so it is important to choose the most appropriate. This can be determined by the cost, the volume of data to be input and the number of mistakes you can allow to be made.

45

# Keyboard

A keyboard is a typewriter-like set of keys that are used to input data and control commands to the computer. A keyboard has a set of letter and number keys, and may also have a calculator-like numerical keypad, as well as a set of cursor-movement keys.

Keyboards are good for inputting small quantities of data.

There are three main keyboard layouts: QWERTY, alphabetical and Dvorak. Most keyboards use the QWERTY layout.

**Figure 2.1** Types of keyboard

Keyboards do not always have to have capital letters on them. Primary school keyboards are available with lowercase letters and concept keyboards are programmable.

A concept keyboard/overlay is a sheet that goes over a flat pad and allows you to create your own individual keys. These are used in bars and restaurants where the keys represent items for sale, such as drinks and meals.

Concept keyboards are good in situations where language is a problem (pre-school, physically impaired) or there is a set number of options (on tills).

**Figure 2.2** Using a concept keyboard

Keyboard design has evolved over the last few years and now there are several different ergonomic varieties. These include curved keyboards, split keyboards and complete keyboard desks to ensure good posture.

**< Activity >**

Create a concept keyboard which could be used in your school canteen by the till operator.

## Mouse

A mouse is a pointing device that can be used to select items on a screen. It has buttons on top to make the selection and a sensor underneath which allows the pointer (cursor) to move on the screen following the physical movement of the mouse.

The mouse shapes have evolved over the last few years and it is now possible to get ergonomically shaped mice that fit into the palm of the hand. The movement is sensed by a ball and rollers, or by using an optical sensor.

A mouse needs some surface area to operate on. This is not always convenient with laptops, so these are fitted with touch pads which sense the movement of the user's finger.

Alternative pointing devices include the trackerball and the joystick. Both of these devices remain stationary on the desk surface.

The tracker ball is effectively an upside-down mouse, so the ball is moved directly by the user instead of moving it along a surface.

The joystick directly controls the cursor on the screen. Ergonomic joysticks are moulded to fit the hand. They are commonly used for games software and flight simulators.

## Scanner

A scanner translates information into a form the computer can use. There are many different types of scanner, for example:

- Bar code. This reads the bar codes and translates the bars into numbers. Bar codes are used to identify an item, for example products in supermarkets so stock and price can be analysed, or on parcels, so that the location of a delivery can be tracked.
- Optical Mark Reader (OMR). This detects the presence or absence of a mark in a predefined area on a page and translates it into a value, for example on Lotto number selection forms, school registers and multiple choice questions.

**Identify an appropriate input device for a given situation and justify the choice made**

- Magnetic card reader. This can take the information on a magnetic stripe and convert it into usable data, for example on credit cards and secure access cards.
- Flatbed scanner. This digitises an image so that it can be processed later as a picture or, by using optical charcter recognition (OCR), as editable text.
- Magnetic Ink Character Recognition (MICR). This detects magnetic ink marks and turns them into numbers. The are used to read bank details on cheques.

**Figure 2.3** OMR, MICR and bar code

## Graphics tablet

A graphics tablet is a flat working area like a sheet of paper with a stylus that resembles a pen. Both have evolved ergonomically in recent years. The movement of the stylus is detected by the tablet so the user can manipulate images on a screen and create free-hand drawings. Classroom interactive whiteboards can be thought of as very large graphics tablets.

Graphics tablets are used by designers and anyone involved in drawing directly on a computer.

## Digitiser

Any device that converts analogue data to digital data is a digitiser. It is a generic description of many devices. A scanner, digital camera and graphics tablet are all types of digitiser.

### < Activity >

1 There are many other data input devices that have not been covered above. Research the following devices, focusing on their purpose and ergonomic features:

- Digital camera
- Touch screen
- Microphone
- Switch
- Sensor

2 Investigate the use of biometric devices as input devices. Describe the devices and list their advantages and disadvantages.

**QUESTIONS**

1 Why are keyboards not suitable for inputting large amounts of data?
2 What are the advantages of concept keyboards?
3 Describe a digitiser.
4 Describe **two** different types of scanner and give examples of where they should be used.
5 What is the most efficient input device for a newspaper reporter and why?

# Identify an appropriate output device for a given situation and justify the choice made

Output devices are used to display the result of processing to the user. They are designed to get data from within the computer to outside of the computer system. As we move towards the paperless society there is less reliance on hard copy and a lot of output is now being produced electronically (emails, transferred to CDR/RW, etc.).

There are many different output devices and it is not possible to list them all. Different output devices are suitable for different uses, so it is important to choose the most appropriate.

## Monitor

A monitor is a device that takes signals from a computer and displays them on a screen. Monitors come in a variety of sizes and resolutions. The resolution is the maximum number of dots (pixels) that can be displayed on the screen at any one time. A screen resolution is given as the number of horizontal dots and then the number of vertical dots, for example $800 \times 600$ or $1024 \times 768$.

Traditional monitors were built around a 'tube' (cathode ray tube – CRT) like an old television, but similarly, they are increasingly available as flat screens (LCD/plasma), which weigh a lot less than a CRT and take up a lot less space on the desktop. The flat screen has no flicker and thus may cause less health problems for users, but the image is often poorer than a CRT.

Large monitors are used by graphic designers and newspaper editors, who need a lot of material displayed on the screen at a time.

## Printer

Printers produce hard copy output (most often on paper). There are several different types of printer.

## Dot matrix

These are impact printers. This means there is physical contact between the print head and the paper through an inked ribbon. Dot-matrix printers can print in colour as well as black and white and their main advantage is that they will print on multi-part stationery (carbon forms).

## Ink jet

These spray ink onto the paper and are relatively quiet. They are available in black and white or colour. They are relatively cheap to run as the only replaceable component is the cartridge. They are used in homes and offices where the cost of a colour laser can be prohibitive.

## Laser

These are high-resolution non-impact printers that use a similar process to photocopiers. A laser printer uses a rotating mirror to reflect laser beams onto a photosensitive drum, where the image of the page is converted into an electrostatic charge that attracts and holds the toner (ink). A piece of charged paper is then rolled against the drum to transfer the image, and heat is applied to fuse the toner and paper together to create the final image.

They are reliable and produce excellent quality in both colour and black and white. Toner will frequently need replacing so running costs are high. Drum and fuser unit replacements are also expensive.

Laser printers are used where high-quality fast output is required. Once mainly found in businesses, they are becoming cheaper to buy and are now often used in homes. Colour laser printers are often now found in schools.

### < Activity >

1 Fill in the following table.

| Printer | Description | Advantages | Disadvantages |
| --- | --- | --- | --- |
| Dot-matrix | | | |
| Ink-jet | | | |
| Laser | | | |

2 There are other types of printer. Research the following types of printer:

- Daisy wheel
- Line
- Thermal

There are several factors that need to be taken into account when choosing a printer.

How much output?

What speed is needed?
Is heavy-duty equipment necessary?

Quality of output needed?

Letter quality?
Near letter quality?
Draft?

Location of printer?

How big a footprint can be handled (i.e. what surface area does the printer cover)?
Is noise level important?

Multiple copies needed?

Colour print needed?

## Plotter

A plotter is a mechanical device which produces printout using vector or coordinate graphics. They are used to draw accurate lines diagrams, such as maps and building plans.

There are two types of plotter: the flat-bed plotter where the paper stays still and the pens move, and the drum plotter where the paper is on a drum which moves in one direction while the pens move across it at right angles.

**Figure 2.4** Flat bed and drum plotters

**< Activity >**

1 There are many other data output devices that have not been covered above. Research the following devices, focusing on their purpose:

■ Loudspeaker
■ Lights

2 Research the modem as an input/ouput device.

Identify an appropriate output device for a given situation and justify the choice made

# Identify an appropriate storage device for a given situation and justify the choice made

Storage devices are used to hold data and programs. They are non-volatile (they keep the stored data after the computer has been switched off). Storage capacity is measured in bytes.

| | |
|---|---|
| kilobyte (kB) | 1024 bytes |
| megabyte (MB) | 1024 kB |
| gigabyte (GB) | 1024 MB |
| terabyte (TB) | 1024 GB |

There are many different types of storage device on the market. The main ones are discussed here.

## ■ Floppy disk

This is a portable magnetic disk on which data and programs can be stored. Although housed in a rigid plastic case, the magnetic disk itself is made from flexible plastic (the name is derived from early floppy disks which were in a cardboard sleeve and so were less robust). They have a storage capacity of 1.44 MB and are useful for transferring small files. They are less useful today because of their small storage capacity and many computers, laptops in particular, are now sold without floppy disk drives.

## Hard disks

Hard disks are the main storage devices for a computer and hold the data and programs.

A hard disk uses similar technology as the floppy disk, but with a far greater storage capacity (terabyte disks are available today). It comprises a flat, circular, rigid plate with a surface that can be magnetised on one or both sides and on which data can be stored. The disk is sealed in a case to prevent dirt entering and potentially crashing the drive read/write heads. Hard disk drives can be internal (fixed in the computer) or removable. Portable hard disks allow large amounts of data to be transferred easily between machines (which perhaps are located far apart), and they are often used as external back-up units.

## Optical discs

### CD-ROM
The CD-ROM (compact disc-read only memory) are similar to music CDs. They have a storage capacity of about 700 MB and come in two varieties: a CD-R (recordable) and CD-RW (rewritable). CD-Rs are WORM (Write-Once, Read-Many) storage devices, and once the data has been written to them it is fixed and cannot be removed. CDs that you buy in shops (music, games and program CDs) have already been written. You can buy blank CD-Rs and copy data (write) to your own CDs. CD-RWs can be written to, erased and rewritten many times.

### DVD
The DVD (digital versatile disc) again looks similar to the CD. It has a storage capacity of 4.7 GB (or more) and, like CDs, come in recordable (DVD-R) and rewritable (DVD-RW) forms.

## Tape drive

Tape drives use tape cassettes to store data and have very high storage capacity. They are used for backing up large amounts of data.

## Memory sticks

These are a series of solid state devices. They were originally developed for digital cameras but have found a market replacing the floppy disk. They have a large storage capacity and come in a variety of formats.

< Activity >

**1** Fill in the following table.

| Media | Description | Use | Capacity | Transfer speed | Cost per megabyte |
|---|---|---|---|---|---|
| Floppy disk | | | | | |
| Hard disk | | | | | |
| CD | | | | | |
| DVD | | | | | |
| Tape | | | | | |
| Memory stick | | | | | |

**2** Describe five characteristics that you should be looking for in order to make a comparison between devices when choosing a storage device.

**QUESTIONS**

**1** Describe the different types of CD and their uses.
**2** Describe **three** different criteria to be used to compare memory sticks.
**3** Why is tape suitable to use for backing up data?
**4** How is a removable hard disk different from a portable hard disk?

# Describe specialist hardware devices for physically disabled users: puff-suck switch, foot mouse, eye typer, Braille printers and keyboards, speakers and microphones

There are a number of input and output devices for physically disabled people. There are two main groups of physically disabled who require special devices to use a computer: the visually impaired and the motor impaired.

## Devices to help the visually impaired

A person might have a total loss of vision in one or both eyes (blindness) or a partial loss. Hardware devices that can assist include:

- a Braille keyboard (a keyboard with Braille dots on the keys)
- a microphone (an input device used with voice recognition software)
- a loudspeaker (an output device for hearing signals and text read out for someone who cannot see it)
- a Braille printer (an impact printer that can create Braille on a page).

**< Activity >**

Investigate other hardware devices that have been created for visually impaired people and copy and complete the following table:

| Device | Use |
| --- | --- |
|  |  |

## Devices to help the motor impaired

Motor impairment is a loss or limitation of function in muscle control or movement, or a limitation in mobility. This can include hands that are too large or small for a keyboard, shakiness, arthritis, paralysis and loss of limb.

Hardware devices that can assist include:

- a mouth-stick (a stick to control input controlled with the mouth)
- a puff-suck switch (or blow-suck tube – a tube placed in the mouth and blown/sucked through)
- a tongue-activated joystick (placed in the mouth and manipulated with the tongue)
- an eye-typer (a device that fits onto the muscles around the eye and when the eye is moved a pointer on the screen moves)
- a foot mouse (a mouse that is controlled by the foot)

**Figure 2.5** Helping the impaired

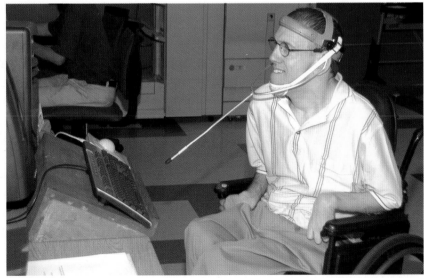

**QUESTIONS**

1 Describe **two** input devices that can be used by a visually impaired person.
2 Describe **two** input devices that can be used by a motor impaired person.
3 Describe how a foot mouse works.
4 Describe how an eye-typer works.

# Describe specialist software for physically disabled users: predictive text, sticky keys, zoom, voice recognition

One way of making the computer more usable for physically disabled individuals is to install specialist software. Some software comes pre-installed with computers.

The most common aid for the visually impaired is a screen reader: a program that reads out a computer display. The screen reader can read text that appears in dialogue boxes, menus, icons, and text-editing windows. The screen reader may output information in Braille, use voice output or use other audio signals to indicate graphics on the screen.

Other tools that can be useful in place of or in addition to a screen reader include:

- Text-to-speech system. This takes written text and outputs it using a speech synthesiser. A text-to-speech system is useful for the visually impaired and in situations where users are not able to view the computer screen at all times, for example when driving.
- Speech-to-text system. This takes the spoken words and inputs them into the computer, where they can be used to run commands or they can be converted to text in a word processor.
- Auditory feedback system. This plays sounds in response to user activity, for example noises for key presses, opening windows and menus, deleting files, etc. This is useful as it confirms an action.
- Screen magnifier. This is a utility that can zoom in on portions of the screen to make it easier for the visually impaired to view information on computer monitors.
- Predictive text. This suggests the required word as the letters are typed so the user does not have to type the whole word.

- Sticky keys. These are useful for people who find it difficult to hold down more than one key at a time. Sticky keys allow keys to be pressed once and the system to act as if is was being held down.

< Activity >

Investigate the software that is pre-installed on a standard computer. Experiment with the software and consider whether it is useful only to physically disabled users or if other people could also benefit.

**QUESTIONS**

1 Explain how software could be used by a visually impaired person to improve their computer use.
2 Describe **two** items of software that could be useful to a motor impaired person.
3 Describe how a voice recognition system works.
4 Explain how the use of specialist software for disabled users could be used to improve computer use for the elderly.

# Describe different types of software (operating systems, user interfaces, utilities, applications software) and give examples of how and where each type of software would be used

Software is a computer program which provides the instructions enabling the computer hardware to work.

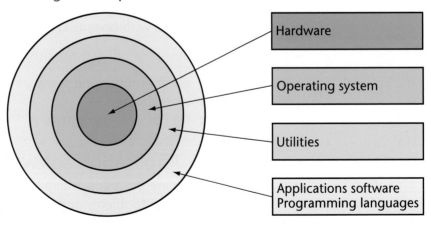

Hardware

Operating system

Utilities

Applications software
Programming languages

**Figure 2.6**

There are various types of software.

## ■ Operating system

The operating system is software that controls the allocation and use of hardware resources, such as memory, central processing unit (CPU) time, hard disk space and peripheral devices (like speakers or a mouse). It performs basic data management tasks, such as recognising input from the keyboard, sending output to the display screen, and keeping track of files and directories on the hard disk.

The operating system is the core software on which programs depend. There are many different operating systems available, for example Microsoft Windows, BEOS, Linux and Unix.

## User interface

The user interface is the means by which the user can interact with an application or operating system.

There are different types of user interface:

- Menu: an on-screen list of options
- Form: an on-screen form in which to type data
- Command line: a space to type instructions
- Natural language: a voice-based interface

A user interface is often termed as being a GUI and a WIMP interface.

A GUI (graphical user interface) is the term for an interface that is based on graphics and pictures rather than text.

A WIMP (Windows Icons Mouse Pointer) interface is a particular type of GUI. Not all GUIs use windows, icons, menus and pointers, but might use one or two of them.

All WIMPs are also GUIs, but not all GUIs are WIMPs.

## Utility

A utility program is a small program that assists in the monitoring and maintaining of the computer system. Many utilities are now included with operating systems.

Examples of utility programs include:

- printer monitoring software
- virus checkers
- file compression software.

## Application software

These are programs that allow the computer to be used to solve particular problems or perform particular tasks for the end user. Application software includes programs such as:

- word processors
- spreadsheets
- databases
- communications (email)
- graphics packages.

< Activity >

1 List as many pieces of software as you can.

2 Using an athletics club as the scenario, copy and complete the following table (an example has already been done). You can use the same type of software more than once.

| Name of software | Type | Use |
|---|---|---|
| Word processor | Application | Writing letters to members letting them know when the next meeting is to be held. |

## QUESTIONS

1 What is the role of the operating system?
2 Identify **two** different types of application software.
3 Describe **two** different user interfaces.
4 What does WIMP stand for?
5 What is a GUI?
6 Describe **two** different utility programmes.
7 How could a library make use of a spreadsheet, database and word processor?

# Describe the characteristics of different styles of user interface (command-based, forms, dialogue, natural language, WIMP) and their appropriate uses

The user interface is the method by which the user communicates with the computer. When deciding which user interface to implement, the situation where it is going to be used and who is going to be using it must be considered.

## Command-based

The user types instructions at a command prompt to control what the computer does. This means that you need to have a good knowledge of the commands and the effect of those commands. It is possible to do a lot of damage to the computer because the operating system can often be controlled directly unlike through a GUI. The screenshot example on page 60 shows the MS-DOS command dir/p typed at the command prompt C:\> to output a directory listing of a computer's C: drive, pausing after each page length is displayed.

**Figure 2.7** A command-based instruction

The commands available will depend on the operating system, but often allow instructions to:

- output a directory listing
- show the difference between two files
- display environment variables.

If the interface is command based only, then it takes up less memory than a GUI and so has the effect of running the commands faster.

A large number of commands have switches. These are parameters (additional commands) that can be added to the end of the main command to slightly change how it operates. In the screenshot example /p is a switch to output the directory one page at a time.

Command-based systems are used by expert users with a good understanding of the operating system. They are useful for running commands which cannot be accessed from a menu or form.

**< Activity >**

Investigate **five** different commands from two different operating systems. Describe what the command does and its syntax, including the switches.

## ■ Forms

A form is a limited area on screen with boxes to fill in.

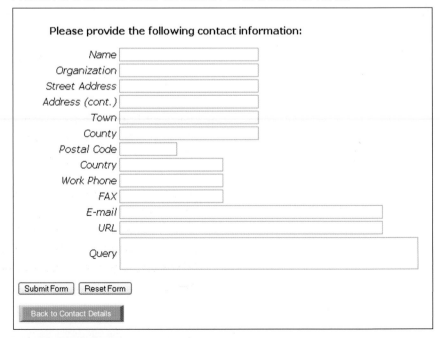

**Figure 2.8** An on-screen form

A form has labels to give help to the user (for example stating what data to type in the box) and spaces to enter data. The latter might be drop-down boxes giving choices or open text boxes for free-form type. The form might also include option buttons to give further choices.

Forms can guide the user through typing relevant information in a structured manner. It can include the default options for the user and give context-based assistance. The data entry boxes can also be validated.

Sometimes an on-screen form is designed to look like a paper-based form. This can make entering data easier.

**< Activity >**

Design a form to be used for entering a customer order when purchasing a car.

Another type of interface which makes use of forms is a dialogue interface. This is one which asks questions and requires a response before continuing. Error messages that appear and must be dealt with are part of a dialogue interface.

**Figure 2.10** A file menu

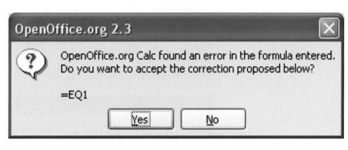

**Figure 2.9** An on-screen error message

## Menus

- Menus are a series of related items that can be selected. Menus are either pop up (when you press a button or key a menu appears next to the cursor) or pull down (when you click a heading the rest of the menu appears below the heading).
- Menus are usually structured. This means that the menu items are categorised by the top word in a pull-down menu which gives an indication of what the menu is about. For example, 'File' contains all aspects to do with the file itself, 'Format' is about changing the appearance.
- Menus can be cascaded, that is one menu leads to another menu. Items on menus can appear faded to show they cannot be used in a particular context.
- Menus can also be context sensitive. Depending on what you are doing within the application, a different set of menus might appear. If you are working with tables you will get a menu for tables and if you are working with pictures you get a picture menu.

- Menus can use a GUI or be text-based.
- Menus are part of a WIMP interface.

---

**< Activity >**

1 Investigate the history of the WIMP interface.

2 The Apple Mac and Microsoft Windows computers both use a WIMP interface. Compare and contrast the interfaces on both types of computer.

---

## Natural language

Natural language interfaces allow the users to use their own language to communicate with the computer. To some extent, this type of interface is still being researched and current offerings are still in their infancy.

There are two main types of natural language interface: spoken and written. Spoken interfaces are typified by voice recognition software which allows you to speak words into a word processor. Typed natural language interfaces include Microsoft Help and Ask.com. Software is also available for tablet PCs and Portable Digital Assistants (PDAs) that recognises handwriting.

When natural language interfaces eventually become common place they will allow users of all abilities to access computers and this will revolutionise ICT.

---

**< Activity >**

Investigate and write a report on the problems of voice recognition and using voice-activated software.

---

**QUESTIONS**

1 Describe **three** advantages of using a command-based interface.
2 Where would the use of a forms interface be appropriate?
3 What are the disadvantages of a natural language voice interface?
4 Describe **three** characteristics of a menu interface.

## Summary

**The difference between hardware and software**
Hardware: something you can touch
Software: the programs used on the computer
Examples: NOT proprietary

**Standardisation and its impact**
Incompatibilities and cost implications

**Input, output and storage devices**
Input: getting data external to the system into the system
   Keyboard
   Mouse
   Graphics tablet
   Scanner
   Digitiser
   Microphone
Output: getting data within the system out of the system
   Printer  Plotter
   Monitor  Speakers
Storage: holding data
   Internal and external hard disk drives
   CD / CD-R / CD-RW / DVD / DVD-R / DVD-RW
   Memory stick
   Tape

**Specialist hardware devices**
Puff-suck switch
Mouth stick
Foot mouse
Eye-typer
Braille printer
Braille keyboard

**Specialist software**
Text-to-speech
Magnifier
Predictive text
Sticky keys

**Different types of software**
Operating system: core software
Utilities: additional programs to make the use of the computer easier
User interface: method by which the user communicates with the computer
Applications software: programs which solve particular problems and replace manual methods

**Characteristics of different user interfaces**
Command line: types commands at a prompt, can use switches, low memory overheads but specialist knowledge required
Forms: structured areas for responses, validated and logical
Menus: drop-down, pop-up and context sensitive, can be part of WIMP
Natural language: written or spoken everyday language, computer translates into commands needed to operate.

## Test 1

A local newspaper has many computers advertised for sale within it.

1 The computers have hardware and software. Describe, with examples, the difference between hardware and software. [4]

2 One of the adverts claims that an advantage of buying a PC from them is that they conform to industry standards. Explain the problems that would be brought about by a lack of standardisation in hardware. [4]

3 Physically disabled users can purchase specialist input devices for the computers. Identify and describe **three** specialist hardware input devices. [6]

4 Describe and state how a home user would make use of **three** different output devices. [6]

5 Identify **two** different utilities that could be found on a PC. For each utility state how it would be used. [4]

6 Describe **two** characteristics of a command line interface. [4]

## Test 2

An employee of an insurance company has recently been given the opportunity to work from home.

1 The software used at home is often different to the software used at work. Describe **two** problems that might arise as a result of this lack of standardisation. [4]

2 The employee has been given a QWERTY keyboard. Give **two** reasons why this is a more appropriate keyboard layout than DVORAK or alphabetical. [4]

3 Identify **three** different input devices that could be used by the employee, and for each one give an example of its use. [6]

4 Describe **two** items of software appropriate for a physically disabled user. [4]

5 How would the employee make use of:
a) a rewritable DVD [2]
b) a memory stick? [2]

6 Identify **three** different types of software found on a computer. [3]

7 Describe **three** different types of interface found on a computer and, for each, give an appropriate use. [9]

# Characteristics of standard applications software and application areas

## Introduction

This chapter covers the characteristics, purposes and uses of the commonly used standard applications software. You will need to make sure that you understand the specific purposes, characteristics and uses of each type. You should also be able to apply your knowledge to a specified scenario.

This chapter covers:

- **Types of software used for basic tasks**
- **Characteristics of applications**
- **Wizards, styles, templates and macros**
- **Design considerations and tailoring of data-entry screens**
- **House style**
- **Master documents and slides**
- **Transfer of data between applications**

## Identify basic tasks that standard/generic software can be readily used for

### Word processor

A word processor is a generic applications package that allows the entry, editing and formatting of text to create a range of documents. Word-processing packages are among the most commonly used computer software. We use the term 'word processing' to mean the activity of writing with the aid of a computer. Writing, when used in association with word processing, is generally used to mean the production of business or personal documents. These documents may include:

- letters
- memos
- reports.

The use of word-processing packages has replaced the use of pen and paper and typewriters in many businesses. These packages enable the user to enter data using a keyboard so that the data appears on the monitor as though on a piece of paper. The data may also be input by speaking into a microphone. The text on the screen can then be formatted to meet the needs of the user, edited, saved and printed.

Most word-processing packages have WYSIWYG (pronounced 'wizzy-wig') features. This means:

**What You See Is What You Get**

WYSIWYG means that the user can be sure that the screen layout will match the printed layout.

## Desktop publishing

Desktop publishing (DTP) packages allow users to combine images and text to create publications.

The main difference between a word-processing package and a DTP package is that of emphasis. A word-processing package focuses on the creation of text-based documents while a DTP package focuses on the manipulation and accurate positioning of graphical objects on the page, including text, to create a composite publication.

A DTP package incorporates specific features to enable the end user to design, create and produce professional looking publications.

Among the publications that can be produced using a DTP package are:

- flyers
- brochures
- posters
- business cards.

There are many similarities between word processing and DTP packages. Many of the features, such as style sheets, wizards, templates and macros, found in a word-processing package are also found in DTP packages, and other packages such as spreadsheets, databases and presentations. However, the options presented to the user are likely to be different and will depend on the package being used.

## Spreadsheet

Spreadsheet packages enable the user to produce both mathematical and financial models, and to produce graphs to diagrammatically represent the data. They display and process data and are capable of performing a wide range of calculations and so are generally used to process numerical data. However, a spreadsheet package can also handle text. They are used to create graphs, to make 'What if...?' calculations and for goal seeking, forecasting (including trend lines) and data pattern analysis. Any task that involves the manipulation of numbers is suitable for a spreadsheet. (Chapter 4 gives more detailed explanations on the use and purpose of spreadsheets.)

## Database

Database packages enable the user to handle data, such as sorting and searching. The data can be split into tables and relationships created between the tables to allow the data to be joined together. The data can be sorted by different methods and different fields – one field, or more than one, as required. (Chapter 5 gives more detailed explanations on the use and purpose of databases.)

Spreadsheet and database packages can be linked with a word-processing package to complete the process of mail merge. The process of mail merge is discussed in Chapter 6.

## Web authoring

Web authoring, the creation of web pages, can be achieved through the use of a web-authoring package or by using a word-processing package and converting the document produced to a web page. Web-authoring software has built-in functions to enable well-designed web pages to be created with a variety of features to meet the needs of the users.

The user interface of web-authoring software is similar to that of a standard applications package but there are some functions that are different, for example changing the font style. Some technical ability is therefore needed and training may be required to use the software.

Web pages are visual representations of code, generally HTML (Hypertext Mark-up Language). Most web-authoring software packages do not require the user to write any code as pages are created using a graphical interface where objects are dragged and dropped on to a page template. It is then possible to access and amend the code, to tidy it up and make it more efficient, if the user has sufficient knowledge.

The majority of web-authoring software packages are aimed at the general user. Templates are available in the packages (usually an outline website structure that just requires details to be added) and wizards (a series of questions/dialogue boxes that take the user through a procedure one step at a time).

The user can determine the final look and structure of a web page by formatting. Most web-authoring software packages offer formatting facilities such as:

- colour options for background, text, lines and boxes
- font and point size options for text
- the positioning of objects on the web page and layout items such as columns, tables and forms.

As well as text and layout items, web pages contain graphical objects. A web-authoring software package will allow the user to access these objects, for example by providing a clipart library. The user can then import these graphics into a web page and manipulate them, so they meet the needs of the web page and its users. Other objects, such as animation, video and sound clips, can also be used in the creation of web pages.

Web pages normally contain links to other pages within the site or to other related and linked sites. These are hyperlinks. When the user activates these hyperlinks, a request is sent for the page to be downloaded. The web-authoring software package will allow the user to create and add new links to their page(s). The hyperlinks may show the URL (Uniform Resource Locator) that is being activated or may be activated by clicking a graphic.

Many web pages allow user interaction. The web page may contain an interactive form. This form may allow the user of the web page to, for example, register their details or place an order. This facility requires the use of CGI (Common Gateway Interface) script. Most web-authoring software packages will enable the creator of the web page to produce forms without having to write any code.

Another approach to creating web pages is to use a standard application package and use the built-in facility to convert the document to a web page. This is a quick and simple method of distributing a document on a website, and it requires very little knowledge of web authoring and HTML. Also, as very little technical ability is needed and it is likely that a standard applications package will be used, no training will be involved.

The pages are created in the standard applications package, saved using the web page option and then viewed using a browser. This screenshot shows the option of saving a document as a web page.

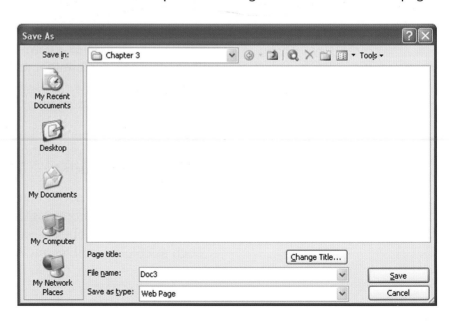

**Figure 3.1** Saving as html

Some of the benefits and limitations of using web-authoring software rather than other applications are given in the next table.

| Advantages | Disadvantages |
|---|---|
| ■ The exact effects required can be developed.<br>■ Wizards for specific tasks are built in, for example creating HTML tables.<br>■ WYSIWYG. Some web-authoring software also allows the representation of different screen sizes and different browsers.<br>■ Some packages include website management tools, for example to help the user to check versions of pages.<br>■ A site manager can be used – if the name of a page is changed then all links to that page within the site are automatically updated.<br>■ Specialist software, code samples/scripting language, can be integrated and tested. These can then be integrated into other packages within the authoring software, for example you can integrate Adobe Flash and Fireworks into Adobe Dreamweaver.<br>■ Editing of the code can be done by either using the WYSIWYG feature or editing the HTML directly. | ■ Some degree of knowledge and technical ability are required as not all concepts from word processing will apply (e.g. changing the size of the font).<br>■ Often more expensive to purchase than a standard applications packages. |

Some of the benefits and limitations of using standard application software rather than web-authoring software are given in the next table.

| Advantages | Disadvantages |
|---|---|
| ■ Very little technical knowledge is required. If a standard word processor can be used then a web page can be easily created and saved using the automatic conversion facility.<br>■ It is likely that a standard applications package is already installed, so there will not be an additional cost. | ■ It is very difficult to get the page to look exactly how it is wanted, as this method of creating web pages is not true WYSIWYG.<br>■ The code that is created is 'messy'. It is bloated and often not very good or compatible with all browsers.<br>■ Available tool sets are limited – there is likely to be no site management or uploading tool, very few wizards and no tools to assist in script generation. |

## QUESTIONS

**1** What are the advantages of using a word processor to create web pages?

**2** What are the advantages of using web-authoring software to create web pages?

Identify basic tasks that standard/generic software can be readily used for

**69**

## Presentation

Presentation software can be used to produce presentations to be shown, on printed acetate or by using a computer and projector, to a target audience. They can be for kiosk applications or presentations for speeches. They can run without intervention on a timer or with user intervention. Presentation software, its use and purpose is discussed in Chapter 6.

# Describe the characteristics of a range of applications

There are many common applications that are used in business, commerce and education. The characteristics of each of these are generally specific to the task for which they are used.

## School administration systems

These are systems used within schools and colleges to assist in the day-to-day running of the establishment. Administration can be related to students or staff and it has three distinct features:

- A database to hold records – the system must:
  - be able to store students' personal details such as next of kin, doctor, mode of transport to school
  - have a unique identification number, a UPN (Unique Pupil Number), that follows a student through their school career.
- A facility to record student marks – the system must:
  - record subject marks against students
  - store historical data against the student
  - prepare reports based on students' results.
- An attendance monitoring facility – the system must be able to:
  - record student attendance, absence and type of absence
  - summarise attendance
  - produce lists of outstanding absences
  - produce required averages for school documentation.

## Stock control system

This is a system that knows how much of each item is in stock, when orders are due and how much stock is required on certain days. If necessary it can order stock and update the stock records when the stock is delivered. It therefore needs to have links to suppliers. Many organisations have moved over to JIT (Just In Time) ordering. If a lot of stock is being held that stock needs to have been paid for and it is not producing profit until it is sold. JIT ordering works on the principle of keeping the stock that is held to a minimum and through the use of ICT and logistics (transportation systems) to have the materials delivered either on the day they are required, or, at the very least, the day before.

There are two main users of stock control: shops and manufacturers. Shops try to keep their shelves stocked but they do not want too much, particularly if the goods are perishable. Stock control systems for the shops need to be linked to the sales system to try to identify trends. They also need to know of special offers and other events that may increase sales. Manufacturing stock control systems need to know all the components that are required to create a product. They need to be linked into the ordering system so that they can see how much stock they require to meet demand. They also, as with the shops, need to be linked to the sales so that they can identify trends and prepare for surges in sales, for example Christmas and forthcoming promotions. The system must:

- have a list of all stock items and the suppliers
- have a list of all components for the item if the stock is manufactured
- know the minimum and maximum stock levels
- work out how much to order
- know the delivery times for stock items that have been ordered
- have links to the orders database
- update the stock records when deliveries are received
- link with the budgeting system
- store previous sales figures
- predict stock requirements based on previous sales
- have manual override on items being ordered.

## Booking systems

There are many different things that can be booked, for example rail tickets, theatre tickets, cinema tickets, doctor's appointments, etc. There are three main ways of booking: the telephone, the Internet and by person/post/fax. Booking systems require an event, a person and a date and time. Booking via the Internet is becoming more popular. The combination of emails to notify individuals of events, with direct links to booking systems and the ability of the online systems to retain settings, means that mailshots can be tailored to individual choice.

A booking system must allow the user to:

- select a time and date
- select an event
- specify number (adults, children)
- check availability of event for time, date and number
- check price of selected booking
- change options
- confirm and pay (via email or booking number).

What are the advantages and disadvantages of booking via the Internet as opposed to in person/by post?

## Route-finders

These are pieces of software that allow the user to enter a variety of information about the starting and destination places and will plot a route between the two. This can be done prior to the journey and printed out, requested and printed from an organisation's website or through the use of in-car navigation systems. With the in-car system, using GPS, it is possible to change the route while in the middle of it, for instance if during a journey the driver becomes aware that a road is blocked, the route can be changed to avoid the road. Some new systems can automatically receive the traffic information and change the route accordingly without driver input. The system must enable the user to:

- specify the location you are leaving from and going to
- specify places and roads you want to pass through or avoid
- specify type of journey, for example scenic, fastest or cheapest
- save and print a route in a number of formats, for example text and maps.

Compare the use of a software-based route finder with using a map.

## Customer records/accounts

All companies have customers and need to keep records of them and finances. The records need to include contact details and ordering details. Invoicing and accounts for the customer need to be accurate so they can be audited. Customer systems for storing records and accounts are extremely common and essential to the running of a business. If any records are incorrect, then customers are likely to lose confidence and go elsewhere. The Data Protection Act (1998) has implications with regard to storing customer information and how that information is used. The system must enable the user to:

- store contact details of customers
- have a unique ID for each customer
- store orders with a unique number
- store orders against customers
- generate invoices / credit notes for orders
- store customer payments against the customer and the invoice
- produce customer statements and outstanding invoices
- produce a list of products available
- handle discounts and returns.

< Activity >

Investigate the following common applications, giving a description of their use and the tasks which they should enable the user to complete:

a) Online banking

b) Travel timetables

c) Online training systems.

# Describe the purpose and characteristics of wizards, templates, styles and macros describing the advantages and disadvantages of their use

Most standard/generic applications packages have features that can assist the user. The purpose and characteristics of these features are, generally, the same but the use of the features will vary depending on which package they are in.

## Wizards

A wizard facility helps the user to produce the final product, which might be, for example, a document, a presentation master slide or a database. The wizard found in each application will present options to the user which apply to that application.

The next screenshot shows the options that can be selected and completed by the user using a wizard to produce a letter using a word-processing package.

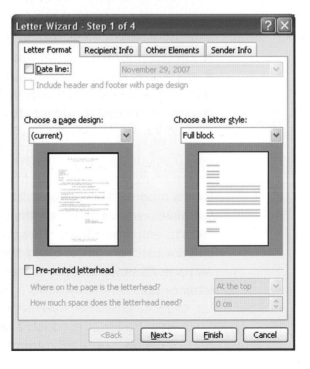

**Figure 3.2** A letter wizard

A wizard offers the user a range of screens where they can make choices and enter information. Having completed all the wizard stages, the user is presented with the completed document (or other requirement) containing the information in a pre-set format. A wizard helps a user who is unfamiliar with a particular task, however there are a limited number of options available in wizards. This may result in the end result produced by the wizard not meeting the exact needs of the user, but it can often be close needing only minor editing/formatting to get it exactly right.

There are a number of advantages and disadvantages to using wizards.

| Advantages | Disadvantages |
|---|---|
| ■ They save time for the inexperienced user.<br>■ They ensure that no important information is forgotten.<br>■ Standard formats can be used.<br>■ There is an element of user friendliness. | ■ There is no individuality to the end result. All documents can end up looking exactly the same.<br>■ The end result may not fully meet the needs of the user.<br>■ It is harder for documents to be tailored to meet the needs of the targeted audience. |

**< Activity >**

Investigate the wizards available in the database, presentation and DTP packages available at your centre. Describe the advantages and disadvantages of using the wizard in each package.

## ■ Templates

A template provides standard pre-set layouts and formats. For example, in a word-processing package a template will determine the basic structure and settings of a document and includes:

■ character formatting (font size, colour, type of font, etc.)
■ page formatting (margins, size, layout, etc.)
■ text insert (standard words, date, time, etc.)
■ graphics inserts (standard logo, position, etc.).

Every word-processed document is based on a template: when a new blank document is created the package's pre-set template option is selected by default. Many word-processing packages also have a range of templates which can be selected by the user. The templates cover a range of different documents including memos, reports, letters and faxes. These templates have pre-set formats and the user can simply insert the text required. The screenshot on page 75 shows the pre-set templates available for producing a letter or fax.

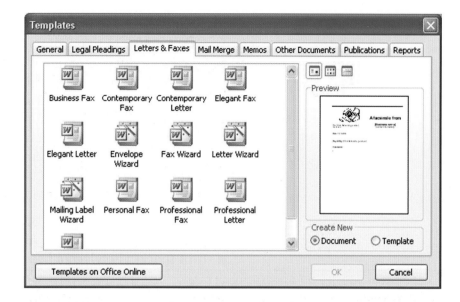

**Figure 3.3** Templates

**QUESTION**

Identify **three** features of a word-processed document that can be set by the template.

In presentation software a template will specify the colour scheme as well as the master slide and master title slide layouts with custom formatting and fonts. These are all designed to create a particular look. When a design template is applied to a presentation, the master slide, master title slide and colour scheme of the new template replace the existing design of the presentation. When a design template is applied, each new slide will follow the same custom look.

Most presentation software comes with a wide variety of professionally designed templates, but a design template can also be created. If an original design template is created then it can be saved as a template to be used again.

A variety of pre-designed colour schemes are also available in most presentation software packages. These are sets of balanced colours designed for use as the main colours of a slide presentation. They detail the colours to be used for text, background, fill and accents. Each colour in the pre-designed scheme will be used automatically for the appropriate element on the slide. A colour scheme can be selected for an individual slide or for an entire presentation. When a pre-set design template is applied to a presentation then the presentation software will offer a set of pre-designed colour schemes made to go with that design template.

**QUESTION**

Describe the disadvantages of using design templates in the production of a presentation.

## Styles

Styles are similar to templates and are used to set out layouts. Styles can also be referred to as master documents. Styles usually relate to word-processed documents or those produced using a desktop publishing (DTP) package. Styles refer to complete documents. The use of a style ensures that all documents produced conform to a pre-determined layout yet still give the producer of the documents some scope for creativity. For example, a company may decide that its newsletter should be simply styled with:

- headings in Arial, font size 32, bold and centred
- body text in two columns, Arial, font size 13 and justified
- 14pt spacing between a heading and the following text.

The styles used in a book can be extensive, ensuring consistency throughout all formatting features.

Here are some advantages and disadvantages of using pre-determined styles.

| Advantages | Disadvantages |
|---|---|
| ■ Documents and other material are produced to a consistent house style.<br>■ Different people can work on parts of the same documents but, because of the use of styles, the end results will be consistent and conform to the house style. | ■ Someone needs to develop the style before it can be set as a template. |

**< Activity >**

Collect a range of business documents. Describe the styles which have been used and whether they make the document 'fit for purpose'.

## Macros

A macro is a set of stored commands that can be replayed by pressing a combination of keys or by pressing a button. A macro enables the user to automate tasks that are performed on a regular basis. This is done by recording a series of commands to be run whenever that task needs to be performed. The complexity of the macro is only limited by the task requirements and the ability of the programmer.

For example, in a word-processing package a macro may be recorded to add a name as a header to documents.

In a spreadsheet package macros can be used to give additional functionality to the spreadsheet and increase the customisation of the interface. The macro can be attached to a button, for example, to open a worksheet or to initiate an event (such as a cell becoming a particular value). Some examples include:

- moving to a different part of the spreadsheet or a different worksheet
- running a calculation
- closing the application
- printing the application
- adding a header and footer to the spreadsheet.

Once the macro has been recorded then it can be run by pressing the keys assigned when it was recorded. Macros can also be activated through the use of a button placed on the toolbar. A macro will only run when the application program to which it is associated is being used. A macro will not run on its own or with a different application program.

Some advantages and disadvantage of macros are given in the next table.

| Advantages | Disadvantages |
| --- | --- |
| ■ A repetitive task can be performed using a simple instruction (e.g. key press, button click).<br>■ Errors may be reduced as the instructions included in the macro are run automatically and are the same every time.<br>■ Inexperienced users can perform complex tasks by using a pre-recorded macro. | ■ Errors may occur if the conditions when the macro is run are different from those when it was recorded.<br>■ Users must know and remember the key combination to run the macro.<br>■ Inflexible – the macro may not do precisely what the user wants.<br>■ If the macro is run from a different starting point than intended then it may go wrong.<br>■ To correct any errors the user must have some knowledge of how the macro was recorded. |

### QUESTION

What are the advantages of using macros?

# Describe the design considerations for tailored data-entry screens

Data-entry screens can be tailored to meet the needs of the end-user. This can be in either a database or a spreadsheet package. The type of application being used to enter the data is irrelevant – the design considerations stay the same.

When a data-entry screen is being designed there are some aspects that must be considered:

- A consistent layout should be used which should follow the house-style or corporate image.

- The text should be easily readable. The colours used should be carefully selected so they do not clash and obscure the text. The font, style and size should be chosen for clarity.
- Graphics and animation should be selected to meet the needs of the users. Any images selected should be fit for purpose with their number kept to a minimum.
- Any help messages should be useful, clear and in simple language.
- The on-screen information should be presented in a logical order and flow down the screen.
- The interface should be easy to learn and use. This will minimise the training required and the amount of instructions that have to be remembered by the users.
- Clearly marked exits should be given in clear language. Commonly used functions should be given a shortcut/button/menu option.
- The expertise of the users must also be considered.

In database packages, by the nature of the application, the general interface provided is often not user friendly enough for the average user to complete the required tasks. This is more of an issue in databases than in other applications.

The end-user's ability and the task they will be doing must be prime considerations when designing and creating any data-entry screen.

## Design considerations for forms

The interface for a standard database is aimed at the developer not the user. The implication is that the developer will use the tools available to build an appropriate interface for the user. This is done through the use of forms. These forms can be created:

- within the application
- using web-based forms
- using third-party programs, such as a programming language, to access and manipulate the data.

When designing and creating forms there are several elements that need to be taken into consideration.

### Consistency

If there are several forms, then the user will expect buttons that do similar things to be in the same place and look the same. If a date is to be entered in several places then the format it is entered in must be the same every time.

If the data being entered into the computer form comes from a paper form then there needs to be consistency between them: they need to look the same. This will help the user and speed up the data entry time.

The interface should also be consistent with other applications. Menus, labels and interface actions should correspond with the user's idea of what will happen and their previous experience. This will assist the usability and reduce the time it takes the user to learn how to use the interface.

### Relevance

The interface should not ask for redundant material. It should require the minimum of input and user actions. The information provided on-screen should not be excessive. It should be concise and useful.

Every task should require the minimum of keystrokes to complete. This is linked to memory and learning.

### Supportiveness

There needs to be a balance between too little and too much information being given to the user. The user does not want redundant information but they need enough to feel supported in the task.

### Visual and audible cues

There needs to be feedback, audible and visual, to confirm actions. The user needs some reassurance that what they are doing is correct or has been accepted by the system. This can be done through visual cues (e.g. by messages, green lights at correct responses, etc). If they have made a mistake, error messages should be displayed informing the user of the error and how to solve it. There could also be audible cues (e.g. beeps).

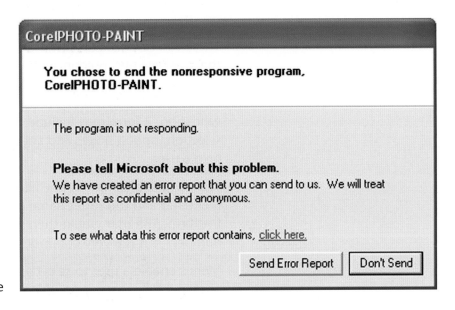

**Figure 3.4** Example error message

**Intuitiveness**

It is unlikely that the user will use the system only once, so the interface needs to be designed in such a way that the user can remember what they have done. This is linked to naturalness – the interface must appear appropriate for completing the task and reflect the user's knowledge and understanding. If the user can relate to items within the design, this will help them use the interface.

# Describe how standard/generic applications software can be tailored using buttons, forms, form controls, menus and templates and give examples of the use of each

An interface can be tailored to meet a user's needs through the custom use of buttons, forms, menus and macros.

## Buttons

These can be used to take the user to a specified page or to run a selected action/command. A macro can be run when the user clicks a button. For example, a command button can be added to a database user interface to run a search, or to sort or edit data. A button can also display pictures or text.

## Forms

These can be used to assist in the entry of data. A form can give the user help and guidance on what data should be input. Instructions to the user and error messages can be included on forms. It is also possible to include on the form some data validation. A form may include drop-down boxes for data selection, option boxes and automatic fill-in boxes, which can help a user.

An example of an automatic fill-in box might be when a postcode is entered and the street name and town automatically appear on the form. The user would then simply have to input the house number. This is a very common feature in business today.

Menus enable a user to select actions. There are three main types of menu: full-screen, pop-up and pull-down. Each type of menu gives the user choices of actions in a particular context.

Form controls are generally used to increase the interactivity with the user and improve usability. Here are some of the form controls that might be available.

Button: the user can click the button to start an event. The button can be linked to a macro.

Check box: the user can tick an option, for example an invoice has been paid.

Group/Frame: Form controls can be grouped together. For example, if you have two related options buttons, by grouping them you can make them into choice buttons so only one can be selected at a time.

Option button: options can be selected and given values.

Text box: this allows text to be written and picked up and used in the application.

Combo box: items can be selected from a drop-down box.

List box: this gives a list of items – either single or multiple items can be selected.

Image: a picture can be inserted.

Label: instruction labels or titles can be added.

### QUESTIONS

1 Identify **three** different controls that can be used to customise the user interface.
2 What are the disadvantages of customising a user interface?
3 What are the benefits of using buttons and forms to customise a user interface?

# Explain the advantages and disadvantages of tailoring standard/generic applications software

There are benefits and problems with tailoring applications software.

The benefits include the simplification of user data entry. This leads to fewer mistakes by the user. By using forms, buttons, menus and macros the time taken to enter data can also be speeded up, users can become more productive, and the data entered can be validated. Complexity is removed, which simplifies the interface for novice users.

The main problem with customising a user interface is the level of technical knowledge required to create and test the interface. If changes are required, for example to meet the evolving needs of the business or organisation, then this may take time. If the software on which the interface is built is upgraded then there is no guarantee that the interface will still perform as required. If a problem occurs with the interface or an option is not available on the button or menu then the users may not be able to complete the tasks.

# Explain why an organisation needs a consistent house style

**Figure 3.5** Well-known logos

House-style or corporate image refers to a company or organisation's standard method of presentation of documents and other forms of communicating information. A house style is a set of rules followed on all documents sent out by a company or organisation to maintain a consistent appearance. The public will become familiar with an organisation's 'look' and will recognise it immediately. A company will pay a team to design a consistent house style.

Logos are part of a house style. Many companies are immediately recognisable by their logo.

Templates and macros can be set up to make it easy to use a house style, so headed paper always shows a logo and specific colour schemes, fonts and other layout features are applied on all a company's documents.

A house style template can also mean that it is less likely that important information will be missed off documents. Different people can work on parts of the same document and use the same style and templates. This allows the integration of several documents from different teams to be integrated into a final document or presentation.

# Describe how master documents/slides, style sheets and templates can be used to create a consistent house style

A consistent house style can be maintained through the use of master documents/slides, style sheets and templates. This will, as discussed in the previous section, enable a company or organisation to maintain their house style while different people work on the production of the document or presentation.

## Master documents/slide

In presentation software, a master slide enables a team of people to work on the same presentation separately. When the presentation is collated, all the elements of the presentation follow exactly the same format. The master slide will show:

- the theme to be used for the presentation
- the position of any graphics to be shown on each slide in the presentation (e.g. a company logo)
- the position of any information which must appear on each slide, such as the date, slide number and any footer/header text.

The master slide also controls certain text formatting (the 'master text'), such as font type, size, and colour, as well as background colour and certain special effects, such as shadowing and bullet style. Objects appear on slides in the same location as they do on the master slide.

The master slide contains text placeholders and placeholders for footers, such as the date, time and slide number. When a global change is needed (i.e. a change to all the slides in the presentation), each slide does not have to be changed individually. The change is made on the master slide and the presentation software automatically updates the existing slides and applies the changes to any new slides added to the presentation. The formatting of the text can also be changed on the master slide by selecting the text in the placeholders and making the changes required. For example if the colour of the placeholder text is changed to blue, the corresponding text on the existing and any new slides will be changed to blue automatically.

The master slide can be used to:

- add a graphic
- change the background theme
- adjust the size of the placeholders
- change font style, size and colour.

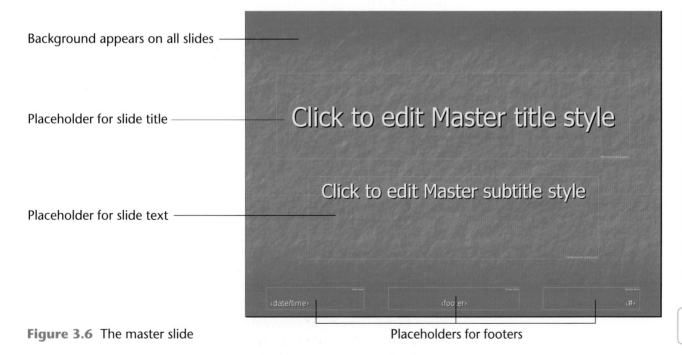

Background appears on all slides

Placeholder for slide title

Click to edit Master title style

Click to edit Master subtitle style

Placeholder for slide text

‹date/time›     ‹footer›     ‹#›

**Figure 3.6** The master slide

Placeholders for footers

It is possible for a team to work on the development of a presentation. By using templates and master slides, a team can work individually on different parts of the presentation and then collate their work once it is finished.

| QUESTION |
|---|
| What is a master slide? |

In a word-processing package, a master document is a collection or set of separate files or sub-documents. A master document can be used to set up and manage a multipart document, such as this book or a company report, that has several sections or chapters. The master document can be used to organise and manage a long document by separating it into smaller manageable sections or chapters. These are known as sub-documents. This enables several different people within an organisation to work on a long document and still maintain a consistent house style.

By using a master document a table of contents, index, references and headers and footers can be created for all sub-documents. Once created, the master document also lets the authors:

- expand or collapse sub-documents or change views to show or hide detail
- quickly change the structure of the document by adding, removing, combining, splitting, renaming, and re-arranging sub-documents.

The template used for the master document can control the styles used when the entire document is being viewed or printed. Different templates, or different settings within the templates, can be used for the master document and for individual sub-documents.

As any changes are made to the sub-documents these are automatically updated in the master document. This means that if any changes have to be made to part of a company report then the specific sub-section can be changed without having to recreate the whole document.

## Style sheets

Style sheets are similar to templates and are used to set out the layout of documents. Style sheets can also be referred to as master documents. Style sheets can relate to word-processed documents or those produced using a desktop publishing (DTP) package. Style sheets are very similar to paragraph styles except that they refer to complete documents. The use of a style sheet ensures that all documents produced conform to a pre-determined layout yet still give the producer of the documents some scope for creativity. For example a company may decide that the company newsletter should be formatted with:

- headings in Arial, font size 32, bold and centred
- body text in two columns, Arial, font size 13 and justified.

Some benefits and limitations of using pre-determined paragraph styles and style sheets are listed in this table.

| Advantages | Disadvantages |
| --- | --- |
| <ul><li>All company documents are produced to a consistent house style, making them recognisable.</li><li>Different people can work on parts of the same documents, but the end results will be consistent and conform to the house style.</li></ul> | <ul><li>All documents can end up looking exactly the same.</li><li>It is harder to tailor documents to meet the needs of the targeted audience.</li><li>Designers need to be paid to develop a corporate style.</li></ul> |

## Templates

A template provides standard pre-set layouts and formats. For example, in a word-processing package a template will determine the basic structure and settings of a document and includes:

- character formatting (font size, colour, type of font, etc.)
- page formatting (margins, size, layout, etc.)
- text insert (standard words, date, time, etc.)
- graphics inserts (standard logo, position, etc.).

Every word-processed document is based on a template: when a new blank document is created the package's pre-set template option is selected by default. Many word-processing packages also have a range of templates which can be selected by the user. The templates cover a range of different documents including memos, reports, letters and faxes. These templates have pre-set formats and the user can simply insert the text required. The screenshot below shows the pre-set templates available for producing a letter or fax.

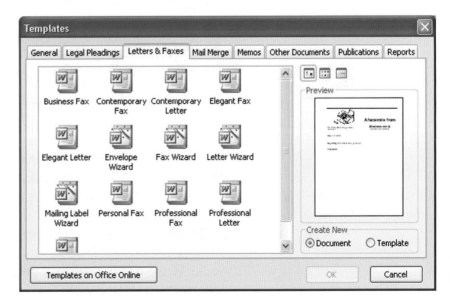

**Figure 3.7** Letter and fax templates

In presentation software a template will specify the colour scheme as well as the master slide and master title slide layouts with custom formatting and fonts. These are all designed to create a particular look. When a design template is applied to a presentation, the master slide, master title slide and colour scheme of the new template replace the existing design of the presentation. When a design template is applied, each new slide will follow the same custom look.

Most presentation software comes with a wide variety of professionally designed templates, but a design template can also be created. If an original design template is created then it can be saved as a template to be used again.

A variety of pre-designed colour schemes are also available in most presentation software packages. These are sets of balanced colours designed for use as the main colours of a slide presentation. They detail the colours to be used for text, background, fill and accents. Each colour in the pre-designed scheme will be used automatically for the appropriate element on the slide. A colour scheme can be selected for an individual slide or for an entire presentation. When a pre-set design template is applied to a presentation then the presentation software will offer a set of pre-designed colour schemes made to go with that design template.

# Describe how to import/export files between standard/generic applications with no common format

Output from different software providers is often saved in different formats. Different applications from the same provider will also save the files in different formats. This is because different file types are suited to different applications. For example, Microsoft uses the doc file extension for word-processed documents, the xls extension for spreadsheets, and the mdb extension for databases, but, respectively, OpenOffice uses the odt, ods and odb extensions.

Another reason for having different file types is that operating systems recognise the file extensions and associate them with particular programs. This ensures the correct program is opened if a user clicks a file.

Knowing the file extension or the type of file can help when searching for files. For example to search for a letter saved in Microsoft Word, the user can start by searching for all files with a doc extension (*.doc).

If data is saved in one application but the user needs to use it in a different application then the data will need to be converted. The applications may be completely different (e.g. from a word-processed document to a spreadsheet file), they may be the same type of application (e.g from Microsoft Word to Corel WordPerfect), or they may be different versions of the same application (e.g from Microsoft Word 2003 to Word 2007). Files can also be converted across different computer systems (e.g. from PC to Apple Mac).

Some file types are universally recognised:

- txt and rtf (rich text format) for documents
- CSV (comma separated variable) and TSV (tab separated variable) for spreadsheets or tables of data
- dbf and CSV for databases.

If these file types are used to save the file then it is easier to share the data across similar applications.

There are two standard procedures for converting files from one format to another. For example, a file saved in Package A needs to be read in Package B.

Option 1: Package A can save the file in Package B's format.
Procedure: 1 Open the file in Package A.
2 Save as or export to the Package B format.
3 Open in Package B and save.

Option 2: Package A cannot save to Package B's format. In this case, in step 2, the file should be saved to a different format common to both A and B, that is one that Package A can export (save) to and Package B can import from (open).

---

**QUESTIONS**

1 Why are there so many different file types?
2 How can a file from one software package be converted so it can be read by another software package?

---

# Explain the needs of different users of standard/generic applications software

Different users need different things from the software they use. For example, a secretary, a translator and a technical author will have very different requirements for a word processor.

A secretary will be working with many different people and many documents, and so will need a wide range of fonts, a spelling and grammar checking facility and templates. Functions that are commonly used will need to be easily available. The secretary is likely to need to keep copies of all letters and to send out mailings using a mail merge facility.

A translator will take a document from one language and convert it to another language. The translator will need a language specific dictionary with the ability to insert specialist characters.

A technical author will need a technical dictionary and thesaurus, automatic section numbering and indexing, specialist graphics, the facility to import and export, and the facility to automatically format work into a report style.

These are only three examples of different users of generic software. There are many more.

---

**< Activity >**

Identify three users of one other standard/generic applications package. For each user define the features they will need in the software.

---

## Summary

**Standard application/generic software**
Word-processing
    Letter writing
    Memos
    Reports
Desktop publishing (DTP)
    Flyers
    Brochures
    Posters
    Business cards
Spreadsheet
    Graphs
    Modelling data – mathematical and objects
    Forecasting
Database
    Handling data – searching and sorting
Web page authoring
    Producing web pages
Presentation
    Create slides – acetates or electronic

**Application areas**
School administration and teaching systems
Stock control
Booking systems
Online training systems
Timetabling and route finding systems
Customer records systems
Online banking systems

**Characteristics and purposes**
Wizards
Styles
Templates
Macros

**Design considerations**
Consistent layout/house style
Font style, font size
Colours
Error messages
Flow of information required
Validation of information
On-screen help (e.g. pop-ups and clear exits)

**Customising applications**
Buttons
Forms
Form controls
Macros

## House style
Recognition by clients and customers
Pre-defined colours/font style and size
Consistency across all company documentation
   Achieved by using:
      Master documents
      Master slides
Style sheets
Templates

## Transferring files
To transfer a file from Package A (the source) to Package B (the destination):
1 Open the file in Package A.
2 Save as or export to Package B's format.
3 Open the file in Package B.
Alternatively, if Package A cannot save the file in the destination format, then in step 2 save in a format that is common to both the source and the destination, so Package B can open it.
Sometimes, steps 1 and 2 can be missed out, as the destination software can be set to open the source format directly.

**Different users of standard/generic applications packages have different needs.**

## Test 1
A company has recently introduced a telephone ordering system.

1  Describe **three** design considerations that should be taken into account when designing data-entry screens to input customers' orders.   [6]

2  The data-entry screens are to follow the company house style. Explain what is meant by house style.   [4]

3  A stock-control system is to be linked to the telephone ordering system. Describe the characteristics of a stock control system.   [6]

4  Describe how a master document could be used during the production of the user guide for the telephone ordering system.   [4]

## Test 2
A company selling antique furniture is updating the systems it currently uses.

1  The company logo is saved using a graphics package. Describe how this logo could be imported to a word-processing package without using cut/copy and paste.   [4]

2  Explain why it is important to have the company logo on every document produced by the company.   [4]

3  The owner of the company uses a route finding system when he is travelling in his car. Describe the characteristics of a route finding system.   [6]

4  A template is used to create a brochure for the company. Describe **two** advantages and **one** disadvantage of using a template to create the brochure.   [6]

## Introduction

This chapter covers the basic concepts relating to spreadsheets and how spreadsheets can be used. You will need to make sure you understand the use of spreadsheets in a variety of situations and are able to apply this knowledge.

This chapter covers:

- Characteristics of modelling software
- Variables, formulae, functions and rules
- Worksheets, workbooks, rows, columns, cells and ranges
- Absolute and relative referencing

## Describe the characteristics of modelling software and give reasons why a model might be used

There are two main types of modelling used in ICT:

- Modelling of objects (rooms, buildings, cars, etc.)
- Mathematical modelling (financial, calculations, spreadsheets, etc.)

### ■ Modelling of objects

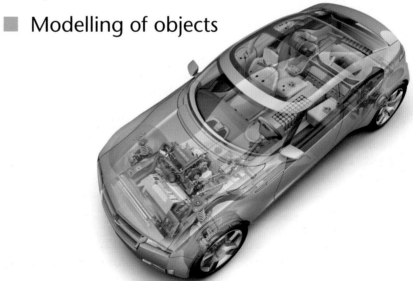

**Figure 4.1** Computer modelling

Computer models allow you to create a virtual representation of the item within the computer. You can model large items such as buildings and look at the effect on them from different external influences, for example earthquakes, fire or explosions.

It is possible to see different layers: external view, electrical wiring view, basic frame and so on. The model can be rotated so that different aspects can be viewed. It is possible to zoom in on a particular part, for example in a model of a vehicle, individual nuts and bolts can be viewed. How individual components will react to different circumstances can also be seen.

An important characteristic of software used to model objects is the ability to ask questions of the model: to change the components and see how it reacts, to move an item and try a different design. The effects can be gauged at the touch of a button, without having to take the risk of building the real thing.

## ■ Mathematical modelling

| | A | B | C | D | E | F | G | |
|---|---|---|---|---|---|---|---|---|
| 1 | | | | | | | | |
| 2 | | | | | | | | |
| 3 | | | | | | | | |
| 4 | | SA income | | | | | UK Savings | |
| 5 | Month 0 | ZAR 27,840.00 | | | | | | |
| 6 | Month 1 | ZAR 3,652.00 | ZAR 27,000.00 | to UK at | 14 | ZAR/£ | £1,928.57 | |
| 7 | Month 2 | ZAR 6,464.00 | | | saving at | 5.5% | £1,656.04 | |
| 8 | Month 3 | ZAR 9,276.00 | | | | 5.5% | £1,382.52 | |
| 9 | Month 4 | ZAR 12,088.00 | | | | 5.5% | £1,107.98 | |
| 10 | Month 5 | ZAR 14,900.00 | | | | 5.5% | £832.45 | |
| 11 | Month 6 | ZAR 17,712.00 | | | | 5.5% | £555.90 | |
| 12 | Month 7 | ZAR 524.00 | ZAR 20,000.00 | to UK at | 14 | 5.5% | £1,706.91 | |
| 13 | Month 8 | ZAR 3,336.00 | | | | 5.5% | £1,433.57 | |
| 14 | Month 9 | ZAR 6,148.00 | | | | 5.5% | £1,159.22 | |
| 15 | Month 10 | ZAR 8,960.00 | | | | 5.5% | £883.87 | |
| 16 | Month 11 | ZAR 11,772.00 | | | | 5.5% | £607.52 | |
| 17 | Month 12 | ZAR 14,584.00 | | | | 5.5% | £330.14 | |
| 18 | Month 13 | ZAR 396.00 | ZAR 17,000.00 | to UK at | 14 | 5.5% | £1,266.04 | |
| 19 | Month 14 | ZAR 3,208.00 | | | | 5.5% | £991.08 | |
| 20 | Month 15 | ZAR 6,020.00 | | | | 5.5% | £715.12 | |
| 21 | Month 16 | ZAR 8,832.00 | | | | 5.5% | £438.14 | |
| 22 | Month 17 | ZAR 11,644.00 | | | | 5.5% | £160.14 | |
| 23 | Month 18 | ZAR 14,456.00 | | | | 5.5% | -£118.87 | |
| 24 | Month 19 | ZAR 268.00 | ZAR 17,000.00 | to UK at | 14 | 5.5% | £815.38 | |
| 25 | Month 20 | ZAR 3,080.00 | | | | 5.5% | £538.77 | |
| 26 | Month 21 | ZAR 5,892.00 | | | | 5.5% | £261.15 | |
| 27 | Month 22 | ZAR 8,704.00 | | | | 5.5% | -£17.50 | |
| 28 | Month 23 | ZAR 11,516.00 | | | | 5.5% | -£297.16 | |
| 29 | Month 24 | ZAR 14,328.00 | | | | 5.5% | -£577.85 | |
| 30 | | | | | | | | |

**Figure 4.2** Example spreadsheet

Tasks with mathematical elements, such as finance, are commonly modelled with spreadsheets.

Spreadsheets are based on a layout of rows and columns. This layout assists financial modelling. It allows items to be laid out in a logical and easy-to-follow format. The use of rows and columns leads to the use of sequencing and replication. Replication is the copying of a cell either horizontally or vertically. The value of the cell can be incremented. If the value is an item in a list, the next item in the list can be given in the next cell, for example, days of the week or months of the year. Formulae can also be copied and cell references automatically adjusted.

Spreadsheets have many features to help when modelling. They can be based on functions and formulae, which allow numbers to be input into the spreadsheet and for any changes to be automatically recalculated. This means that many different scenarios can be tried out using a single model.

'What if...?' questions allow a user to change values and see what the effect would be on end results. An alternative method of asking questions is to start with the result and to see what would need to happen for that result to occur – this is known as goal seeking.

Spreadsheets can use variables and constants. A variable is a changeable value that is entered into a cell that is then used in a formula. The variable can be changed by a user when required, and the change will lead to a re-calculation of figures based on that variable. For example, a cell contains a formula to calculate a currency conversion. The conversion will depend on the rate of exchange at a given time. The user will need to enter the rate of change and amount to be converted: these are the variables. The cell containing the conversion formula will be updated depending on the figures entered as the variables. Constants are values which are used in formulae but which cannot be changed by a user. For example, a company finance department uses a spreadsheet to calculate the VAT owing at the end of each quarter. The VAT rate is a constant (17.5%) and will be used in every purchase or sale figure.

In spreadsheets individual cells or ranges of cells can be given names to make them easier to remember. For example, instead of referring to cell C10, you can give the cell a name relating to its contents, for example VAT_RATE, which can then be used to refer to the cell. This makes formulae easier to understand.

Other features include the use of multiple worksheets and graphical representation of data.

## ■ Why is computer modelling used?

There are many reasons why computer modelling is used.

- It is less risky (safer and cheaper) to test a model of a design (financial or an object) than to create it in reality and test it. For example, to build an aircraft, test it and to have it go wrong could cost human life.
- Only one model needs to be created in a computer. The model can be altered and changed. If a real model or the real thing was to be created, a new one would need to be created for each different alteration. This would cost time and money.
- A computer model can be backed up and shared. Since it is stored electronically, it can be backed up on a disk. It can be emailed or sent to others who can also work on the model.

■ Computer models can be accelerated or slowed down to see effects that could not be viewed in reality. For example, an explosion happens very quickly. A computer model can slow the process down so that its different stages can be analysed. The creation of the universe happened over a long period of time. A computer model can speed this process up so that it can be used effectively for research purposes.

It should be remembered that ultimately, all modelling is based on mathematics. The creation and manipulation of objects in the model is mathematical, as is the modelling of purely mathematical simulations such as financial models.

## QUESTIONS

**1** Describe **three** characteristics of software used to model objects.
**2** Why is software used to model objects?
**3** What are the disadvantages of using software to model objects?
**4** Describe **three** characteristics of software used to model financial data.
**5** What are the advantages of using a software modelling package to model next year's accounts?
**6** Describe the similarities between software used to model objects and software used to model financial data.

# Explain how variables, formulae, rules and functions are used in modelling software

A model has four main characteristics that allow it to manipulate numbers and text. These features allow the model to recalculate values when a number changes, questions to be asked and answered with the minimum amount of effort, and different scenarios to be tested. These features are:

■ variables
■ formulae
■ rules
■ functions.

## ■ Variables

A variable is an identifier associated with a particular cell. Within the cell, there will be a value. The variable could be a cell reference (e.g. D4) or the cell could have a name (e.g. VAT_RATE). When the variable is used in a spreadsheet, it is the value contained within the variable that is used.

# Formulae

A formula is the way that a calculation is represented in a spreadsheet. Formulae use numbers, addresses of cells (either references such as A12 or names) and mathematical operators (such as + / * -).

An example of a formula is:

**A12+(A12*VAT_RATE)**

# Rules

Rules are a set of procedures that must be followed. For example, if a calculation requires two values, then these values must be supplied. A validation rule can be applied to make sure that the value is given.

A rule can also be the sequence of events required for the calculation to work. For example, to work out an exam grade:

> **For each candidate**
> > **For each module**
> > > **Enter a UMS mark**
> **Add all the marks together**
> **Look up the mark in the grade table**
> **Return a grade**

This set of rules will enable the procedure to be followed by different people and a comparable result obtained.

# Functions

A function is used to represent a formula that is too complex or too long to expect an ordinary user to enter. A function uses reserved words that are built into the spreadsheet. Examples include:

- SUM: Adds a range of cells and gives the total.
- MAX: Gives the maximum value from a list.
- LOOKUP: Gives a value from an array based on a given value.

You may need to give examples of variables, formulae, rules and functions. The example you give must be relevant to the context of the question being asked in the examination. So, if a question is about garages, give an example to do with garages.

## QUESTIONS

1 Define the term variable.
2 Give an advantage of naming a cell.
3 Describe **two** differences between functions and formulae.
4 Give an example of a function and a rule that perform the same action.
5 In the context of modelling, what is a rule?
6 Describe the rule required to work out the age of a person on a given date.

# Describe how a data model may be used for answering 'What if…?' questions and explain the advantages of being able to answer such questions using a spreadsheet

A 'What if…?' question is an attempt to find out what is going to happen in the future. It requires a value to be changed so other values are re-calculated.

Examples include:

- How much do I need to increase the price of a certain brand of sportswear by for my profit to increase by 5%?
- What would happen to the number of accidents on a certain road if we reduced the speed limit to 20 mph?
- If I was to add a second staircase to the building, then how many extra people could get out within three minutes of a fire alarm going off?

Models contain calculations, formulae, functions and rules. They contain cell references and named cells. They can re-calculate automatically and present data in a variety of formats: textually, numerically and graphically. Custom interfaces can be built to increase the usability of models. All these features assist in answering 'What if…?' questions.

The benefits of using the model include re-calculation: the model can be changed many times and many different values and figures looked at. The only cost involved is time. Once the model has been created it will answer as many 'What if…?' questions as you want it to.

The cost and time involved in using a model are both likely to be less than creating physical models. To answer 'What if…?' questions using physical models will require a new model to be created for each question, especially if the test ends in the model's destruction as might happen when testing a building for earthquake resilience. Virtual models of buildings can be tested in many different scenarios without being destroyed.

If there is an error in the model, it is simpler and faster to alter it on a computer than in a physical model. It may only require the re-writing of a rule or function, which can be done quickly.

# Explain the advantages and disadvantages of using a spreadsheet to create and run simulations

A computer model comprises a set of data about something and a set of rules that control what the data does. You have already seen that there are two main types of modelling:

- mathematical modelling
- object modelling.

A model is an artificial re-creation of an object or event that should behave in the same way as the real thing. For example, a model of a bridge should enable the designers to simulate what will happen to the bridge under different conditions.

There are advantages and disadvantage to using a spreadsheet to create and run simulations/models of both objects and mathematical situations.

| Advantages | Disadvantages |
|---|---|
| ■ 'What if…?' questions can be asked without rebuilding a model from scratch each time a test is run.<br>■ Automatic re-calculation: if a change is made then all related formulae and values change.<br>■ Graphs can be produced: these will automaticallychange as any values change.<br>■ Variables and constants can be used: this enablesthe entire model to be changed by changing one or more values.<br>■ The model can be saved and backed up: if the original is lost or corrupted there is a copy.<br>■ The model can be shared between different people in different locations.<br>■ No additional software is required: spreadsheets are standard business software. Most people are able to use a spreadsheet, so no specialist training is needed.<br>■ It might be quicker and cheaper to build a computer model than a physical model.<br>■ Only one model needs to be built, which can then be changed. If a physical model is built then a different one will be needed each time a change is made.<br>■ It can be safer to run a simulation / model under extreme conditions than to build an actual model and test it. For example, testing a ship in storm conditions and risking it sinking.<br>■ Computer-based models can be speeded up or slowed down to see effects that are difficult to see in real life. | ■ The model may not be an accurate representation of the real world. The real world is complex!<br>■ If the model relates to people then an accurate result may not be given. For example, if a model is constructed to show the time taken to evacuate a building, it might not take into account the fact that people panic.<br>■ Many variables may need to be considered and it is easy to miss things out! This may lead to misleading results.<br>■ Producing an effective model may be time consuming and running the model may need expensive hardware and software. |

# Describe and explain the purpose and use of worksheets, workbooks, rows, columns, cells and ranges in spreadsheet software

A spreadsheet is made up of different parts. Each part has a different function and purpose.

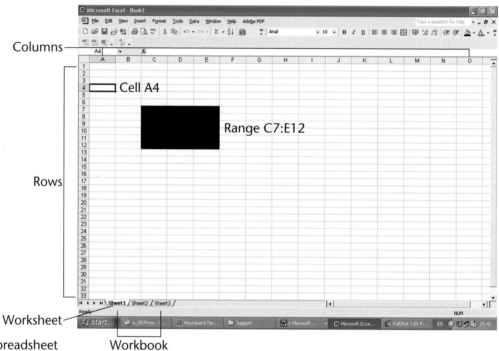

**Figure 4.3** Parts of a spreadsheet

## Worksheet

A worksheet (called a sheet or spreadsheet in some applications) is a large grid of cells on a single sheet. A worksheet can be used to hold data on a single area of the business. For example, it can hold the sales data, the expenditure or the stock. Worksheets can be given names.

## Workbook

A workbook is a collection of more than one worksheet in the same spreadsheet. Separate worksheets could contain financial figures for different areas of a business. Together they comprise a workbook, and contain the figures for the whole business.

For example, a workbook might contain worksheets on income, expenditure, stock and a summary (four worksheets within the workbook).

Workbooks can be used to divide data up into different categories and organise it. For example, the owner of a chain of shops might have a workbook on each shop, or a worksheet on each shop and a single workbook for all of them.

One advantage of using workbooks is that data that is changed on one worksheet will be reflected across the whole workbook. Another advantage is that different access rights can be given to different worksheets. For example, if a workbook contained several worksheets and each worksheet contained data relating to a single shop, you could allow the manager of each shop access only to their shop's worksheet.

As a workbook is saved as a single entity, it is easy to back-up, copy and send to other people. All the data required is in a single location.

## Rows and columns

A row is a range of cells that goes across the spreadsheet.
A column is a range of cells that goes down the spreadsheet. In most packages, rows are given numbers and columns are given letters.

Rows and columns are used to organise the data. They can hold headings to show where the data is stored and they can be used to hold the data within a tabular structure.

| | A | B | C | D | E |
|---|---|---|---|---|---|
| 1 | Sales by Groups of Item Each Quarter | | | | |
| 2 | | | | | |
| 3 | | 1st quarter | 2nd quarter | 3rd quarter | 4th quarter |
| 4 | Pens | 576 | 454 | 876 | 343 |
| 5 | Pencils | 345 | 232 | 545 | 323 |
| 6 | Pads of paper | 54 | 45 | 76 | 43 |

**Figure 4.4** Rows and columns

The width and height of rows and columns can be altered, for example columns can be widened to fit the text.

If necessary, rows and columns can be hidden. If a set of columns contained some calculations that you did not want to be shown, you could hide them from the user.

Describe and explain the purpose and use of worksheets, workbooks, rows, columns, cells and ranges in spreadsheet software

99

## Cell

A cell is an individual data store identified by a column and row indicator, in that order, for example A4, BJ100, etc. Every cell in the spreadsheet can be uniquely identified. Cells can also be given names as unique identifiers.

Cells can be formatted. Each individual cell can be formatted independently of the others, to change, for example, background colour, font, font size, validation, alignment and conditional formatting.

Cells can also be protected to stop the data within them being altered without a password.

## Range

A range is a group of cells. The group can be given a name or just known by its cell references. A range is usually given top left to bottom right and separated by a colon. For example A4:B6, C7:G12, etc.

A range is used when the cells within it contain similar data. They may contain grades, marks for an exam or names of stock items. Ranges are often used in formulae and functions. They make it easier to understand the spreadsheet and how it is working and allow the same formatting to be applied at the same time (instead of individually to a cell).

### < Tip >

You may need to give examples of worksheets, workbooks, rows, columns, cells and ranges. The example you give must be relevant to the context of the question being asked in the examination, so, for example, if the question is about shops, give an example to do with shops.

### QUESTIONS

1 Describe how a cell could be used in a financial spreadsheet.
2 What is a range? Give an example of how a range could be used in a sports league spreadsheet.
3 Describe the benefits of using a worksheet for a sweet shop.
4 Describe how a furniture shop could use a workbook.

# Describe absolute and relative cell referencing, and give examples of uses of each method

Referencing in spreadsheets is the use of cell identifiers to include the value contained within the cell in a formula or function. For example the formula C2+D2 uses two cell references and the cell containing the formula would show the result of adding the contents of the cells C2 and D2.

When you copy formulae or functions in a spreadsheet there are two ways the cell reference can be affected. It can move in relation to the direction of the copy (relative referencing) or it can stay the same (absolute referencing).

## ▇ Relative referencing

Relative cell referencing is when the cell referenced in a spreadsheet formula changes when the formula is copied to other cells. This means that when a formula or function is copied the cell reference within the formula or function will move.

In the example, the formula in cell A3 has been copied to the right into cells B3, C3 and D3. Each time, relative addressing ensures that the columns referenced in the formula are also changed by the same amount so the correct result is shown in each formula cell.

| | A | B | C | D |
|---|---|---|---|---|
| 1 | 23 | 43 | 54 | 23 |
| 2 | 34 | 54 | 2 | 12 |
| 3 | =A1+A2 | =B1+B2 | =C1+C2 | =D1+D2 |

**Figure 4.5** Relative addressing

Relative addressing also works to ensure the correct cells are referenced when cells are copied to new rows.

Relative referencing is used when you want the cell reference to change when you copy the cell.

## ▇ Absolute referencing

Absolute referencing is used when a referenced cell in a spreadsheet formula needs to remain exactly the same when the formula is copied to other cells. For example, a cell might contain a constant value such as the VAT rate, so this cell will always be referred to in calculations that use it, even if the cell containing the calculation is copied. This means that when a formula or function is copied the cell reference within the formula of function will not change.

This is used when you have a value entered into a single cell that the formula or function refers to, for example:

- VAT: all individual figures need to be multiplied by the VAT rate
- postage: all individual sales totals have the same postage added on.

Using the previous example, suppose each value contained in cells A2, B2, C2 and D2 is to be added to the value in cell A1. Relative referencing will give the incorrect answer because it will use the values in cells B1, C1 and D1 in the calculation. Clearly this is wrong as cell A1 needs to be 'locked' so it doesn't move as the formula is copied. This is achieved by putting a dollar sign ($) before the column and row parts of the cell reference as shown.

| | A | B | C | D |
|---|---|---|---|---|
| 1 | 23 | | | |
| 2 | 34 | 54 | 2 | 12 |
| 3 | =$A$1+A2 | =$A$1+B2 | =$A$1+C2 | =$A$1+D2 |

**Figure 4.6** Absolute addressing using the $ symbol

Absolute referencing can also be done using the name of a cell.

| | A | B | C |
|---|---|---|---|
| 1 | P&P (£) | 1.99 | |
| 2 | | | |
| 3 | Order number | Order total (£) | Total with P&P (£) |
| 4 | A123B1 | 45.33 | =B4+Post |
| 5 | B432H7 | 27.54 | =B5+Post |
| 6 | J345U9 | 19.99 | =B6+Post |
| 7 | F342K8 | 56.87 | =B4+Post |

**Figure 4.7** Absolute addressing using names

In the example, B1 has been given the name of 'Post'. When Post is used in the formula it refers to cell B1 and because it is not incremented when copied: the name makes it an absolute reference.

The main advantage of absolute references is that if you want to change the cost of P&P, you only need to change the value in B1 and all formulae that use the value it contains will re-calculate.

Absolute referencing is used when a value is used in the same formula or function many times.

## QUESTIONS

1 What is meant by referencing?
2 Using an example, describe relative referencing.
3 Give **two** advantages of relative referencing.
4 Using an example, describe absolute referencing.
5 Give **two** advantages of absolute referencing.

## Summary

### Characteristics of modelling software
Used to model objects
   Virtual representation
   Use of layers
   Questions can be asked
Used for financial modelling
   Based on functions and formulae
   Variables and constants can be used
   'What if...?' questions can be asked

### Variables, formulae, rules and functions
In a spreadsheet:
- a variable is an identifier associated with a particular cell and within the cell there will be a value
- a formula is a calculation which uses numbers, addresses of cells and mathematical operators
- rules are a set of procedures that must be followed and can also be the sequence of events required for the calculation to work
- a function represents a complex formula that uses reserved words.

### Worksheets, workbooks, rows, columns, cells and ranges
Worksheets consist of all of the cells on a sheet.
A workbook is a collection of worksheets.
A row is a range of cells, denoted by numbers that go across a spreadsheet.
A column is a range of cells, denoted by letters, that go down a spreadsheet.
A range is a group of cells denoted by either a name or cell references.

### Absolute and relative referencing
Relative referencing: the cell referenced in a formula changes when the formula is copied to other cells.
Absolute referencing: the cell referenced in a formula remains exactly the same when the formula is copied to other cells.

### Test 1
Mrs Burns has four shops. At present the accounts for the shops are done on paper.

1  Describe **three** characteristics of modelling software that could help Mrs Burns with her accounts. [6]

2  Use an example to show how Mrs Burns would use relative and absolute referencing. [4]

3  Describe **two** differences between a formula and a function. [4]

4  How could Mrs Burns make use of:
   a) a workbook
   b) a range? [8]

5  Describe **two** advantages of being able to give a cell a name instead of using the column and row identifier. [4]

## Test 2

An estate agency is moving to bigger premises.

1   Describe **two** characteristics of modelling software that could assist the estate agency in creating a virtual model of the new premises.                                                              [4]

2   Describe **three** benefits to the estate agency of using a virtual model instead of a physical model.                                                                                                                        [6]

3   The estate agency is going to use a spreadsheet to work out the cost of the move.
    a) Describe how 'What if...?' questions could be used.                                                            [2]
    b) Describe **three** features of spreadsheet modelling software that allow it to be used to answer 'What if...?' questions.                                                                               [6]

4   Describe how the estate agency would use a range in the spreadsheet.                               [2]

5   Explain, using examples, the difference between absolute and relative referencing.            [6]

# Relational database concepts

## Introduction

This chapter covers the database element of ICT. There is a large amount of theory that is required before the practical elements can be attempted.

This chapter covers:

- Terms used when describing databases
- Entity relationship diagrams
- Data dictionaries
- Characteristics of data in first, second and third normal form
- Advantages and disadvantages of normalisation
- Selecting appropriate data types
- Simple and complex queries using static and dynamic parameters

## Describe the terms typically used in relational database terminology

Databases involve a large amount of terminology and it is essential that the key terms are understood before progressing to the later sections of this chapter.

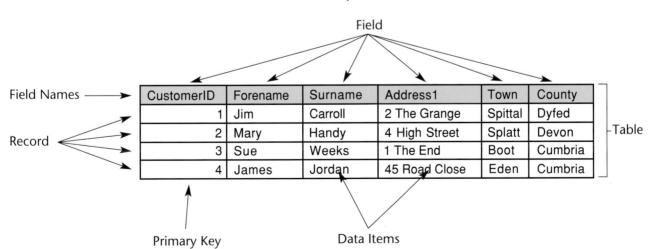

**Figure 5.1** Database terminology

A table is made up of records, records are made up of fields and fields are made up of characters.

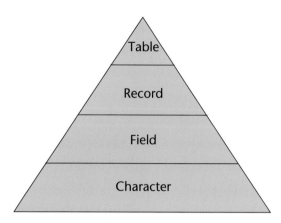

Figure 5.2  Parts of a table

## Table

Tables contain data about 'things', for example students, orders, events, purchases, customers, suppliers, etc. A table is a data structure made up of rows and columns that contains data about the items.

A table is a very specific and regulated item within a database. The following requirements must be met for the data structure to be called a table:

- The table must have a unique name.
- Each field/column must have a unique name.
- Each record/row must be unique.
- Each data item within a field must contain only a single data item.

The order of the records within the table does not matter. The order of the fields does not matter.

## Record

A record is a single row within a table. It is a collection of data about a single item or a single event. For example, a record might be about an individual, such as a customer, an order that has been placed, an item in stock or an appointment, etc.

Records are made up of fields and can contain different data types. In a table, each record must be unique.

## Field

A field is an individual data item within a record. Each field within a record should have a unique name. A field should only contain a single data item.

Fields have individual data types and can have their own validation.

## ■ Key

There are several different keys that can be applied to a table. The most important key is the primary key. This is a field, in the table, that allows each record to be uniquely identified. Every value of the primary key must be unique.

| Forename | Surname |
|----------|---------|
| Charlie | Smith |
| Lacey | Adams |
| Charlie | Smith |
| Jim | Carroll |
| Jan | Jordan |

Wrong.
Neither of these fields is suitable as a primary key as there are duplicate values.

| ID | Forename | Surname |
|----|----------|---------|
| 1 | Charlie | Smith |
| 2 | Lacey | Adams |
| 3 | Charlie | Smith |
| 4 | Jim | Carroll |
| 5 | Jan | Jordan |

**Figure 5.3**
Simple primary key

Correct.
ID can be the primary key as it has a unique value in each record.

The primary key can be of two types:

- simple
- compound/composite.

A simple primary key is one which is made up of a single field only, like ID in the example. A compound primary key is one which combines more than one field to make a unique value.

In the next example, a student can only be in one place at a time. Therefore combining the student name, date and period gives a unique value. These three fields could be combined to make a composite primary key.

| Student | Date | Period | Present |
|---------|------|--------|---------|
| H Top | 12/12/2008 | 1 | Y |
| S Small | 12/12/2008 | 1 | Y |
| P Andres | 12/12/2008 | 1 | N |
| H Top | 12/12/2008 | 2 | Y |

**Figure 5.4** Composite primary key

### Secondary key

A secondary key is a field that is identified as being suitable for indexing the data. It is used to sort the data in a different order to the primary key. A table can have many secondary keys – every field could be a secondary key.

### Foreign key

A foreign key is used to link tables together. A foreign key is a field in one table that is linked to a primary key in another table. The data types of the fields that are linked must be the same.

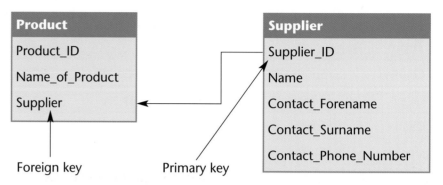

**Figure 5.5** Foreign key

Foreign key

Primary key

| QUESTIONS |
| --- |
| 1 Identify the **four** requirements of a table. |
| 2 What is the difference between a field and a record? |
| 3 Identify **three** properties of a field. |
| 4 What is the role of the primary key? |
| 5 Describe the difference between a simple primary key and a composite/compound primary key. |
| 6 What is the role of a secondary key? |
| 7 Using an example, describe how a foreign key works. |

# Relationships between entities

Entities are difficult to define. Chen, who introduced the entity relationship model, defined an entity as 'a thing which can be distinctly identified'. The idea of an entity is central to understanding entity relationship models. There are some general observations we can make about entities that can help.

- The world is made up of entities.
- Entities can be classified into entity types.
  - For example, we can identify EMPLOYEE as an entity and instances (records) of the entity EMPLOYEE would be individual employees.
- Each entity of the same type has a set of properties that can be applied to the entity type.
  - For example, each instance of the entity EMPLOYEE has a salary and a department where they work. This applies to every entity type.
- Entities can be linked to each other by means of a relationship.

## ■ Relationships

There are three types of relationship that can be identified as existing between entities.

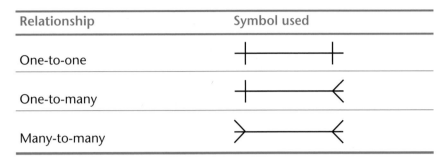

| Relationship | Symbol used |
|---|---|
| One-to-one | |
| One-to-many | |
| Many-to-many | |

### One-to-one relationship

If it is true that any instance of the entity X can be associated with only one instance of entity Y, then the relationship is one-to-one.

When determining one-to-one relationships you need to consider the timescale and not be concerned with historical values.

For example:

A school can only have one headteacher and a headteacher can only be a headteacher of one school.

Historically, a school is likely to have had many headteachers and a headteacher may have held a post as a headteacher at a previous school. It is therefore easier to discount what can happen historically when considering relationships.

Here are some other examples of one-to-one relationships.

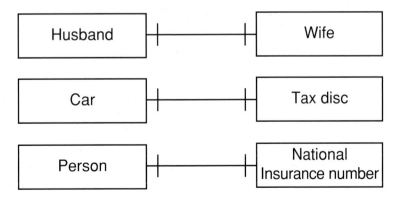

Figure 5.6

Figure 5.7

In database design it is uncommon to find a one-to-one relationship. If there is a one-to-one relationship then it is likely (but not always so) that the tables would be combined.

## One-to-many relationship

This is the most common type of relationship between entities. A single instance of an entity can be associated with many instances of another entity. Within the relationship it is true that many instances of an entity are associated with only a single instance of another entity.

When looking at entities and relationships it is necessary to look in detail at the situation as the relationship between similar entities could be different in different situations.

Here are some examples of one-to-many relationships.

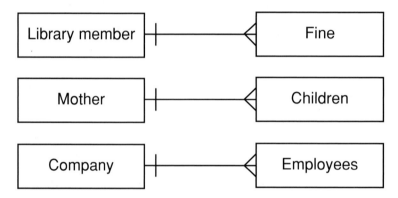

**Figure 5.8**

A library member could have several fines at the same time for different books. However, each fine is only owed by a single member.

A mother can have several children, but every child has only one mother.

A company has many employees but (in this situation at least) each employee is only employed by the one company.

## Many-to-many relationship

Many instances of an entity can be associated with many instances of another entity.

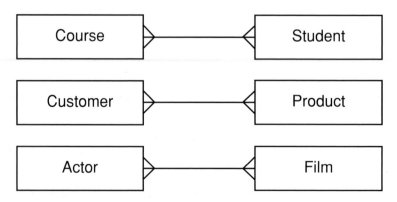

**Figure 5.9**

A student in a school takes many courses. A course has many students registered on it.

A customer can purchase many products and a product can be purchased by many customers.

An actor has been in many films and a film has many actors.

Many-to-many relationships break the rules of normalisation. There should be no many-to-many relationships in a normalised database.

If you have a many-to-many relationship, a link entity needs to be added. This is an entity that sits between the two current entities and has a one-to-many relationship with each.

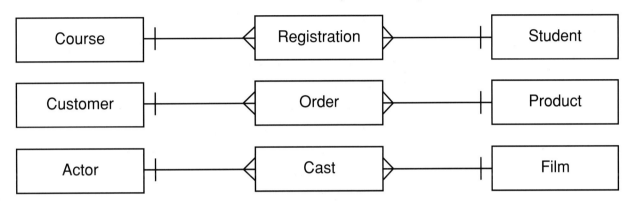

Figure 5.10 Link entities

Each course has many students registered on it and a student is in many registration books.

A customer can place many orders and a product can appear in many orders.

An actor can be one of many in a cast and a film has many cast members.

When resolving many-to-many relationships, the foreign key is on the many side, and the primary key is on the one side.

> **QUESTIONS**
>
> 1 Describe the degree of the relationship between:
>    a) a person and a birth certificate
>    b) a film and an Academy Award
>    c) a car and an owner
>    d) a teacher and a school.
>    Explain your reasoning for each.
> 2 Resolve the following many-to-many relationships:
>    a) additives to plants
>    b) books to authors
>    c) library member to books.
>    Explain your reasoning for each.
> 3 Describe the characteristics of an entity.
> 4 Describe the **three** types of relationship.

Databases require a good understanding of the technical aspects and language. It is important to learn the terms used, so the following revisits the definitions and places them within a practical context.

Consider the following scenario: The owner of a very successful but disorganised company that sells paint has decided to create a database for the business.

## Entities and attributes

Having examined the business the owner finds that he has:

- a list of all the paints in stock (amounts, prices, etc.)
- a list of where he gets the paints from
- a list of customers
- a list of which customer has bought which paint.

These four collections of data are the entities. An entity is a name for a logical or physical storage unit. In simpler terms, an entity is the name given to anything that you store data about. A list of all the paints in stock is an entity. All the data items refer to the same thing: paint.

Entities are referred to singularly and when written out, always in capitals. Ideally, entity names should be single words. If a two-word name must be used, then the words should be joined by an underscore (_).

The four entities identified might be called:

PAINT
SUPPLIER
CUSTOMER
ORDER

### < Activity >

Identify the entities contained in the scenario below and give reasons why they are entities.

**A library holds details on all the books, CDs and tapes in the library. It also has details on all its borrowers and which books/tapes/CDs they have borrowed.**

We need to add some details to the entities. We know the entities hold information, but we need to decide what information.

The paint shop has details on customers. We need to identify all the different details about the customers that will need to go into the database, that is:

- name of the customer
- address of the customer
- phone number of customer.

Having come up with the details, it is good practice to reduce them to a single identifiable word:

- Name
- Address
- Phone

It is also good practice to reduce the contents to single pieces of data. This means that name and address need to be broken down:

- Forename
- Surname
- Address Line 1
- Address Line 2
- Town
- County
- Postcode
- Phone

The results are known as attributes. An attribute is a characteristic of an entity.

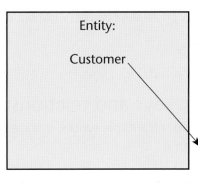

| Entity: |
| Customer |

| Attributes: |
| Forename |
| Surname |
| Company name |
| Address line 1… |

| Details about that person |

**Figure 5.11** Example of an entity and its attributes

Every entity has attributes.

**< Activity >**

For the SUPPLIER, PAINT and ORDER entities, write down the information that will be stored in each and then break those down into single word attributes.

So far, we have been dealing with a theoretical database. When it comes to actually creating the database, the entities will become tables and the attributes will become fields.

## ▤ Tables and fields

A database table is made up of fields. The field holds an individual item of information. The field is identified by the name (usually the same as the name of the attribute) and is given a data type. Validation rules can also be applied to fields. A table such as this is useful when planning a database:

| Table Name: | Tbl_Customer | |
|---|---|---|
| **Field name** | **Data Type** | **Validation** |
| Forename | Text | Length |
| Surname | Text | Length |
| Address Line 1 | Text | Length |
| Town | Text | Length |
| County | Text | Choice |
| Postcode | Text | Picture |
| Phone | Text | Type, Length, Picture |

**< Activity >**

For the library example used earlier, write out the tables and field names.

## ▤ Records, keys and relationships

In order to see how the table works, it is necessary to look at the table with data in it.

| Forename | Surname | Address Line 1 | Town | County | Postcode | Phone |
|---|---|---|---|---|---|---|
| John | Green | 43 The Grove | Chatham | Kent | ME1 2AB | 01634 12345 |
| Harry | Blue | 18 Hilltop | Chatham | Kent | ME1 3AB | 01634 22345 |
| Susan | White | 23 The Street | Chatham | Kent | ME1 4AB | 01634 32345 |
| John | Green | 43 The Grove | Chatham | Kent | ME1 2AB | 01634 12345 |

Each line is known as a record. The example above has four records in it. (The top line containing the headings is not a record.) A record is a collection of fields that all relate to the same topic.

There are rules for tables. In order for the table to conform to the rules, every row needs to be unique.

In the example above, every row is not unique: the first and last have the same details. These may refer to the same customer, but they may refer to different customers (two people who live at the same address with the same name).

To make the records unique, we need to have a primary key. The primary key is a field that makes each record uniquely identifiable.

Primary keys are usually numeric and, in many database systems, the data type can be set to Autonumber. This is a number field which the database will start at 1 and automatically increment for each new record.

| Customer ID | Forename | Surname | Address Line 1 | Town | County | Postcode | Phone |
|---|---|---|---|---|---|---|---|
| 1 | John | Green | 43 The Grove | Chatham | Kent | ME1 2AB | 01634 12345 |
| 2 | Harry | Blue | 18 Hilltop | Chatham | Kent | ME1 3AB | 01634 22345 |
| 3 | Susan | White | 23 The Street | Chatham | Kent | ME1 4AB | 01634 32345 |
| 4 | John | Green | 43 The Grove | Chatham | Kent | ME1 2AB | 01634 12345 |

As you can see, the primary key is just a number, but it now makes every record unique: no two records will have the same primary key.

One of the advantages of a relational database is that it removes duplicate data. Imagine if you had to write out the customer's name and address every time they placed an order. If they placed 50 orders that is a lot of data that is duplicated. Would it not be better to store their name and address once and link it to their order?

If we go back to the original scenario it will help find the links between tables:

- Each paint has a supplier.
- Each customer orders a paint.

Look at the tables and field names. The following field names are repeated in different tables.

- In the PAINT table there is **SupplierID** (also in the SUPPLIER table).
- In the ORDER table there is **CustomerID** (from CUSTOMER table) and **PaintID** (from PAINT table).

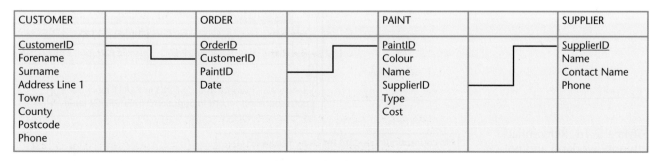

**Figure 5.12** Entity diagram with attributes and links

Notice how one of the sides of the link is always a primary key and the other is just a field. This is important. The one that is just a field but is part of the link is called a foreign key.

A foreign key is a field in one table that is also a primary key in another table and is used to create a link between the two.

Look at the tables below showing the PAINT and SUPPLIER tables. The value of the primary key of SUPPLIER matches the value of the foreign key in PAINT allowing a link between the two tables and the data to be matched between them.

| PaintID | Colour | Name | SupplierID | Cost | Type |
|---------|--------|------|------------|------|------|
| 1 | Blue | Sky During Day | 1 | £14.99 | Gloss |
| 2 | Green | Rough Sea | 1 | £12.99 | Matt |
| 3 | Yellow | Jaundice | 2 | £12.99 | Matt |
| 4 | White | Bright Light | 2 | £15.99 | Gloss |

| SupplierID | Name | Contact Name | Phone |
|------------|------|--------------|-------|
| 1 | Natural Colours | Jordan Carroll | 012 345 |
| 2 | Radiant Paints | Sylvia Farrant | 012 346 |

**Figure 5.13** Entity with data showing links

**< Activity >**

Complete the tables and attributes for the library and draw out a diagram showing the links between tables.

## ■ Referential integrity

Looking at the paint shop example, it is possible to have a supplier in the database who did not supply the company with any paints. They may have done so in the past but you do not stock any of their paints now. However, it is impossible to have paints in the database which do not have any supplier. Referential integrity makes sure that it is impossible to enter a reference to a link which does not exist.

Paint:

| PaintID | Colour | Name | Cost | SupplierID | Type |
|---------|--------|------|------|------------|------|
| 1 | Blue | Sky During Day | £14.99 | 1 | Gloss |
| 2 | Green | Rough Sea | £12.99 | 1 | Matt |
| 3 | Yellow | Jaundice | £12.99 | 2 | Matt |
| 4 | White | Bright Light | £15.99 | 2 | Gloss |
| 5 | Purple | Plum Island | £18.99 | 3 | Gloss |

Supplier:

| SupplierID | Name | Contact Name | Phone |
|------------|------|--------------|-------|
| 1 | Natural Colours | Jordan Carroll | 012 345 |
| 2 | Radiant Paints | Sylvia Farrant | 012 346 |

Referential integrity as SupplierID in PAINT table has a corresponding record in SupplierID in SUPPLIER table

No corresponding record for Paint 5 (supplier 3) – therefore referential integrity has been broken

**Figure 5.14** Referential integrity working and not working

< Activity >

**QUESTIONS**

1 Describe the following database terms:
   a) database
   b) record
   c) field.
2 Describe the difference between an entity and a table.
3 Using an example, describe the primary key and explain why it is needed.
4 Using an example, describe the foreign key and explain why it is needed.
5 What is referential integrity and why is it important?

# First, second and third normal form

< Tip >

You will not be required to carry out the actual process of normalisation during the examination. However, you will be required to know the rules of normalisation and be able to identify which normal form data is in, with reasons. This section does not, therefore, cover how to normalise data but it does describe what to look for in each normal form.

## ■ Normalisation

Data is normalised in order to reduce redundancy and inconsistency, and to make it easier to use and maintain. There are specific rules attached to each normal form.

Before a table gets to 'first normal' form it is in 'unnormalised' form – UNF or 0NF.

The next example is based on a local authority requiring exam results from all students within its area.

| StudentNo | Student Name | School Code | School Name | School Location | ExamID | Exam Name | Exam Date | Exam Result |
|-----------|--------------|-------------|-------------|-----------------|--------|-----------|-----------|-------------|
| AB12 | Jo May | PT1 | Prior Taylor | Chatham | HI1 | History GCSE | 24/05/07 | A* |
| AB12 | Jo May | PT1 | Prior Taylor | Chatham | MA1 | Maths GCSE | 20/05/07 | A |
| AC15 | Phil Sept | HT1 | Hall Taylor | Rainham | FR2 | French AS | 13/05/07 | B |
| AC15 | Phil Sept | HT1 | Hall Taylor | Rainham | IT2 | IT AS | 10/05/07 | C |

### First normal form (1NF)

A table is in 1NF if every data value in a field is atomic and each record does not contain repeating data.

Atomic means that the data value cannot be broken down any further. The **Student Name** and **Exam Name** fields are not atomic as they both contain two data items each. **Student Name** contains 'forename' and 'surname' and **Exam Name** contains 'subject' and 'level'.

To make a start on normalising this table we need to make each field contain only atomic data.

| Student No | Student Forename | Student Surname | School Code | School Name | School Location | Exam ID | Exam Name | Exam Level | Exam Date | Exam Result |
|---|---|---|---|---|---|---|---|---|---|---|
| AB12 | Jo | May | PT1 | Prior Taylor | Chatham | HI1 | History | GCSE | 24/05/07 | A* |
| AB12 | Jo | May | PT1 | Prior Taylor | Chatham | MA1 | Maths | GCSE | 20/05/07 | A |
| AC15 | Phil | Sept | HT1 | Hall Taylor | Rainham | FR2 | French | AS | 13/05/07 | B |
| AC15 | Phil | Sept | HT1 | Hall Taylor | Rainham | IT2 | IT | AS | 10/05/07 | C |

As defined earlier, a table has its own set of characteristics:

- Each row must be uniquely identifiable.
- Each field name must be unique.

For each row to be uniquely identifiable it needs a primary key. (When showing a table with data in it, the primary key is identified by putting an * next to the field name.)

All the field names used in a table must be unique: they cannot be copied.

| Student No* | Student Forename | Student Surname | School Code | School Name | School Location | Exam ID* | Exam Name | Exam Level | Exam Date | Exam Result |
|---|---|---|---|---|---|---|---|---|---|---|
| AB12 | Jo | May | PT1 | Prior Taylor | Chatham | HI1 | History | GCSE | 24/05/07 | A* |
| AB12 | Jo | May | PT1 | Prior Taylor | Chatham | MA1 | Maths | GCSE | 20/05/07 | A |
| AC15 | Phil | Sept | HT1 | Hall Taylor | Rainham | FR2 | French | AS | 13/05/07 | B |
| AC15 | Phil | Sept | HT1 | Hall Taylor | Rainham | IT2 | IT | AS | 10/05/07 | C |

Note the use of the composite primary key: **StudentNo** and **ExamID**. This uniquely identifies each record because a student only takes each exam once (in this scenario).

Checks for 1NF:

- Does the table have a primary key?
- Is each field name unique?
- Are there any repeating fields in a single record?
- Is all the data within a field atomic?

### Second normal form (2NF)

A table is in 2NF if it is 1NF and all its non-key attributes are dependent on the entire primary key (or there are no partial key dependencies).

2NF is based on functional dependence. A data item Y is functionally dependent on data item Z if, once you know the value of Z there is only one possible value for Y at a given time. For example I am told the **StudentNo** is AB12, therefore I know the forename is Joe because there is only one AB12.

Another way of looking at this is that second normal form is about the removal of some redundant data.

| Student No* | Student Forename | Student Surname | School Code | School Name | School Location | Exam ID* | Exam Name | Exam Level | Exam Date | Exam Result |
|---|---|---|---|---|---|---|---|---|---|---|
| AB12 | Jo | May | PT1 | Prior Taylor | Chatham | HI1 | History | GCSE | 24/05/07 | A* |
| AB12 | Jo | May | PT1 | Prior Taylor | Chatham | MA1 | Maths | GCSE | 20/05/07 | A |
| AC15 | Phil | Sept | HT1 | Hall Taylor | Rainham | FR2 | French | AS | 13/05/07 | B |
| AC15 | Phil | Sept | HT1 | Hall Taylor | Rainham | IT2 | IT | AS | 10/05/07 | C |

In the table above, the primary key is made up of the student number and the exam ID. This makes sense because the exam date and exam result will be different for every student/exam combination. As these form a composite key, each one of these fields is a 'partial key'. We need to remove dependencies upon these 'partial keys'.

**Student Forename** and **Student Surname** depend only on **StudentNo** (a partial key). The same forename and surname will appear (and be redundant) every time the student number appears in the main table.

Although **School Name** and **School Location** are dependent upon **School Code**, **School Code** is not a partial key and therefore they are really dependent upon **StudentNo**.

**Exam Name** and **Exam Level** depend only on **ExamID** (a partial key). The same exam name and exam level will appear (and be redundant) every time its ID appears in the main table.

To achieve second normal form, we need to separate the attributes depending on both parts of the key from those depending only on the partial keys (**ExamID** and **StudentNo**).

If we break the table into three:

■ Exams, which gives the name for each **ExamID**
■ Students, which gives the name for each **StudentNo**
■ StudentExams which lists the exams taken by each student

then we have separated the attributes.

## STUDENTEXAM

| StudentNo* | ExamID* | Exam Date | Exam Result |
|---|---|---|---|
| AB12 | HI1 | 24/05/07 | A* |
| AB12 | MA1 | 20/05/07 | A |
| AC15 | FR2 | 13/05/07 | B |
| AC15 | IT2 | 10/05/07 | C |

## EXAM

| ExamID* | Exam Name | Exam Level |
|---|---|---|
| HI1 | History | GCSE |
| MA1 | Maths | GCSE |
| FR2 | French | AS |
| IT2 | IT | AS |

## STUDENT

| StudentNo* | Student Forename | Student Surname | School Code | School Name | School Location |
|---|---|---|---|---|---|
| AB12 | Jo | May | PT1 | Prior Taylor | Chatham |
| AC15 | Phil | Sept | HT1 | Hall Taylor | Rainham |

The rule here is that a new table needs to be created for each partial key dependency that is found.

Checks for 2NF:

- Is the table in 1NF?
- Can all of the non-key fields be found out by using the entire primary key?

### Third normal form

A table is in third normal form if it is in 2NF and there is no functional dependency between non-key items (or there are no non-key dependencies). In simple terms, the question 'Are any of the non-key fields dependent on any other non-key fields?' can be asked. If the answer is 'no', then the table is in 3NF.

The STUDENTEXAM and EXAM tables are not only in 2NF but they are also in 3NF because each non-key field is fully dependent upon the primary key.

The STUDENT table is not currently in 3NF because the school information is dependent on the school code and not the student number.

We therefore need to create a school table.

| StudentNo* | Student Forename | Student Surname | School Code |
|---|---|---|---|
| AB12 | Jo | May | PT1 |
| AC15 | Phil | Sept | HT1 |

| School Code* | School Name | School Location |
|---|---|---|
| PT1 | Prior Taylor | Chatham |
| HT1 | Hall Taylor | Rainham |

All non-key items are now fully dependent on the primary key, so all tables are now in 3NF.

The rule here is that a new table needs to be created for each new dependency.

Checks for 3NF:

- Is the table in 2NF (and also, therefore, in 1NF)?
- Are all non-key items fully dependent on the primary key?

## The correct notation for table structures

When writing data structures there is a notation that is universally understood and should be used.

The table name should be in capitals and the attributes (field names) in brackets separated by a comma. The primary key is underlined and foreign keys are overlined.

For example:

STUDENT(StudentNo, StudentForename, StudentSurname, SchoolCode)

SCHOOL(SchoolCode, SchoolName, SchoolLocation)

EXAM(ExamID, ExamName, ExamLevel)

STUDENTEXAM(StudentNo, ExamID, ExamDate, ExamResult)

**QUESTIONS**

1 Describe first normal form.
2 Explain why the following data structure is not in first normal form.

| StudentName | Year | Classes | Games | Games |
|---|---|---|---|---|
| Fred Smith | 11 | 11ICT 10Ma2 | Football | Rugby |
| Heather Phipps | 11 | 11MA4, 11Mu | Netball | Lacrosse |
| Maggie Stuart | 10 | 11En1, 11Ma1 | Hockey | Rugby |

**3** Describe second normal form.

**4** Explain why the following data structure is not in second normal form.

| SeatNumber* | Performance | Date* | Time* | Customer Forename | Customer Surname |
|---|---|---|---|---|---|
| A1 | We Will Rock You | 27/12/2004 | 2.30 | John | May |
| B1 | We Will Rock You | 27/12/2004 | 2.30 | Fred | Deacon |
| C1 | We Will Rock You | 27/12/2004 | 2.30 | Brian | Taylor |
| A1 | We Will Rock You | 27/12/2004 | 7.30 | Roger | Mercury |

(The primary key is a compound key: Seat Number, Date and Time.)

**5** Describe third normal form.

**6** Explain why the following data structure is not in third normal form.

| ID* | Forename | Surname | HouseName/Number | Town | County | Postcode |
|---|---|---|---|---|---|---|
| 1 | John | Davies | 18 Bright Road | Nottingham | Notts | NG8 5EP |
| 2 | Alice | Hall | 24 Halls Avenue | Nottingham | Notts | NG8 5ET |
| 3 | Joan | Stevenson | 19 Walbrook Close | Nottingham | Notts | NG8 5EZ |

**7** Explain why it is an advantage to have a standard notation for tables.

## ◼ Advantages of normalisation

The normalisation process gives many advantages to the database that emerges at the end.

The final tables will have no redundant data within them, as normalisation removes redundant data from the tables. The process also removes duplicate data. This saves on storage space and makes the data consistent. If you are holding multiple copies of the data and only update one of them, they will become unsynchronised. If this happens, the data has lost consistency and it has lost integrity. You will not know which data is the right data.

A normalised data structure is easier to maintain than one that has not be normalised. If the data is not duplicated then an update on a single piece of data will mean that any process that uses the data can be relied upon.

The data that is stored at the end of the process is stored in an efficient structure. This means that, as every data item is atomic, it is possible to combine the data in any desired format. If multiple data items were stored in a single field and only part of the field was required, a lot of programming would have to be done to extract the item required.

The database structure is very flexible. This means that if the requirements of the organisation using the data alter, the database can adapt without a major redesign of the structure.

The advantages of normalisation can be summarised as follows:

- Removes redundancy
- Increases consistency
- Increases integrity
- Easier maintenance
- Flexibility for future expansion

## Disadvantages of normalisation

There are some disadvantages to normalising a database. The main one is reduced database performance. When a query of an action is sent to the database, there are a large number of factors involved. These include CPU usage, memory and input/output. A normalised database requires greater use of those resources as it must locate the requested information from across different tables, join the data from the tables and even from within the same table. This takes more time than from an unnormalised database.

How the database will be used will affect whether it is necessary to have a normalised or unnormalised database. Databases have two main purposes, transaction and reporting. Transaction databases require a lot of inserting, editing and deleting of data, whereas reporting presents data but rarely changes it. Unnormalised data is better for reporting systems because it is likely that the data is in a structure suitable for the reports required and can be presented quicker and with less processing and memory requirements. Normalisation is vital for transactional databases to ensuring data integrity and for increasing the speed with which records can be added, edited, and deleted.

Databases that are required to store historical data need to break the rules of normalisation. In a normalised database, the price of a purchase (invoice), for example, is calculated. In the future, if the price of an item changes then the invoice total will change. If you needed to go back and look at a historical invoice, it would be based on today's values, not the ones at the time. It is therefore, in certain circumstances, necessary to store calculated values.

# Components of a data dictionary

A data dictionary is often called a database about a database. It contains metadata (data about data). Different database packages will contain slightly different information in the data dictionary. The list below is the basic data that would be expected in them all.

The data dictionary holds:

| Data | Description |
|---|---|
| Table name | The name of the table. A unique name for each table in the database. |
| Field name | Each field is identified. |
| Field data type | The data type allocated to each field: text/string/date/Boolean, etc. |
| Field length | The number of characters allocated for the contents of the field. |
| Field default value | If a field has a default value that automatically appears on the creation of a new record. |
| Field validation | Any validation applied to the field. |
| Table security | Who has access to write, update, edit, delete, etc. values to and from the table. |
| Keys | Primary and foreign keys are identified. |
| Indexes | Any field which is indexed. |
| Relationships | Relationships between tables identified: one-to-one, etc. |

**QUESTIONS**

1 Describe **three** items found in a data dictionary that relate to fields.
2 Describe **three** items found in a data dictionary that relate to tables.
3 How would a designer use the data dictionary?

# Select appropriate data types for a given set of data

The main data types available are:

- Text/string – Any key on the keyboard. It can be used to store text (Mr Jones), text and numbers (TN18 7PU), or just numbers (54).

  Numbers are only stored as text if they are not to be manipulated as numbers (i.e. if no addition, subtraction, etc. is to be done).

  Telephone numbers do not have mathematical functions applied to them so they are stored as text. Telephone numbers also have spaces within them and start with a 0 (e.g. 01234 56789), which makes them text based not numeric.

- Integer/Real – Numbers. Integer without decimal places and real with decimal places. When assessing the data to be stored it is necessary to look at examples of data and decide the data type.

  Currency is usually stored as a real number (e.g. £43.00). The symbol, although text, is stored separately. However, consider the appropriateness of storing house prices as real.

- Boolean – Boolean fields can store one of only two possible values (e.g. yes/no, true/false) that can be used to represent any question with two possible outcomes (male/female, video/dvd, etc.).
- Date/Time

The advantages and disadvantages of using the data types are related to their use within a given scenario and what the data will be used for. For example, if the data for a field 'Does the house have a garden?' has only two possible options: yes or no. This is appropriate for a Boolean data type, because it takes up the minimal amount of memory space and can be validated to ensure the data stored is one of those two values. It also enables easier searching of the data.

---

**QUESTIONS**

1 Describe the **five** main data types.
2 When should numbers be used?
3 What are the advantage of using the Boolean data type?

---

# Simple and complex queries using static and dynamic parameters

The ability of databases to run queries is what makes them particularly useful.

Parameter queries return fields from tables where the value of the parameter is matched.

The parameter is the value that is used by the query to select records. The next table shows a selection of records from the PRODUCT table. Each product has a supplier. Some suppliers supply more than one product.

| Product_ID | Name_of_Product | Supplier |
|---|---|---|
| 1 | Red pens | Jones the PenMaker |
| 2 | Red pens | No Frill Quills |
| 3 | Lined A4 | The PaperMaker |
| 4 | Blue pens | Jones the PenMaker |
| 5 | Purple pens | Jones the PenMaker |
| 6 | Plain A4 | The PaperMaker |
| 7 | A4 book covers | The Paper Place |
| 8 | Green pens | Jones the PenMaker |
| 9 | Spiral notebook | The PaperMaker |
| 10 | Propelling pencils | Pencils 4 All |
| 11 | Blue pens | No Frill Quills |
| 12 | HB pencils | Pencils 4 All |
| 0 | | |

**Figure 5.15**

## Simple query

Using a parameter query, all the suppliers of a particular product could be shown.

To find all the suppliers of blue pens, the Name_of_Product column needs to be searched to match the text 'Blue pens'. The other fields to be displayed also need to be selected.

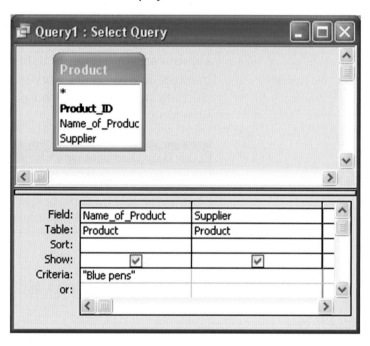

**Figure 5.16** Simple query

The results of the query will display two fields and two records.

| Name_of_Product | Supplier |
| --- | --- |
| Blue pens | Jones the PenMaker |
| Blue pens | No Frill Quills |

**Figure 5.17** Results of query in Figure 5.16

In the query above, the parameter has been 'hard coded'. This means that the query cannot be changed: whenever it is run it will always and only search for blue pens. This is known as a static parameter query. There will be occasions where the user will want to search for different products. It would not be efficient to have separate queries for every product because not every product is likely to be known when the database is being designed.

Parameter queries can be created which ask the user for the value to search for. These are known as dynamic parameter queries. A dialogue box can be created which takes a value from the user and uses that value in the query:

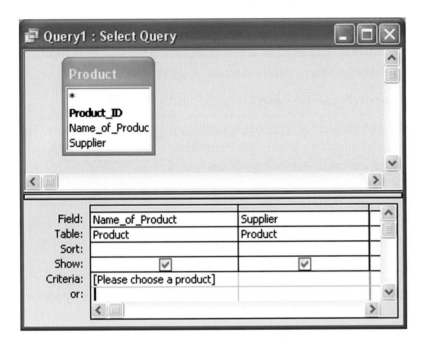

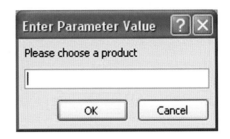

**Figure 5.18** Query with parameter

The parameter value in the query asks a question. The user enters a value in the dialogue box. This value is used. This makes the query more useful than hard coding the value.

## ■ Complex queries

A complex query is a parameter query that searches using more than one parameter value, that is two or more criteria. Suppose you know that Jones the PenMaker supplies you with green pens and you want to order some new stock but you don't know the product ID, then you can search the database with a complex query.

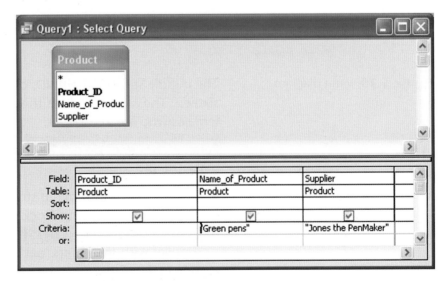

**Figure 5.19** Complex query

The query above shows that the product ID for green pens supplied by Jones the PenMaker is 8.

You can have as many parameters as you like in a query.

The parameters can be joined together in three ways:

- AND – to include all records found from both queries. Only records containing Jones The Penmaker as the supplier AND a product called Green pens will be found.
- OR – to find records that match one or the other or both searches. Searching for Jones The Penmaker OR product will find green pens not supplied by Jones the PenMaker and every product supplied by Jones The Penmaker whether or not they are green pens.
- NOT – an inverse query. Searching for products NOT supplied by Jones The Penmaker removes all products supplied by Jones The Penmaker.

Complex parameter queries can be represented using a Venn diagram

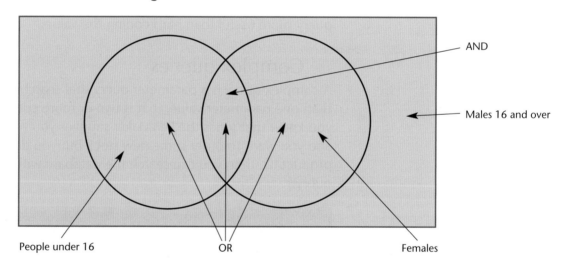

**Figure 5.20** Venn diagram

The middle section, the AND, contains females who are under sixteen. The area outside of the circles contains all the non-females who are 16 or over.

Parameter queries do not have to match values exactly, they can make use of:

- Greater than – number in stock > 500
- Less Than – number in stock < 10
- Contains – supplier = *per* (* is a wildcard so this will find any supplier with the letters 'per' together in the name)
- Starts with – supplier = F*
- Ends with – supplier = *g

## Summary

**Database terminology**

Tables
    Contain data about items
    Made up of records and fields
    Must have a unique name
Records
    Single row within the table
    Collection of data about a single item or event
Fields
    Individual items of data in a record
    Each field can be individually validated
    Also known as attributes
Keys
    Primary key
    Single field – unique identifier for the record
Composite primary key
    Where two or more fields are joined together to make a unique identifier for the record
Foreign key
    Primary key in one table, field in another table, used to join tables together
Secondary key
    Used to index a field

**Entities**

Single objects or processes
Information about things
Each entity becomes a table
Entities linked by relationships

**Relationships**

Links between entities/tables
    One-to-one – where one record in a table is only linked to one record in another table
    One-to-many – one record in a table is linked to many records in a second table
    Many-to-many – the many link goes both ways between two tables

## Referential integrity
Ensuring that, for every record in a table with a foreign key, there is a record in the corresponding table with the primary key

## Normalisation
Process applied to data structures
Decreases redundancy
Increases integrity
First normal form
  Every data value is atomic
  No repeating data
  Primary key
Second normal form
  Must be in 1NF
  Non-key attributes are dependent on the entire primary key
Third normal form
  Must be in 2NF
  No functional dependency between non-key items
Advantages of normalisation
  Removes redundancy
  Increases consistency
  Increases integrity
  Easier maintenance
  Flexibility for future expansion
Disadvantages of normalisation
  Reduced database performance
  Problems with historical calculations

## Data dictionary
Database about a database
Contains design details about the database
Includes table name, field name, data type, length, validation relationships, security

## Data types
Text/string – anything not requiring a calculation
Integer – whole numbers only, NOT telephone numbers
Real – numbers with decimal places
Boolean – one of two values
Date/Time – store age, dates, times
Look to see what the data is going to be used for

## Parameter
Simple
  A query where there is only one parameter
Complex
  A query with more than one parameter
  Makes use of AND, OR and NOT to join parameters
Static
  Parameter is hard coded into the query and cannot be changed by the end user
Dynamic
  Request for the parameter given to the end user at run time, usually by a dialogue box

## Test 1

A small corner shop runs a newspaper round. Until now, the details about the newspaper round have been stored manually. The shop wants to computerise its records. The shop will require a database.

1 Describe the following database terms:
   a) Table
   b) Record
   c) Field [6]

2 The database will contain relationships and foreign keys to ensure referential integrity is maintained.
   Using an example, describe the terms relationship, foreign key and referential integrity. [6]

3 The first designs for the data structure included the following table. Explain, giving reasons, why the following table is not in first normal form (1NF).
   CUSTOMER (Customer name, customer address, newspaper, newspaper, newspaper, delivery round) [5]

4 The following entities have been established:
   Customer
   Newspaper
   Round
   Delivery Person
   Order
   Draw out the entity relationship diagram for the tables and explain the degree of the relationship between each entity. [8]

5 Describe **two** advantages of normalisation. [4]

6 Give an example of the following queries that the corner shop could use:
   a) Simple parameter query
   b) Complex parameter query [2]

7 Using examples related to the corner shop, describe the difference between a static and a dynamic parameter query. [4]

## Test 2

An estate agent currently stores all the data about the business on paper. She wants to computerise her systems and has employed a database expert to assist her.

1 The final database will have tables, fields and records.
   Describe, using examples from the estate agency, the terms tables, fields and records. [6]

2 From the following database design, identify the primary and foreign keys:
   CUSTOMER (CustomerID, Forename, Surname)
   PROPERTY (PropertyID, Address, Price, Seller)
   SELLER (Forename, Surname, SellerID, Address, Postcode, Age, Phone)
   OFFER (CustomerID, PropertyID, Price, Date, Accepted) [6]

3 Identify the characteristics of data in second normal form. [2]

4 Explain, giving reasons, why the following table is not in second normal form (2NF). This is an attendance table showing whether an employee arrived to work on time, late and whether there was a reason.

ATTENDANCE (EmployeeID, OfficeID, Date, Attendance, TrafficCondition, Reason) [4]

5 Identify **three** components of the data dictionary for the estate agent's database and, for each component, explain how it would be used in the creation of the database. [6]

6 The information that is held on SELLERS includes:

Forename, Surname, Phone, Age, Address and Postcode.

For each piece of information, give an appropriate data type and a reason why that data type is appropriate. [6]

7 The table for SELLER contains the following structure:

SELLER(Forename, Surname, Phone, Age, Address and Postcode, SellerID)

Explain why this is not in 1NF and redefine the data structures so that it is. [4]

# Application software used for presentation and communication of data

## Introduction

This chapter covers the basic concepts relating to presentations and the communication of data. You will need to make sure you understand the features of application software used for presentations and communicating data and are able to apply this knowledge to a variety of situations.

This chapter covers:

- **Characteristics of documents**
- **Mail merge**
- **Reformatting documents to meet the needs of an application**
- **Clip art and thumbnail images**
- **Vector and bitmap graphics**
- **Graphic libraries**
- **Features of presentation software**

## Describe the characteristics of documents and how they should be used

All documents have common characteristics that can be used in their production. The characteristics used may be dictated by the house style of the organisation they are being produced for or to meet the needs of the target audience.

The main characteristics of documents are:

- characters
- paragraphs
- sections
- frames
- headers
- footers
- footnotes
- pages.

## Character

A character is any letter, number or symbol used in a document.

## Paragraph

Paragraphs are generally used when a long document is being created. They are generally defined by the use of a carriage return at the end of the text.

The paragraph may have a style that could be pre-defined through the use of a corporate or house style or that may be defined by the user. A paragraph style defines the features of the text. These features may include the paragraph alignment (left, right, centred or justified), indentations, line spacing, font size and style and bullets or numbering. Styles are generally applied to paragraphs and headings but may also be applied to frames and tables. Here is an example paragraph style definition:

Style: Heading 3
Font: Verdana, 20 pt
Format: Bold
Paragraph alignment: Centred
Spacing before: 12 pt
Spacing after: 6 pt

## Section

A section is a portion of a document in which page-formatting options can be set. A new section can be created when properties such as line numbering, number of columns, or headers and footers need to be changed. Until section breaks are inserted the word-processing package will treat a document as a single section. Sections can be used to allow the layout of a document to be varied within a page or between pages. Section breaks are inserted to divide the document into sections, and then each section can be formatted to meet the needs of the user.

## Frame

A frame is an area of a page that can contain text or graphics. The frames can be positioned anywhere on the page. Changes to the content of one frame will not affect the content of another. A DTP package usually makes use of frames.

Word-processing packages can use frames but are not exclusively frame based. Therefore, the position of each object on the page depends on the position of everything else. For example, if a paragraph or sentence is deleted, everything else moves to take its place.

Word-processing packages are not frame based.

The position of each object on the page depends on the position of everything else.

For example if a paragraph or sentence is deleted then everything else move to take its place.

If this paragraph is deleted then everything else moves up to take its place.

Word-processing packages are not frame based.

For example if a paragraph or sentence is deleted then everything else move to take its place.

This paragraph has now moved up to fill the space.

**Figure 6.1** Deleting a paragraph in a word-processed document

In a DTP package each individual frame can be easily moved or resized. This means that a page in a DTP publication can be edited by changing the size or position of the frames. A frame can also be moved from one page to another.

Each block of text or graphic is in its own frame so it can be moved separately to other frames.
Once an empty frame has had text or a graphic inserted it can be called an object.

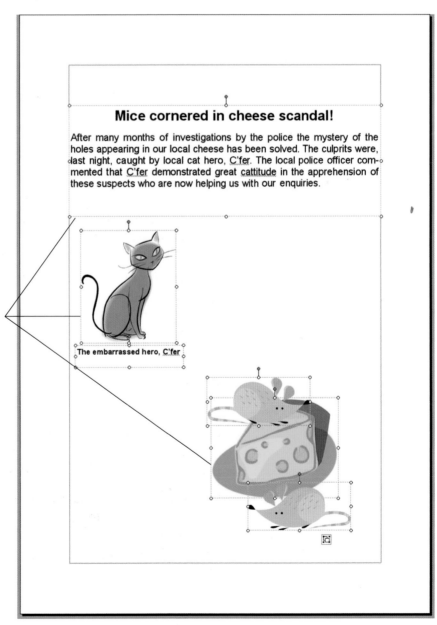

**Mice cornered in cheese scandal!**

After many months of investigations by the police the mystery of the holes appearing in our local cheese has been solved. The culprits were, last night, caught by local cat hero, C'fer. The local police officer commented that C'fer demonstrated great cattitude in the apprehension of these suspects who are now helping us with our enquiries.

The embarrassed hero, C'fer

**Figure 6.2** Using frames in a DTP package

Text, as well as graphics, can be positioned in a frame. Once a text frame has been created, it can be positioned and resized. Text is typed or imported into the frame. Ususally, frames can be linked so if all the text does not fit in the original frame, the excess text flows into the next. The DTP package may do this automatically. Alternatively, the text may need to be edited to fit the original frame.

**QUESTION**

Describe, giving an example of its use, what is meant by a frame.

## ■ Header and footer

A header is text which appears on a document in the top margin of every page. A header may include the creator's name, title and date. A footer is text which appears on a document in the bottom margin of every page. The general rule is that the footer contains the page numbering, date or file name.

You can use the same header and footer throughout a document or change the header and footer for part of the document. For example, you can use a unique header or footer on the first page, or leave the header or footer off the first page. You can also use different headers and footers on odd and even pages or for part of a document.

**QUESTION**

Describe, giving an example of its use, what is meant by a footer.

## ■ Footnote

Footnotes are used to briefly explain a word or phrase without including the explanation in the body of the text. A reference number is placed next to the word or phrase and the explanation is placed at the 'foot' of the page which is identified by the same reference number. Here is an example to explain the word footnote.[1]

**QUESTION**

Describe, giving an example of its use, what is meant by a footnote.

[1] A footnote is found at the foot of the page.

## ■ Page

Pages are each printed side of paper containing the components of a document. The components may include, for example, text, graphics, tables or the contents page. (A website also contains pages.) Each page contains a pre-defined amount of content. This may be defined by the use of a house style or by the user. Pages can also be used to break a long document, such as this book, into chapters, with each page being numbered.

### < Activity >

Collect a range of business documents. Describe the characteristics which have been used and whether they make the document 'fit for purpose'.

# Describe how word-processing and desktop publishing (DTP) software can be used with data from a spreadsheet or database for mail merge, and describe the advantages of using this technique

A standard document created in a word-processing or DTP package can be combined with information from a spreadsheet or database. Mail merging allows the user to create and send a personalised version of the same document to many different people or organisations (recipients).

A data source is created containing all the information to be included in the document. The data source may be created specifically for the mail merge process or it may be an existing data source, for example customer records or student records.

The standard document/template is then produced including merge fields. These are based on the fields in the spreadsheet or database that is being used as the data source. An example would be **Dear <title> <lastname>** where title and lastname are fields in the data source. The standard document can be a letter, address label or envelope.

The data source and the standard document/template are then linked and merged. The software merges the data by inserting the appropriate fields from the data source to produce the personalised documents.

The personalised documents can be sent to a printer or used to create a new file.

If there are 100 customer records held in the data source then the mail merge process would produce 100 documents.

The advantages of using the mail merge process include:

- documents can be produced very quickly
- only one copy of the document needs to be proofread to ensure that all the others are correct
- the data source can be used for many different mail merge processes
- the standard letter/template can be saved and reused.

**QUESTIONS**

**1** What is mail merge?

**2** What are the advantages of mail merge?

# Describe how a document can be reformatted to suit the needs of a given application

Word-processing packages have many other features that can help users format the documents being produced to exactly meet their needs. Users can format the attributes of documents including:

- page size, settings and orientation
- text position, size and style.

## ■ Page size, settings and orientation

The size of the page and the size of the paper to be printed on can be selected by the user to meet their needs. The example below shows the A5 page size selected in Microsoft Word.

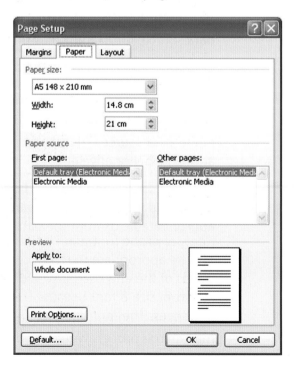

**Figure 6.3** Setting page size in Microsoft Word

Page margins are the blank space around the edges of the page. In general, text and graphics are positioned in the printable area surrounded by the margins. However, some items can be positioned in the margins, for example headers, footers and page numbers.

The user can also select the orientation of the page: either portrait or landscape. The example below shows the landscape orientation selected.

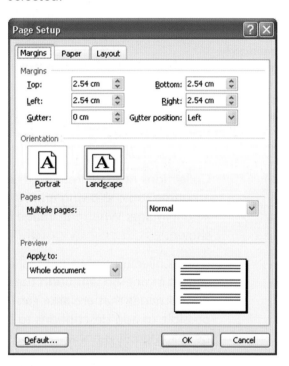

**Figure 6.4** Setting margins in Microsoft Word

## ■ Text position, size and style

Text position is also known as alignment. The user can select the most appropriate alignment to meet their needs. Headings are often centred, but the user may also choose left, right or justified alignment.

A user may also select the font to use. There are many different fonts to choose from. Some fonts are easy to read, such as **Verdana**, **Arial** and Times New Roman. Other fonts are very difficult to read, such as *Pristina*, *Palace Script MT* and *Mistral*.
A user may also choose to highlight some words or phrases through the use of bold, italic or underline features. The style of font selected must be appropriate to the document being produced and the needs of the end users.

The size of the font may also be selected. The size of the font must also be appropriate to the document being produced and the needs of the end user. It would be very difficult to read a business report in size 8 font because the end user would have to strain their eyes. The font size used for this text is size 11.

# Discuss the advantages and disadvantages of using clip art images and collections of thumbnail images

Clip art images are either supplied free with other software packages or at a cost from a software manufacturer. Clip art images can be edited or used as they are.

| Advantages | Disadvantages |
|---|---|
| ■ Images are readily available.<br>■ Images are available immediately.<br>■ The use of clip art can reduce the cost of the design process, for example when designing a logo a designer does not have to be employed.<br>■ Extra equipment, such as scanners and digital cameras, does not have to be purchased. | ■ Choice of images is limited to what is available.<br>■ The quality of the images ranges from very poor to good.<br>■ Clip art is not original or unique.<br>■ Clip art images, especially from Internet sources, may be subject to copyright. |

Collections of small images, thumbnails, are generally based around a topic showing a preview or a representation of the actual image. When the image is clicked then the actual image is shown.

Using collections of thumbnail images enables many images to be shown in one go, although the quality of the images may be poor. Images that are alike can be grouped together. It is also possible to add descriptions to the images so that they can then be searched. It is not always possible to tell whether the actual image is of a better quality or a larger size than the preview or thumbnail image. If the image library holds a large number of images then it can take a long time to download.

**< Activity >**

List the advantages and disadvantages of using a collection of thumbnail images.

| Advantages | Disadvantages |
|---|---|
| | |

# Describe the differences between vector and bitmap graphics and evaluate their suitability for given applications

There are two main ways in which graphics can be stored: as bitmap graphics and as vector graphics.

## ■ Bitmap graphics

These are also known as raster graphics. A bitmap graphic is made up of pixels. In a true black and white graphic each pixel is represented by one bit which is either switched on or off (1 or 0). The more bits representing each pixel, then the more colours can be displayed. If a pixel is represented by four bits in a black and white graphic then 16 different shades of grey are available, while eight bits per pixel means that 256 different shades of grey can be used.

Most graphics are stored in colour. These graphics combine the primary colours of red, green and blue to produce a palette of different shades. Each primary colour, if represented by eight bits, can have a value between 0 and 256. When combined, this gives $256 \times 256 \times 256 = 16\,777\,216$ (i.e. more than 16 million) possible shades.

The table below shows how the values of red, green and blue could be allocated to a specific pixel.

| Primary colour | Value |
| --- | --- |
| Red | 190 |
| Green | 55 |
| Blue | 137 |

Each pixel has two key properties associated with it: a position on the grid which makes up the image and a colour value. These properties are stored as data in the computer's memory. When the graphic needs to be displayed, the data held in the bitmapped file is used to reconstruct the graphic.

A bitmap graphic is produced when an image is taken from a scanner or a digital camera.

Bitmapped files appear in a number of different formats. Some of these are shown in the table.

| Format | Description |
| --- | --- |
| BMP | Windows bitmap. The standard file format used with Windows applications. |
| GIF | Graphics Interchange Format. These files are often used on websites, especially as animated GIFs. They have a 256 colour limit (8 bits per pixel) and use a lossless compression algorithm to save on the amount of memory used. |
| JPEG | Joint Photographic Experts Group. These are also frequently used on websites. JPEGs are often used when good-quality photographic images need to be stored, as they can store 24 bits per pixel and have the capability to store 16 million colours. There are different JPEG formats, which relate to the level of compression used. |
| TIF/TIFF | Tagged Image File Format. The file structure is more complex than some of the other formats but this format can be used on several different platforms. |

## ■ Vector graphics

Vector-based graphics are also known as object-orientated graphics and work in a different way to bitmap graphics. Rather than being stored as data relating to a grid of pixels, this type of graphic is stored as geometric-based data. The file for a vector-based graphic contains mathematical data that defines the key properties of every element in the graphic. Instead of individual pixels storing the required data, vector graphics work on the basis of lines, where drawing starts from a certain point which is central to the image.

If, for example, there is a straight line in the graphic then the data in the file will define its starting point, length, thickness, location within the graphic, etc. The file data, also known as the display list, will also specify the order in which each component will be displayed. This is also known as the hierarchy of the objects.

Although a vector graphic is stored according to its mathematical properties, it is still displayed as a temporary bitmapped graphic.

Vector-based graphics are mainly used for design purposes and are usually used in CAD programs. Vector graphics are used by architects and designers who need to adjust the size, perspective and proportions of their diagrams. A vector-based graphic can be resized without distortion. Vector graphics are essential when CAD/CAM systems are being used. This is when the whole or part of the graphic is being used as the basis for instructions to automated machines.

## ■ Bitmap or vector graphic?

The next table shows the main differences between vector and bitmap graphics.

| Vector | Bitmap |
| --- | --- |
| Can be re-sized or re-scaled with no loss of definition. | When resized there is a lowering of image quality. The image will become blurry and can appear pixellated. |
| The size of a vector graphic file is relatively small compared with a bitmap graphic file for the same size of image. | As each pixel in the image has to be saved individually, a bitmap graphic file can be very large. |
| Every component of the graphic is described by its features (length, colour, thickness, etc). | The components of the graphic are only stored as pixels with their attributes. |
| Vector graphics can be grouped. This keeps the components in the same position relative to each other. | Bitmap graphics are more consistent with the general computing environment, i.e. display and printing devices tend to use a series of dots to define images and text. |
| The facility for producing simple vector-based graphics is often included as part of a word-processing program. These allow the user to create simple graphics, such as squares and lines, that can enhance the presentation of a document. | Bitmap graphics are popular as they deal well with complex highly detailed images such as photographs. As each pixel is an addressable unit, it is possible to make subtle changes to the properties of a graphic. |
| Vector-based graphic files cannot be compressed. | Bitmap files can be compressed. |
| The processing power required to display a vector-based graphic on display equipment is high. | The screen resolution of the display equipment can affect the display of the colours used in a bitmap graphic. |
| Individual elements that make up a vector-based graphic can be edited independently, e.g. moved, resized, and copied. | Editing of bitmap graphics relates to changing the properties of the pixels in the graphic as a whole or an area of it. |

### QUESTIONS

1 What is a bitmap graphic?
2 What is a vector graphic?
3 An architect has a choice between saving his plans as a vector or a bitmap graphic. Giving reasons, identify which he should use.

**Describe the differences between vector and bitmap graphics and evaluate their suitability for given applications**

# Describe the advantages and disadvantages of using graphics libraries and their use in the following applications: kitchen design, cartography and network design

Graphics software for specialist applications, such as kitchen design, map making (cartography) and network designs, provide libraries of graphical images and symbols that are often used in the application. For example, a kitchen design software package will have standard symbols for cupboards and kitchen appliances (cookers, dishwashers, etc), which are used when planning and designing a kitchen layout. Network design graphics libraries will contain industry-standard symbols for the main components needed in a network, for example servers, routers, cabling, etc.

These specialist software applications are developed with the involvement of manufacturers and professional bodies. For example, specialist cartography software would, most likely, have been developed in consultation with the Ordnance Survey and Land Registry to ensure that industry-standard symbols are available. This approach also means that all software relating to the production of maps uses the same symbols with the same meaning.

The main problem with graphics libraries is keeping them up to date. For example, the continual advances in the IT industry means that sometimes the graphic of a new component may not be included or components are included that are no longer used or available.

However, through the use of graphics libraries the diagrams that are constructed will follow an industry standard and will be recognisable in all parts of the world.

# Describe the features of presentation software: text, images, sound, video, animation, slide transition, hyperlinks, hotspots and buttons

## ■ Text

The text used on a presentation slide must meet the needs of the audience. The text style and size should be selected with the audience in mind and should enable the audience to clearly read the text on each slide. The rules, given at the end of this chapter, must be considered at all times. Fancy text, *like this one* like this one, should be avoided and the amount of text on each slide should also be considered.

## ■ Images

The use of images and graphics on a presentation slide can help to convey a message relating to the presentation or as an aide-memoire for the presenter. Again, it is important that the number of images and graphics used on each slide is kept to a minimum and are of a size that can be clearly seen by the audience. If images and graphics are used then any copyright must also be considered.

## ■ Sound

Sound can be used in many different ways within a presentation. Sound effects can be set with animation effects, for example, they can be used to signify the 'arrival' of a piece of text on the screen. Examples of available sound effects are:

- clapping
- drum roll
- chime.

If used appropriately these sounds can be used to emphasise an important piece of information and add impact to the slide. Sound effects should be used sparingly as they can detract from the information contained on the slide.

Sound can also be used in other forms, such as speech and music. Sound files can be a pre-existing file, such as a company jingle, or downloaded from the Internet. It is also possible to record sound files to meet the specific needs of a particular presentation.

## ■ Video

Video clips can be inserted into a presentation, for example part of a company's advertising commercial. The video clip can be set to play automatically when the slide is shown or can be started by the presenter, (e.g. by clicking a button or pressing a key). Do not use too many video clips in a presentation; like other special effects, they can draw attention away from the content of the presentation.

## ■ Animation

Animation effects are visual effects that can be added to text or other objects, such as a chart or picture. All the elements of a presentation, including text, graphics, movies, charts and other objects, can be animated. By using animation it is possible to control the way that objects appear on each slide. For example, the presenter may want to introduce a bulleted list one item at a time. Each bullet point can be made to appear when the presenter performs an action, for example a mouse click. Text can also be animated to appear one letter, word or paragraph at a time.

Animation emphasises important points, controls the flow of information within a slide and adds interest to a presentation.

Another example of the use of animation may be to change the side that text first appears on the slide. English text is read from left to right, and the animation on bullet points is set up so that they appear from the left, but to emphasise a bullet point, it could be animated to appear from the right. The change will grab the audience's attention, thereby reinforcing the text in that bullet point.

Other effects might be to dim text or objects, or to change an object's colour when a new element appears on the slide.

The order and timing of animations can also be changed. If the presentation is to be shown without a presenter then it is possible to set the animations to occur automatically without any human intervention.

When the animations for a presentation have been set up it is possible to preview the presentation to ensure that all the effects are appropriate and that they do not detract from the content of the presentation.

## ■ Slide transition

Transition effects can be applied to a slide to make the presentation more interesting. Transition effects govern how the presentation software moves from slide to slide. The transition effect can be changed to indicate a new section of a presentation or to emphasise a particular slide.

Presentation software offers a range of transition effects. Some of the effects that may be available are:

- cut
- dissolve
- wipe left.

It is also possible to set the speed at which the transition occurs.

A transition effect can be applied to one particular slide or to the whole presentation. They can also have a sound associated with them. The sound effects connected to each slide transition can be set to occur with one specific transition or within the whole presentation. Sound effects should be used sparingly as they can detract from the presentation and its contents.

### < Activity >

Investigate the different slide transition effects that are available on the presentation software you have access to. Identify the advantages and disadvantages of using transition effects.

## Hyperlinks

A hyperlink is coloured and underlined text or a graphic which, when clicked, takes the user to a file, a location in a file or an HTML page on the World Wide Web or an intranet. Hyperlinks can also link to newsgroups and to Gopher, Telnet and FTP sites.

Hyperlinks can be included on presentation slides and used to move to a variety of locations, for example a specific slide within the presentation, a different presentation, a document or spreadsheet, or an Internet, intranet or email address. Any object, including text, shapes, tables, graphs, and pictures, can be configured as a hyperlink.

**Figure 6.5** Hyperlinks and action buttons

## Hotspots

A hotspot is an area on a screen display which responds to a mouse click. This may be a piece of text or a graphic which will take the user to another page or screen. A hotspot is normally used in a multimedia presentation.

## Buttons

An on-screen button can be used to move from one slide to the next. When this method of navigation is used the presentation is interactive. This means that the presenter or viewer is interacting with the presentation by using it to meet their needs. By using this method the user can select the slides viewed and sometimes select the order of viewing. This method is useful where the user needs to jump to another part of the presentation to view the information they need.

---

**QUESTIONS**

1 Explain the advantages of using video in a presentation.
2 What is meant by slide transition?
3 Explain the disadvantages of using sound in a presentation.
4 How could hyperlinks be used in a presentation?

# Compare delivering a presentation using printed acetate slides with using a computer and projected slides, describing the advantages and disadvantages of each

## ■ Printed acetate versus computer and projector

Presentations can be given using a computer and projector or by using printed acetate slides on an overhead projector. Presentation software can also be used to create and print acetate slides.

### Computer and projector presentations

| Advantages | Disadvantages |
| --- | --- |
| ■ The full rage of features (e.g. special effects, hyperlinks, interactivity, etc.) are available. A presentation does not have to be followed in the slide sequence.<br>■ Once a presentation has been developed and saved then it is relatively easy to edit the presentation, and the slides are immediately ready to be shown.<br>■ The slides do not deteriorate with repeated use. | ■ There is a temptation to overuse special features.<br>■ Requires a computer and a projector. Both are relatively expensive and not all places have a projector (which are not very portable).<br>■ Special software is required to allow the presenter to annotate slides in real time.<br>■ Unless the presenter has kept a paper copy of the presentation, then it cannot be given in the event of a powercut. |

### Overhead projector presentations

| Advantages | Disadvantages |
| --- | --- |
| ■ It is easy to write on the slides to annotate them and explain/highlight items.<br>■ An overhead projector (OHP) is the only equipment needed. OHPs are relatively cheap and most places have access to one. They are simple and robust so they seldom go wrong.<br>■ In the event of a powercut, the presenter is able to read from the acetate slides. | ■ Special effects and interactivity cannot be used (e.g. bullet items in a list will have to be covered and revealed one at a time).<br>■ It can be difficult to jump to a slide that is out of sequence to revisit it or if a different route through a presentation is required.<br>■ When a change is made new acetate slides will have to be printed.<br>■ Slides can deteriorate with repeated handling, possibly becoming unreadable.<br>■ Blank acetate slides have to be bought and then printed on. A high use of colour (e.g. for backgrounds) can quickly use up ink/toner. |

### < Activity >

Investigate how and where presentations are given and, using the advantages and disadvantages described above, and any others you might think of, decribe situations where one presentation method might be chosen in preference to the other.

# Compare and give advantages and disadvantages of different modes of navigation (automatic and manual transition) and identify and give examples of when the use of each method is more suitable

A route through a slide show may be navigated using manual or automatic transition methods.

## ■ Manual transition

Manual transition involves some form of action from the presenter/viewer to move on to the next slide. If the slide contains a number of items then each item can be displayed manually. For example, if the slide contains a bulleted list, using the manual method, the presenter can perform an action to display each bullet point in turn. Manual navigation allows the presentation to run at a speed determined by the presenter or viewer. For example, a speaker to an audience can control when each slide or item is displayed, and can tailor the navigation to meet the needs of the audience. A viewer can move to another slide when they are ready by clicking a button, or they can navigate to somewhere else in the presentation by selecting an item in a menu list.

## ■ Automatic transition

A presentation can be set up to run automatically with no intervention required to move on to the next slide. Timings can be set up so that the next slide is displayed automatically after a pre-specified time period. The timings must be set to give the audience sufficient time to read the information contained on a slide before the presentation moves on to the next one. The presentation can also be set to re-start as soon as it has finished. This navigation method is suitable for presentations where no presenter is involved, such as at an exhibition. Automatic navigation is not suitable for verbal presentations as the presenter may struggle to keep pace with the presentation.

### < Activity >

Using the table headings below, identify the advantages and disadvantages of using manual and automatic navigation methods.

|  | Advantages | Disadvantages |
| --- | --- | --- |
| Manual transition |  |  |
| Automatic transition |  |  |

You may need to be able to identify which method of transition is more suitable for a given situation. The method you identify in the examination must be relevant to the situation in the question.

**QUESTIONS**

**1** Identify an appropriate situation where manual slide transition might be used.

**2** Identify an appropriate situation where automatic slide transition might be used.

# Describe non-linear and hierarchical presentations giving the advantages and disadvantages of each. Identify and give examples of when each may be more suitable

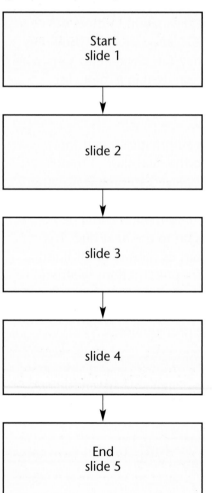

**Figure 6.6** Linear presentation

A presentation is made up of a number of slides. When designing a presentation the structure of the presentation should be developed carefully. The three main structures which a presentation can take are:

- linear
- non-linear
- hierarchical.

The structure of the presentation should be chosen to meet the needs of its content and the target audience. The structure of the presentation will provide the routes that can be taken through the presentation.

A linear presentation is one where slides are shown in a pre-determined order and in which any jump out of this sequence is not allowed, that is the slides follow an ordered line from the beginning to end of the presentation.

A non-linear structure is where slides can be accessed in any order. This structure gives the presenter the option to jump over slides to specific groups or individual slides. It can be represented by a mesh diagram. The user can move through a presentation by going forward to any other slide or by jumping back to any previous slide in the presentation. This structure can become very complicated but can provide a presentation that meets the needs of either the individual user or of a presenter who wishes to use the same presentation for different audiences. Buttons and hyperlinks can be used to jump backwards and forwards to different slides in the presentation.

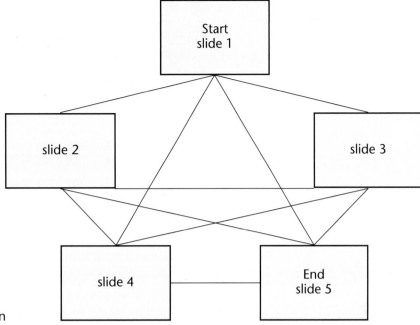

**Figure 6.7** A non-linear presentation

A hierarchical structure allows different, but pre-determined, slides to be jumped to from a slide depending on a option selected (e.g. a menu item or similar), but movement through the slides will follow a pre-determined route and the user cannot jump to any slide, only to those in the path.

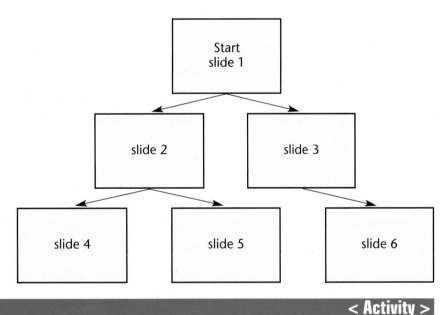

**Figure 6.8** A hierarchical presentation

**< Activity >**

Using the table headings below, identify the advantages and disadvantages of the non-linear and hierarchical structures. Provide an example of when each structure could be used.

|  | Non-linear | Hierarchical |
| --- | --- | --- |
| Advantages |  |  |
| Disadvantages |  |  |
| Example of use |  |  |

**151**

## ■ Rules!

If a presentation is carefully designed then it can be an effective tool to communicate information. There are some rules that must be considered when designing a presentation to ensure that the presentation is effective and meets the needs of the presenter and audience.

1  The style and size of any font used should meet the needs of the presentation and the audience. There should be no more than three different font styles on each slide in the presentation. More than this and the slides will be difficult to read.
2  The size of the text should be large enough for an audience to be able to read from a distance.
3  When an on-screen presentation is being developed, the slide background should contrast with the text colour. Consideration should be given to avoid clashing, garish colour schemes, for example bright green and bright pink, as these can cause eyestrain for the audience and the presenter.
4  The text on the slides should be kept to a minimum. The text contained within the slides should be a summary, with the presenter expanding these points in their talk.
5  Graphics should be very carefully selected. A graphic can add impact to the points being made but if too many graphics are used then they will distract the audience.
6  Animation, sound and transition effects should also be carefully considered. As with graphics, these features can add to the impact of the presentation but if too many are used then they can detract from the content of the presentation.

## Summary

**Characteristics of documents**
Character
Paragraphs
Sections
Frames
Headers
Footers
Footnotes
Pages

## Mail merge
Create data source.
Create template document.
Insert merge fields from data source.
Check merge fields with data.
Complete merge.

## Formatting documents
Page size, settings and orientation
Text position, size and style

## Images and graphics
Bitmap graphic
    Made up of pixels
    Quality is lost on re-sizing
    File sizes very large
    Deal well with complex highly detailed images such as photographs
    Subtle changes can be made to the properties of a graphic
    Files can be compressed
Vector graphic
    Components described by its features (length, colour, thickness, etc.)
    Can be grouped
    Files cannot be compressed
    Individual elements can be edited independently
Clip art
    Readily available
    Available immediately
    Little, if any, extra cost required (e.g. designer or extra equipment, such as scanners)
Thumbnail images/libraries
    Based around a topic
    When preview clicked, image shown
    Lots of thumbnail images can be shown in one go
    Quality of actual image may be poor
    If image library is large, may take a long time to load
Graphics libraries
    Kitchen design
    Network design
    Cartography

## Features of a presentation
Text
Images
Sound
Video
Animation
Slide transition
Hyperlinks
Hotspots
Buttons

**Presentation delivery**
Printed acetates
Computer and projector

**Presentation navigation methods**
Manual
Automatic

**Structure of presentation**
Non-linear
Hierarchical

## Test 1

Answer the following questions in the context of producing a flyer which will be sent with a mail-merged letter to all of a company's customers.

1  Explain the process of mail merging.                                          [4]

2  Clip art images will be used in the flyer. Describe **two** advantages and **one** disadvantage of using clip art in the flyer.                                          [6]

3  The clip art image is a bitmap graphic. Describe bitmap graphics.             [4]

4  The letter includes a header and paragraphs. Describe headers and paragraphs, giving an example of when each could be used.                                          [6]

5  Describe how the page size and orientation could be used to format the letter.  [4]

## Test 2

Answer the following in the context of a school that is setting up a 'healthy eating' snack bar.

1  A logo needs to be created for the snack bar. Describe two advantages and one disadvantage of using an image library to select the logo.                       [6]

2  The logo selected is a vector graphic. Describe vector graphics.              [4]

3  A presentation will be shown advertising the snack bar. Sound and animation will be used in the presentation. Describe sound and animation, giving an example of when each could be used.                                          [6]

4  The presentation is to be shown using a computer and projector. Explain two advantages and one disadvantages of using a computer and projector to show the presentation.                                          [6]

5  The presentation has a linear structure. Describe a linear structure.         [2]

# The role and impact of ICT

## Introduction

This chapter covers the discussion elements of ICT. A large proportion concerns the legal position and Acts of Parliament relating to ICT. You will need to ensure you understand the implications of the laws. This chapter covers the topics you need to know for the discussion question at the end of every examination paper.

This chapter covers:

- The main aspects, purpose and implications of the
  - Data Protection Act
  - Computer Misuse Act
  - Copyright, Designs and Patents Act
  - Regulation of Investigatory Powers Act
  - Electronic Communications Act
  - Freedom of Information Act
- Methods for combating a range of ICT crimes
- The advantages and disadvantages of networking computers
- The required standards and the impact of different standard
- A range of health and safety problems related to working with ICT and measures for avoiding them
- The social impact of ICT upon individuals, organisations and society
- Possible future developments in ICT

## The Data Protection Act (1998)

The Data Protection Act was set up to protect individuals from organisations. There is a lot of information available on individuals and this is collected by many different organisations and government agencies.

### < Activity >

List **three** organisations and **three** government agencies. For each, list all the information on individuals you can think of that might be stored by them.

The Data Protection Act limits the data held by individual organisations to only that which they need. It was meant to stop organisations holding excessive quantities of data on individuals for which they do not have an immediate purpose.

There are a number of terms related to the Data Protection Act.

- **Personal data** – Any data which relates to a living, identifiable individual.
- **Data** – Anything that is held which can be said to be part of a record. This covers both manual and computer data. If you store data on people, such as their health or education records, whether it is on paper or on computer, it is classed as data. Data is also anything stored which is processed by a computer.
- **Processing** – Obtaining, recording or holding the information or data. It also covers any operation performed on the information or data. Operations on the data include organising it (sorting, indexing), changing it, retrieving it (searching) and using it in some way. Operations on the data also include disclosing it (telling someone else or passing it on) and destroying it.

There are several people who are specifically mentioned by the Act and have different rights and responsibilities.

- **Data subject** – The data subject is the living identifiable human being about whom the data is being held.
- **Data controller** –This is the individual within the company who is responsible for making sure that all the provisions of the Data Protection Act are being complied with. This is also the person that you would contact if you had any queries with a company about the Data Proctection Act.
- **Data processor** – This is any person (other than an employee of the Data controller) who processes the data on behalf of the Data controller. This is for companies that hire third parties to process their data for them. Even if the processing is done by a third party, the Data controller retains responsibility for making sure the Data Proctection Act is not contravened.
- **Recipient** – These are individuals who are given the data in order to do some form of processing on it. They are usually employees of the Data controller or are data processors.
- **Third party** – This is the person who receives the data for processing. A company may need to pass on its data to certain people in order to do its job, for example schools give references and information to the government. These people are known as recipients.
- **Information commissioner** – This is the individual who is responsible for ensuring that the Data Protection Act is being adhered to, by giving advice, running training sessions and investigating complaints.

As an individual, you have certain rights under the Data Protection Act. There are six main rights that you possess.

- **Right to subject access** – You are allowed to see what information is being held on you by a company. You need to write to the Data controller and request a copy. You will need to pay an administrative charge. The company must provide the information within a reasonable time of receiving the request (credit agencies 7 days, schools 15 days, other organisations 40 days).

- **Right to prevent processing likely to cause damage or distress** – If the processing of the data is going to cause you damage and distress, you can ask the company to stop. The level of damage and distress needs to be very high and, if the company does not think it is causing damage and distress, it is up to the courts to decide.

- **Right to prevent processing for the purposes of direct marketing** – Direct marketing is mail that is sent to you advertising goods and services. You can request that it be stopped.

- **Rights in relation to automated decision making** – Some decisions are taken by a computer. Credit checks are an example – points are awarded for things such as time in work, owning your own home, etc. and, based on the number of points you get, a decision is made as to whether you can have a credit card or not. You can request that a person takes the decision, not a computer.

- **Right to compensation if damage and distress is suffered by the Act being contravened** – If you can prove that the Data controller did not follow the requirements of the Act and, by not doing so, you suffered both damage and distress, then you are entitled to compensation. Damage can be physical or financial loss. You cannot be compensated for distress on its own.

- **Right to rectify, block or erase incorrect data** – If the data that is held is wrong, then you can get it changed.

The Data Protection Act is very long and complicated. The above discussion is a very simplified version of the main points.

There are some reasons for exemption from the Act. A few of them include:

- national security
- crime and taxation – you cannot see your records
- health, education and social work – if giving the subject access will cause them harm
- domestic purposes – data held on your own computer for your own use, such as a mailing list for Christmas cards.

< Activity >

Investigate and summarise the main exemptions from the Data Protection Act.

**QUESTIONS**

1 Describe what is meant by Data Controller.
2 What is the difference between a recipient and a third party?
3 What are the implications for a company under the Data Protection Act?
4 What does the Data Protection Act mean by data?
5 Who does the Data Protection Act apply to?
6 Describe the rights of the individual under the Data Protection Act.
7 Describe **four** exemptions under the Data Protection Act.

# The main aspects of the Data Protection Act (1998)

The Data Proctection Act has eight principles that must be followed.

1 **Personal data shall be processed fairly and lawfully**
This means that there should be consent for the processing to occur.

2 **Personal data shall be obtained only for one or more specified and lawful purposes, and shall not be further processed in any manner incompatible with that purpose or those purposes**
When a company wants to collect and hold personal data, it must let the Information commissioner know what it is going to hold and what it is going to do with it. The companies can only collect and process data that meets those requirements.

3 **Personal data shall be adequate, relevant and not excessive in relation to the purpose or purposes for which they are processed**
Holding more information than is necessary is not allowed. For example, there is no need for a school to hold information on the pets that your parents had as children. It would not be relevant.

4 **Personal data shall be accurate and, where necessary, kept up to date**
The company must endeavour to ensure that it only has accurate information on you. This may entail them sending out the information they hold for you to check. If they find any inaccurate information, they must correct it.

5 **Personal data processed for any purpose or purposes shall not be kept for longer than is necessary for that purpose or those purposes**

You cannot hold data indefinitely. Eventually it will no longer meet the purpose. For example, a school does not have a need to keep records on pupil detentions from five years ago – it is not needed or consistent with the current purpose. However, schools are required to hold student records for seven years in case of requests for a reference.

6 **Personal data shall be processed in accordance with the rights of data subjects under this Act**

The data subject has certain rights. These include access to the data, the right to correct data if it is wrong, the right to compensation if the processing has caused damage and distress and the right to prevent processing from causing damage and distress.

7 **Appropriate technical and organisational measures shall be taken against unauthorised or unlawful processing of personal data and against accidental loss or destruction of, or damage to, personal data**

The company must ensure that there is sufficient security in place to prevent the data being deleted or being stolen. Back-ups should be taken to restore deleted data.

8 **Personal data shall not be transferred to a country or territory outside the European Economic Area, unless that country or territory ensures an adequate level of protection for the rights and freedoms of data subjects in relation to the processing of personal data**

This is to ensure that data is only given to companies in other countries where there is a similar law to the UK's Data Protection Act. This protects the rights of the data subject. However, if the data subject gives their consent for a transfer then the data can be transferred anywhere.

---

**QUESTIONS**

1 Describe the implications for companies of the seventh principle listed above.
2 What do companies need to do to ensure they comply with the second and third principles listed above?
3 Why is a Data Protection Act necessary?
4 Is the Data Protection Act a workable Act? Describe any problems you can think of with the Data Protection Act.

# The Computer Misuse Act (1990)

## ■ Main provision

The Computer Misuse Act was introduced to protect data held by companies from hackers. It was amended by the Police and Justice Act (2006). It has four main provisions:

- **Unauthorised access to computer material** – This covers entering a computer system without permission by guessing or discovering an individual's password. This is 'hacking' into a computer.
- **Unauthorised access with intent to commit or facilitate the commission of further offences** – This is in addition to entering the computer system. This could be to gain access to a user account and use it to transmit illegal material.
- **Unauthorised acts with intent to impair, or with recklessness as to impairing, operation of a computer** – This is making changes to the contents of a computer or denying access to the computer through Denial of Service attacks.
- **Making, supplying or obtaining articles for use in computer misuse offences (known as 3A)** – This involves malicious scripts or software that will modify original code (i.e. in set top boxes).

## ■ Benefits

Until the introduction of the Computer Misuse Act, theft of electricity was the only crime a hacker could be charged with. The Act allows companies a legal recourse if their security has been compromised.

## ■ Problems

There has to be intent. Accidental intrusion is not a crime. There is also the problem of finding out who is responsible. Just because you can track a computer that is being used for hacking to a property, it does not mean that you know who was responsible. You then need to prove who within the property was using the computer at the point in time that the crime was committed. As with all laws, the Computer Misuse Act is only enforced once the crime has been committed. If a hacker does gain access and obtains confidential information, they could have disseminated it before they are caught. Another problem is that the organisation is the body that determines what is authorised and what is not. This applies in education. If a code of practice for a school indicates that only you are allowed to use your account, if you give your password to your friend and they use your account, technically they have broken the law.

**< Activity >**

1 Discuss the problems for a school and a company of users sharing passwords.

2 Investigate the number of cases of contravention of the Computer Misuse Act that have been brought against people. Why do you think this number is so low?

# The Copyright, Designs and Patents Act (1988)

## ■ Main provision

Among many items, the Act makes it illegal to steal or create unauthorised copies of software. It also covers manuals, books, CDs and music.

## ■ Benefits

A lot of time and effort goes into the production of software, books and music. The people who put in that effort deserve to be rewarded. The reward is in royalties. If the items are copied and distributed then they will not receive any money. The Act allows the individuals and corporations who invest time and money to reap their rewards.

## ■ Problems

When you buy software, you haven't bought the software itself, only a licence to use it. The company who wrote the software continues to own it and allows you to use it under licence on certain conditions. There are many different types of software licence, and these conditions vary depending on the software and the company. Some do not allow the software to be installed and run on more than one machine. Some allow it to be installed on a desktop PC and a laptop, so long as they are not used at the same time. Other types of licence include site and network licences which specify a maximum number of users who can run the software at any given time. Understanding the licences can be difficult and many people wrongly think that because nobody can see then it isn't a crime to copy and distribute software freely. Similarly, copying a CD or downloading copyright music from the Internet is also a crime and the practice damages people's livelihoods and hinders future developments at the end of the chain. 'Microsoft already has too much money, they won't miss me not paying' is a common defence for copying software, but it is still illegal. 'If I had to pay for it I would not buy it' is not an excuse, nor is arguing that everyone does it.

# The Regulation of Investigatory Powers Act (2000)

## ■ Main provision

Nicknamed the 'snoopers' charter', the Regulation of Investigatory Powers Act was introduced to address concerns about the use and misuse of communication interception techniques by public and private organisations. The Act allows for the lawful interception of postal, telecommunications and digital communications. The Act came about because of a court case (Malone vs UK) where the defendant was acquitted and subsequently sued the police for intercepting his phone calls. The case was thrown out and taken to the European Court of Human Rights. They declared that the practice of interception was insufficiently grounded in law. This led to a 1985 Act that was subsequently updated as it did not cover private networks.

The Act makes it a criminal offence to monitor communications without lawful authority. Communications include telephone calls, emails, post, etc.

To be lawful, 'the interception has to be by or with the consent of a person carrying on a business, for purposes relevant to that person's business, and using that business's own telecommunications system.'

Organisations may monitor and record communications:

- to establish the existence of facts to ascertain compliance with regulatory or self-regulatory practices or procedures or to ascertain or demonstrate standards which are or ought to be achieved
- in the interests of national security
- to prevent or detect crime
- to investigate or detect unauthorised use of telecommunications systems
- to secure, or as an inherent part of, effective system operation.

There are some circumstances where the organisation may monitor but not record:

- received communications to determine whether they are business or personal communications
- communications made to anonymous telephone help lines.

Public interceptions can also be made with 'lawful authority'.

## Benefits

The benefits to the company are that it can monitor what its employees are doing. This in turn can ensure that the facilities are only being used for legitimate work and that company secrets are not being revealed or time wasted.

## Problems

Any form of monitoring may be seen as a breach of trust. Some people may say, if we have nothing to hide, we should not be afraid of being monitored, but there is a desire by many to cling onto their privacy. The Regulation of Investigatory Powers Act could be seen as going against that desire. Some people may also be concerned about what controls there may be on organisations who monitor communications.

> **< Activity >**
>
> Research the Regulation of Investigatory Powers Act. Discuss the benefits to companies and what they need to do before they can monitor communications. What is your attitude to someone looking at all your post and emails?

# The Electronic Communications Act (2000)

## Main provision

The government wanted 'to make the UK the best place in the world for e-commerce' and to 'create a legal framework so that people can be sure about the origin and integrity of communications'. In order to achieve this, the Electronic Communications Act was passed.

The legislation is in two main parts:

- **Cryptography service providers** – This allows the government to set up a register of 'approved cryptography suppliers'.
- **Facilitation of electronic commerce, data storage** – This recognises digital signatures, which are now admissible in law.

There is a lot of legislation that is in conflict with digital signatures. The Electronic Communications Act gives ministers the power to make delegated legislation to remove any restrictions in other legislation which prevent use of electronic communications in place of paper.

## ■ Benefits

Contracts that are signed over the Internet have the same legality as those signed by hand. This increases the security with which individuals can engage in e-commerce and the contracts entered into have legal backing.

## ■ Problems

Although there is the legislation in place to remove many of the laws that prevent digital signatures being accepted, this will take time. Conveyancing (buying and selling a house) and wills are two areas where digital signatures will take a long time to be introduced.

There is always a security risk. The first digital signature made by a cabinet minister was effectively hijacked within 24 hours of its creation. A document, digitally signed by the Trade and Industry Minister had an additional statement opposing the government's cryptographic policy inserted into it.

# The Freedom of Information Act (2000)

## ■ Main provision

The Freedom of Information Act came into force at the beginning of 2005. The Act deals with access to official information, that is being able to find out information on any topic from any public authority.

The Act applies to all public authorities, which includes government, the health service (hospitals and doctor's surgeries), schools and police.

**< Activity >**

Research what is meant by 'public authority'. Apart from the ones mentioned above, what other organisations are covered by the Act?

The Act allows anyone to make a request – there are no restrictions on age. A letter to the public authority that you think has the information you want, along with your name, address for them to send the information to and a description of what you want is all that is required. Most requests will be free, however a small charge may be requested to cover photocopying and postage.

Public authorities have 20 working days to comply with your request.

## ■ Benefits

The main benefit is that information which was not accessible to the general public is now available. This increases accountability – the pubic authority cannot take decisions and then hide those decisions. The information is now available to those that request it.

## ■ Problems

It is possible to ask for any information at all. However, this does not mean that you will receive it. Some information might be withheld to protect various interests or it may come under some of the other exemptions.

The Act is part of a set and requesting information under the wrong Act will delay the information being received. For example, information about yourself needs to be requested under the Data Protection Act.

The public authority does not have to confirm or deny the existence of the information you have requested. It does not have to provide it if an exemption applies, if the request is too vague for information to be found, if it is similar to a request previously received, or if the cost of collating and producing the information exceeds an appropriate limit.

### < Activity >

Investigate and report on the exemptions to the Freedom of Information Act.

### QUESTIONS

1 What are the main provisions of the Computer Misuse Act?
2 Explain the disadvantages of implementing the Computer Misuse Act.
3 Explain the problems of enforcing the Copyright, Designs and Patents Act.
4 Describe the main provisions of the Regulation of Investigatory Powers Act.
5 Why do you think there is so much opposition to the Regulation of Investigatory Powers Act? Explain your reasons.
6 What are the benefits of having a Regulation of Investigatory Powers Act?
7 Who benefits the most from the Electronic Communications Act and why?
8 Explain the problems with the Electronic Communications Act.
9 Describe the main provisions of the Freedom of Information Act.
10 Explain why you may not be given the information you have requested under the Freedom of Information Act.

< Tip >

The specification requires you to be aware of any updates and changes to the above Acts. Make sure that you are aware of any changes.

# Describe methods for combating a range of ICT crime

ICT crime is crime involving a computer. It could be the physical theft of the computer or of components from a computer, or using one computer to attempt to gain access to another computer system and commit a crime.

The computer crimes that are seen in films are not usually possible in the real world. Stopping a time clock and stealing money, collecting all the fractions of money and getting them paid to you or hacking into a bank and transferring money to your account all sound easy enough but are extremely rare if not impossible to achieve.

However, crimes involving computers do exist. It can be industrial espionage (finding out what a business competitor is doing), breaking into a computer system or trying to find personal data.

There are two main groups of method for combating computer crime:

- Physical methods
- Logical methods

## ■ Physical methods

Physical methods prevent a person from gaining access to a computer in person. Instead of getting access across the Internet or dialing in, physical access means actually walking in and sitting at a computer yourself.

Ways to protect against physical access include having security guards on the door and giving each employee a pass that the guard checks. You could have an automatic door that responds to a pass given to each employee. The computers could be kept in locked rooms with only specific people given access to them. Security cameras could monitor corridors and rooms.

Physical methods also include the positioning of the screen and keyboard. If the machine is in an open access area, like a reception area, then having the screen so it cannot be seen by the public or the keyboard so they cannot see a password being typed in are sensible precautions.

The use of wireless networks has increased the difficulty of ensuring physical security.

Increasingly biometric measures, such as scanning a person's iris or fingerprint, are being used to provide physical security.

**< Activity >**

For each of the physical methods describe above, give the disadvantages of the method. For example, how might someone determined to get into a building overcome the physical methods?

## ■ Logical methods

These are computer-based methods that can be applied to the computer by a system administrator. They include usernames and passwords, access rights and user groups. Other logical methods include screensaver passwords, so if you leave your desk for any length of time no one else can use the machine, firewalls and anti-virus software, as well as logging actions and analysing these logs.

When you log on to a computer system or network you are asked for two pieces of information:

■ a username or user ID
■ a password.

**Figure 7.1** A network log-on dialogue box

The User ID:

■ is a unique identifier for a user, identifying who the user is to the system
■ can be allocated to groups and those groups can have access rights and programs allocated to them, (e.g. according to which user group they belong to, a user might be only allowed to read a file, while other groups might have edit or delete access)
■ can restrict the user to only logging onto certain machines or at certain times of the day
■ can be used to log what the user is doing.

**Describe methods for combating a range of ICT crime**

A password is a method of restricting access. Unless you know the password, you cannot perform tasks. When used in conjunction with a User ID, the password authenticates who the user is – that they are who the User ID says they are. This assumes that only the user knows the password.

Passwords are the weak link in any system. User IDs tend not be kept secret, but passwords need to be.

The network manager can apply controls to the password to make them harder for other people to find out. Such controls might include:

- using a minimum number of characters
- using a combination of numbers and letters
- not using a word in the dictionary
- changing passwords regularly (e.g. monthly)
- keeping a record of passwords so you cannot reuse one you have already had
- restricting the number of attempts (e.g. three wrong passwords and the account is locked)
- making the password impersonal.

### < Activity >

Create a poster for the ICT rooms explaining password security. Give examples of good and bad passwords.

### QUESTIONS

1 Why are User IDs required?
2 What is a password?
3 What is authentication?
4 Why are User IDs not kept secret?
5 Describe **three** measures the network manager can undertake to ensure passwords remain secure.

Password security is important so users must be instructed not to give out passwords and how to correctly select passwords (not using dictionary words, for example). Educating users about good practice in computer use, such as ensuring they log off, will also increase security.

Preventative methods for combating ICT crime include the threat of legal action. As seen previously, there are several laws that can be broken when using a computer and many of these carry fines or imprisonment as a punishment.

Software releases ensuring that the software is kept up to date and can prevent people getting into the computer through a software vulnerability. Keeping anti-spyware, anti-spam and anti-virus software up to date is just as important.

QUESTIONS

1 Describe **three** physical methods of preventing a computer crime.
2 How can using access rights combat computer crime?
3 Describe **three** laws that would be broken by hacking.
4 Describe **five** different ICT crimes.

Other methods that can be employed to make it more difficult for data to be stolen and used include auditing, firewalls and encryption.

Auditing is a method of looking over logs. Logs can be created for events that occur on the network: user logging in, applications run, websites visited, emails sent, etc. A log can be used to build up a profile of a user.

Software can be used to look at logs to spot patterns of change, for example maybe a user starts logging in at different times or accessing different data. A change in habit might set alarm bells ringing and warrant further investigation in case the username and password are being used by a different person.

A firewall is a hardware and/or software gate between the two networks or between a system and a network that filters the data transferred based on security policies. Firewalls are used on computers that connect to the Internet to prevent unauthorised access to the system or network the computer is part of.

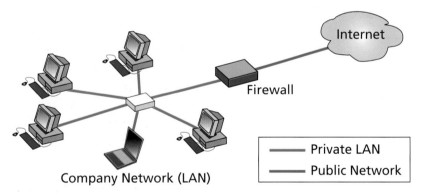

**Figure 7.2** Use of a firewall

Encryption does not prevent the data being stolen. It aims to prevent anyone who has the data being able to understand it without the appropriate key.

Encryption is the process of taking plain text and applying an algorithm to it to turn it into encrypted text. Only someone with a key should be able to convert the encrypted text back into plain text.

**Describe methods for combating a range of ICT crime**

Alphabet ——————→ | A | B | C | D | E | F | G | H | I | J | K | L | M | N | O | P | Q | R | S | T | U | V | W | X | Y | Z |

Alphabet – shifted
four places right ——————→ | W | X | Y | Z | A | B | C | D | E | F | G | H | I | J | K | L | M | N | O | P | Q | R | S | T | U | V |

**Figure 7.3** Simple encryption

CAESAR CIPHER becomes YWAOWN YELDAN

Encryption has been around for a long time: the advent of computers has just made the ciphers more complicated.

< Activity >

Research Pretty Good Privacy (PGP) encryption. Discuss why the US government did not want it widely used. Do you think they were correct?

### QUESTIONS

1 Describe how a network manager might use a log to find a hacker on the system.
2 Give **two** ways a firewall can be used to protect data.
3 What is the difference between encoding and encryption?
4 Describe the disadvantages of using encryption as a method of securing data.

# Describe the advantages and disadvantages of networking

There are many different types of network, the two main ones being:

- peer-to-peer
- client–server.

A peer-to-peer network is a computer network where all of the computers connected to it are of equal status. An example would be linking two home computers together. Any of the computers connected can provide printer or file-sharing resources.

Some benefits and limitations of peer-to-peer networking are listed in the next table.

| Advantages | Disadvantages |
|---|---|
| ■ There is no need to purchase an expensive server. Normal computers can be used.<br>■ Each user manages their own computer. This means that a network manager is not required.<br>■ Set up is done using wizards. No technical knowledge is required.<br>■ There is no reliance on a central server, so the network remains robust if it fails. | ■ Each computer is fulfilling more than one role – it may be printing or file sharing. This increases the load on the systems.<br>■ The data can be stored on any computer, so there is no organisation to data storage.<br>■ Security, anti-virus protection and back-ups are the resposbility of the individual users. |

A client–server network has a powerful controlling computer: the server. This computer controls the peripherals (printers, back-up, etc.) and the network security.

Some benefits and limitations of client–server networking are listed in the next table.

| Advantages | Disadvantages |
|---|---|
| ■ Back-up, security and anti-virus protection are centralised.<br>■ Shared data is centralised and organised.<br>■ The user does not do any of the management of the computers.<br>■ Network processing is done centrally, not at individual computers, freeing them to do what the user wants. | ■ The server and network operating system cost money.<br>■ A network manager is required.<br>■ There is a reliance on the central server. If it fails, no work can be done. |

A computer that is not connected to any other computer (i.e. it is not networked), is said to be stand-alone. The next table gives some of the advantages and disadvantages of networking. The advantages of stand-alone computers are the disadvantages of a network and vice versa.

| Advantages | Disadvantages |
|---|---|
| ■ Peripherals, such as printers and scanners, can be shared by several workstations, reducing the cost (as you do not have to buy one for each). The quality of the device purchased can be better than the quality of the individual devices (as more money can be spent on a better device).<br>■ Data can be shared. This allows standard files, such as templates, to be available from a central source. Data can also be shared by several people in a team allowing them to work on the same document.<br>■ Access to data is controlled by usernames, passwords and associated access rights. The network manager can also log who has used what file and ensure that security is not being breached.<br>■ Access to applications can be controlled from a central area. This can ensure that the use of licences is legal.<br>■ The resources used by individuals can be monitored and logged, allowing access to the resources to be charged to the appropriate department.<br>■ Back-ups and virus checking can be controlled from a central location.<br>■ Users can communicate with email systems and an intranet can disseminate useful information. | ■ All the services a network provides become unavailable if the network fails without adequate contingency in place (which can be expensive).<br>■ The devices that are required to build the network depend on the different topologies.<br>■ If a virus is introduced into a single workstation, then it can use the network to spread to the rest.<br>■ If the network is particularly busy, it may have a detrimental effect on the work that the user can do. |

# Explain why standards are required and the impact of different organisations and networks having different standards

A network is two or more computers connected together so that they can communicate. Without communication between the computers and the peripherals they cannot exchange information – this might be printer data, files or password authentication.

In order for the computers to communicate they need to be talking the same language. This means that they need to be running the same protocol or standard. TCP/IP is one example of a protocol.

A protocol is a set of communication rules. It governs:

- the format of the message
- the type of error checking to be used
- any compression
- how the sending device indicates it has finished sending
- how the receiving device indicates that it has received the message.

There are many different types of protocols available.

**< Activity >**

Investigate and compare **three** different protocols, looking at where they are used and their advantages and disadvantages.

If the computers and organisations are not communicating using the same standard then data transfer will not be possible, or if it does occur, is likely to be incorrect.

QUESTIONS

1 What is a network?
2 Why do computers have to communicate?
3 Identify **three** items that need to be communicated.
4 What is a protocol?
5 Why must the computers have the same protocol running?

# Describe a range of health problems related to working with ICT and measures to avoid them

Working with ICT can be a dangerous activity. There are several problems that can be caused by using computers for long periods of time.

The problems can be divided into two groups: those relating to health and those that cover safety.

Health problems are those based on activities that can cause physical damage to the body due to prolonged use of the computers. Some examples are given below. The causes given are not the only causes.

| Heath problem | Description | Cause | Prevention |
|---|---|---|---|
| Deep vein thrombosis (DVT) | Blood clot, usually in the leg | Sitting in a chair that puts pressure on the back of the knees | Stand up and move around. Ensure correct posture when sitting in a chair. |
| Repetitive strain injury (RSI) | Chronic pain experienced in the arms, shoulder or back | Repetitive actions, poor posture while working, maintaining a fixed forced position | Use correct workstation, keyboard rests, foot stools, adjustable chairs and frequent breaks from continuous activity. |
| Carpal tunnel syndrome | Pressure on the median nerve in the wrist | Repeated wrist movements such as typing | Avoid the repetitive actions. Frequent breaks between the actions. |
| Ulnar neuritis (cubital tunnel syndrome) | Compression of the ulnar nerve in the elbow | Leaning on the elbow for prolonged periods of time | Use wrist rests, adjustable height of chairs and correct desk height. |
| Eye strain | Hazy vision, tired eyes | Looking at a monitor for long periods of time, dehydration of the eyes | Take plenty of fluids and frequent breaks. Use correctly adjusted, flicker-free monitors. |
| Back pain/ache | Muscle spasms | Poor posture, sitting in the same position, forced position | Use correct posture and adjustable chair. |
| Fatigue | Tiredness and lethargy | Continued periods of mental work. | Take a five minute break every hour. Vary the type of work. |
| Stress | State of mental strain | Overwork or software/hardware not doing what you expect. | Take a five minute break every hour. Train in the software. |

Many health problems are caused by incorrect posture.

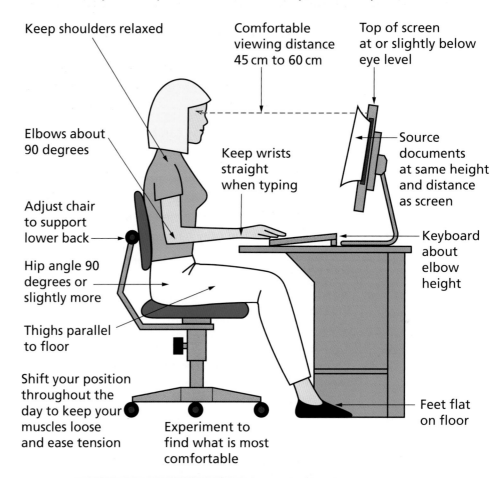

Keep shoulders relaxed

Comfortable viewing distance 45 cm to 60 cm

Top of screen at or slightly below eye level

Elbows about 90 degrees

Keep wrists straight when typing

Source documents at same height and distance as screen

Adjust chair to support lower back

Hip angle 90 degrees or slightly more

Thighs parallel to floor

Shift your position throughout the day to keep your muscles loose and ease tension

Experiment to find what is most comfortable

Keyboard about elbow height

Feet flat on floor

**Figure 7.4** Correct posture at a workstation

< Activity >

Investigate the Health and Safety Regulations for the use of computers. Make a list of the equipment that could be provided by a company to prevent health problems and, for each, explain the problem that it prevents.

# Describe a range of safety problems related to working with ICT and measures to avoid them

Safety hazards are items which can cause injury or damage. They are likely to be immediate rather than built up over time. Some examples are given in the table.

| Safety hazard | Description | Prevention |
|---|---|---|
| Trailing wires | Wires from computers trailing from desks and along floors can cause accidents | Cable management systems to cover wires |
| Fire | Overheating of computers can cause them to catch fire<br>Overloading of plug sockets can cause fire | Adequate ventilation, and clear space around equipment<br>Not overloading plug sockets<br>Correct number of sockets on a breaker<br>Using the correct type of fire extinguisher ($CO_2$) for electrical fire |
| Electric shock | Water and electricity can cause an electric shock (possibly fatal)<br>Bare wires, when touched, can cause electric shock | No drinking near computers<br>No water near computers<br>All wires to be frequently checked and repaired |
| Unstable surfaces and chairs | Desks and surfaces that wobble can cause computer equipment to fall off | All surfaces to be stable before computer equipment is placed on them |
| Food and drink | Liquids can cause shorting and lead to fire. Crumbs from food are a fire hazard | No eating and drinking near computers |

> ### < Activity >
>
> Investigate the room you are sitting in. Make a list of the possible health and safety hazards that exist and, for each, explain how they could be alleviated.

### QUESTIONS

1 What is the difference between a potential health problem and a safety hazard?
2 Describe **three** health problems that could affect a computer operator.
3 For each potential problem described in question 2, suggest an appropriate solution.
4 Describe **three** safety hazards that could be taken into account when installing a new computer room.
5 For each hazard described in question 4, suggest an appropriate solution.

# Discuss the impact of ICT on individuals, organisations and society

**< Tip >**

Discussion questions will appear at the end of every AS paper. It is important that you read the section on examination technique and practise answering discussion questions. You must look at what you have given as an answer and see if you have given an implication: positive or negative. Have you stopped too soon? If you were speaking the same answer to your teacher would they be waiting for you to add something more to the answer? If so, add some more to the written answer.

## ■ Capabilities and limitations of ICT systems

ICT is often put forward as the solution to many problems. It is certainly true that ICT has helped in many areas but it should always be seen as a tool: a tool that we control and we decide when to use. The use of ICT is not always appropriate and there are occasions when its use should be discouraged.

Here are some advantages and disadvantages to the use of ICT systems.

### Advantages

Computers can perform the same actions over and over again, and they can do this very quickly and reliably. For example, calculating interest on bank accounts or working out electricity bills – the same processing is performed on every single account and because of the number of accounts it needs to be done very quickly.

Computers can search large volumes of data and they can do it very quickly. At an ATM the computer needs to search through vast numbers of customer accounts to find yours. You do not want to be standing waiting, so it needs to do it quickly. Consider the amount of data being stored by a company like a bank: every single transaction on every single account – and not just for this year, for previous years as well. It is no good storing the data if you cannot find your way around it and access the required data. Their storage needs to be structured and accessible.

Computers can perform tasks that are impossible or dangerous to humans, for example control systems.

### Disadvantages

There are limitations on the use of ICT. One of the main being the hardware. The speed of hardware development is phenomenal. In 1975, Gordon Moore finalised his prediction for the increase of processing power: the number of components on semiconductor chips with the lowest per-component cost doubles roughly every two years. This has also been applied to storage. Put simply, the same amount of money will purchase twice the speed or twice the storage it did two years previously. For the most part, this has proved, until recently, to be true.

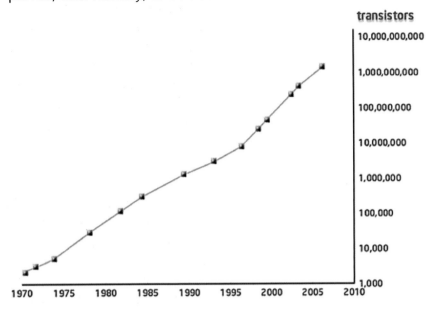

**Figure 7.5** Moore's Law

However, hardware limitations are beginning to have an impact on future developments. People want things done now, not in a few seconds. The interface to the computer, such as the keyboard, is archaic and not useful for entering vast quantities of data quickly.

The software that is used limits what can be done. It can still be cumbersome to use and often requires training. The design and development of software itself can limit what can be done with it.

As we utilise the communications available within computers more and more, so we demand more and more bandwidth. We want video on demand, faster downloads of software, music and movies, and interactive conversations with people on the other side of the world. At the moment this is not possible because of limitations in bandwidth.

**< Activity >**

Describe the ICT and technology that you have seen in films and television programmes recently, for example the ability to manipulate images on a computer screen by hand in *Minority Report*. How realistic is the technology that was used? Do you think that it will eventually be introduced? What are the advantages and disadvantages?

# ■ Communications systems

One of the biggest improvements brought about by technology is in the field of communications. Communications have shrunk the planet: we can send messages in seconds to countries anywhere in the world.

One effect of this is to increase the globalisation of companies. They can retain control over offices and employees from anywhere in the world.

Communications covers a variety of areas: the Internet, intranets, mobile phones, telephone systems and interactive television, to name a few.

### Telephone systems

Telephony is a relatively old method of communication, but it has had a digital upgrade over the last few years. The telephone systems available today allow you to contact other individuals quickly and have an element of personal contact (even if it is only by voice). It is now possible to have conference calls, answer phones, mobile phones, remote access, different ring tones, call forwarding, SMS messaging and many other features. The systems allow you to send documents (either as faxes or as attachments to emails) and emails, and many computers connect to the Internet using telephone systems.

### < Activity >

The use of mobile phones has increased over the last few years. What features are available on a mobile phone and what new features do you want? Describe the advantages and disadvantages of mobile phones.

### The Internet

The Internet is a vast collection of interconnected computers for the purpose of sharing data. One of the biggest benefits and problems of the Internet is that it is outside of any government's control. (Governments can attempt to filter or restrict access but they cannot control the content of websites. Attempts to do so have resulted in the content being relocated to countries with laws that allow that content.) The advantage is that the Internet cannot be turned on or off, or controlled. The disadvantage is that it has security problems, problems with pornography, and it can be used by criminals and terrorists.

### < Activity >

What are the charges relating to the Internet for a user and for someone wishing to set up a website?

The Internet is used to find information. This can be by using websites (which, when taken together, contain the largest encyclopaedia available) or downloading files. The Internet gives access to a large repository of information through the World Wide Web. The Web is useful for technical support: almost every topic has a help page. Drivers for computers can be located, as well as software updates. It is possible to use the Internet to chat with friends and relatives and take part in discussions.

With all the unregulated information on the Web it is sometimes impossible to tell what is true and what is not. Anyone can create a website and put their views and opinions on it. It is necessary to consider carefully all the information posted on the Web and not leap in and believe it all.

The Internet is also an efficient means of transmitting viruses. Downloading files and opening them could infect your machine. It is important that, when using the Internet, you have an appropriate firewall and virus checker.

Identification of individuals is difficult on the Internet. When chatting, how do you know who you are talking to? The person may say they are sixteen and a pupil at a local school but how can you verify this?

Breach of copyright is a problem on the Internet. The ease of posting and availability of files (movies, music and software) makes it difficult to apprehend people who break copyright laws. The location of the server being used to disseminate the data can also cause problems. Governments have little control globally because the laws of one country are different from those of another: crimes in one country may not be crimes in another. The location of the web server may be in a country where it is legal to post certain content that would be illegal elsewhere.

Laws regarding tax and purchases using the Internet are difficult to enforce. If you purchase items from websites and you are getting them from another country then they are subject to taxation and import regulations when they come into the country. Enforcing this is difficult.

### Email
An email is an electronic message sent using the Internet from one person to another located anywhere in the world. Documents, spreadsheets and other files can be attached to an email. Digitally signed emails can be accepted as a contract (see Electronic Communications Act).

< Activity >

There are now many communication methods available to us. Have they shrunk the world or increased physical isolation?

Copy out and fill in the table. Give examples of the advantages and disadvantages of the different communication methods, giving reasons why. Add in other means of communications that have not been covered above.

| Method | Advantages | Disadvantages |
|---|---|---|
| Telephone | | |
| Mobile phone | | |
| Email | | |
| Internet | | |
| | | |
| | | |

## ■ How ICT has changed society

The introduction of ICT into society has brought about some major changes, particularly in the areas of shopping, medicine and health care, disabled people, education and entertainment.

### Shopping

Most high street stores have a web presence. Today, there are some retailers you can only buy from online because they do not have a physical presence which you can walk into to make a purchase. Amazon is perhaps the most well known of this new generation of retailers.

The advantages of Internet shopping for the customer include availability (a website is open 24 hours a day, 365 days a year). It does not matter where the 'shop' is: it could be in this country or on the other side of the world. Currency is not an issue: if you possess a credit or debit card then the conversion is done automatically. There are sites that will compare prices for you to enable you to get the best deal. This is particularly useful for those people who are housebound (the elderly and disabled) or those in remote areas.

However, there are disadvantages to online shopping. How do you know that a website is genuine? How do you know that the site has not been set up purely to get credit card details? You may never see the goods. At least when you go to a shop you come out with the goods at the end of the transaction. You also need to be at home when the item is delivered or arrange to collect it from the delivery company. A buyer also needs a computer and Internet connection to shop online: this can be expensive.

There will be a tendency for people to become lazy and unhealthy. If you can shop without leaving your home, this will reduce the amount of exercise you take and this in turn can lead to an unhealthy lifestyle.

Online food shopping has increased in popularity and websites offering this service allow you to keep a weekly shopping list of staple items that you need every week. However, you are reliant on someone else picking your food and sometimes items you don't want might be substituted for those out of stock.

Companies that have only an online presence do not have to maintain premises and large numbers of staff, however, they will need to employ website designers, technical support and packers.

Delivery firms have benefited from the increase in posted goods, and there are fewer journeys made: one delivery vehicle can take the place of several car journeys. This decreases congestion and pollution.

**< Activity >**

Summarise the advantages and disadvantages of online shopping for both a customer and a company.

## Medicine

Medical improvements are occurring all the time. The impact of ICT in medicine has been in two main areas: treatment and administration. The use of computers in administration has enabled medical staff to have access to patients' notes, treatment records and information on treatments, as well as the latest research. The medical staff can now create care plans, drug administration records and monitor the patient more effectively.

Computers are used to help people with hearing and sight diabilities, they have improved the manufacture of artificial components such as limbs and they have allowed three-dimensional images to be created of the body for surgeons to examine.

Not everywhere has access to medical computing facilities. It is important not to become over-reliant on the technology to the extent that medicine cannot be practised without it.

ICT and the Internet have also made it easier to share research. Universities can pool their findings and collaborate more effectively.

Many people, non-experts, now use medical websites as a first port of call for information on medical conditions, but a little knowledge can be a dangerous thing and information, whether from a book or online, cannot replace a fully-trained medical practitioner. There are medical expert systems that you can consult. They will ask you questions and, based on your answers, recommend treatment or a further consultation with a doctor.

< Activity >

Research and produce a report on all the different parts of the body that can be replaced by an artificial component.

## Education

There are three aspects where ICT has affected education: administration, teachers and students.

Electronic registration is common in many schools. This allows schools to immediately contact parents if their child is absent unexpectledly. Details on students (e.g. exam results, detentions, medical conditions, etc.) can be stored and accessed, and the information gained can be used to give appropriate help and support. Performance can be monitored and any problems picked up before they become serious.

Students benefit from Internet access to a wide range of information, the use of computers to write up and share work given to them, and the use of presentation software and handouts to liven up the lessons! Virtual Learning Environments (VLEs) allow teachers to structure topics and provide all the lesson and testing materials.

Many schools have a facility that lets students access their work stored on the school's computer system from home. This eliminates the need to use portable devices to transfer the work or to forget the work!

Teachers benefit from ICT in lessons by being able to pre-prepare presentation material with handouts. They can also make use of electronic administration aids for registering and recording marks.

Websites give students greater access to material that can be used to support their projects, but plagiarism and submission of ready-made material have become problems.

< Activity >

Only a few aspects of education have been touched on. Think about how students, teachers and admistration staff use ICT in your school. What are the advantages and disadvantages of using ICT?

# ■ The effect of ICT on organisations

Organisations, as well as individuals, are affected by ICT. There was a fear that introducing ICT into offices would mean unemployment. It was argued that with computers, fewer people could do the same job, which meant that fewer people would be required. The actual effect has been to increase employment. ICT has an industry that surrounds it: network managers, technicians, website designers, ICT trainers, etc. Organisations have had to employ more people to install and maintain the ICT equipment. There has been a redistribution of employment.

In retail, if a shop closes to become an online-only shop, it will need website designers, packers and delivery people. These are different to the jobs required when it needed shop assistants and shelf stackers.

Those employees that use ICT in their work have benefited from the advantages of electronic filing systems, the ability to edit a document rather than retype it every time it is needed, and email.

The effect on the organisation has been to increase communication. Email, fax, video conferencing and shared diaries have meant that it is easier to track down and get in touch with people. The workload has not decreased. More work is being done in the same amount of time.

### Structure of the organisation

The structure of organisations has altered. With electronic communications there is no longer the need for a company's headquarters to be in a major city. It can be located anywhere. The company does not even have to have all its departments in the same location: decentralisation of the organisation is partly a result of ICT.

New departments and directors have been created with the advent of ICT. ICT directors, network managers and training departments have all had to be incorporated in the organisational structure.

### Teleworking

One major change in recent years has been teleworking. This is working from home. Employees can spend some or all of their time working from home instead of at a company's premises. Teleworking has also allowed many individuals to set up successful home-based companies.

The advantages of teleworking for an organisation are that a central location for employees to travel to is not required. An organisation can move out of town to places where the rent is cheaper. The size of building required is smaller as there are fewer employees permanently based at the premises.

An organisation keeps control of its workforce, making sure that employees are working effectively, by using email and tracking set targets. Not every person has the right temperament for working from home: it requires self-discipline and the ability to work alone.

The advantages to the employee are that they do not have to commute to work. They can get up later as there is no travel and be back 'at home' earlier. There are no travel costs and less pollution because of the reduction in traffic. More time can be spent with the family, maybe less child care is required (although this has a knock-on effect on the economy).

Disadvantages might include a lack of motivation: if there is no boss it is very easy to put some work off until tomorrow. There may be a lack of social contact: part of working is not about the job itself but the social interaction with our colleagues. Additional equipment may be required: high-speed Internet connection, fax, etc., but this is often provided by the company. A company and its employees also need to be aware of the issues related to keeping commercial and staff information secure, of protecting equipment from theft, and of protecting staff from potential safety hazards.

### < Activity >

Would teleworking suit you? How would you cope with only having deadlines and no imposed structure? As a boss, what would you do to try to make sure your employees were working when at home?

## ■ Dependence on ICT

We rely on ICT a lot more than might first be apparent. Banking, engine management systems in vehicles, alarm clocks, heating systems, etc., all rely on ICT to some degree.

We have become deskilled as a population. This means losing the skills that we did have, but not replacing them with skills that are equally useful. We may have acquired skills in software use, but we have lost some basic survival skills. The majority of us could not survive without ICT. We take ICT for granted, placing our trust in it and getting frustrated when it fails. Consider a supermarket during a power cut: freezers stop working, lighting goes out and the tills cannot be used (no one knows the prices of anything, and even if they did they cannot accept your debit or credit card), and stock control systems fail.

The advent of mobile phone text messages has brought about a new language. Communication is going on but are the traditional language and people skills being lost?

ICT has its advantages. There are places where it has made a large difference, but it is not the solution to all our problems. There are areas where it has caused problems and our reliance on it is an issue that will come to the fore over the next few decades.

< Activity >

Describe a typical day from the moment you get up. List all the ways that ICT directly affects your life, or indirectly affects it. If ICT was not available, what impact would it have on the way you do things?

**QUESTIONS**

1 ICT is used in hospitals. Discuss the effect that ICT has had on patients and medical staff.
2 Explain the advantages to students of teachers using ICT in their lessons.
3 Describe the advantages and disadvantages of teleworking.
4 How can the introduction of ICT affect organisation change?
5 Discuss the impact of ICT on the elderly and the disabled.
6 Explain the advantages for a shop in moving to be an Internet-only shop.
7 Discuss the implications for customers of shopping online.
8 Our reliance on ICT will eventually lead to a decline in our standard of living and a return to an existence similar to that of nineteenth-century Britain. Discuss this statement.

## ■ Future developments in ICT

There have been many predictions about what the future may hold. There have been some ridiculous predictions in the past and it is likely there will be more in the future. A good place to keep up to date about ICT developments and predictions is the BBC's weekly *Click* programme and supporting website.

< Activity >

Produce a presentation about possible future technologies including driverless cars, tracking devices, neural interfaces, and others.

## Summary

**Describe the main aspects, purpose and implications of the**

Data Protection Act
  Set up to protect individuals from organisations
  Allows individuals access to information stored on them
  Eight principles organisations must follow
  Rights of individuals including access and correction
  Several exemptions

Computer Misuse Act
  Protect computer systems from individuals
  Three crimes: unuthorised access, unauthorised access with modification, unauthorised access with intent to commit crime
  Problems: proving an individual is committing the crime

Copyright, Designs and Patents Act
  Illegal to create or steal music, books, CDs, etc. (permission must be given)
  Complex licencing rules (difficult to follow)
  ICT equipment makes copying easy

Regulation of Investigatory Powers Act
  Allows the interception of communications
  Interpretation of 'lawful authority'
  Some things can be monitored and recorded, others just monitored

Electronic Communications Act
  Register of cryptography providers
  Digital signatures admissible in law

Freedom of Information Act
  Information held by public authorities is accessible
  Many exemptions

**Describe methods for combating a range of ICT crimes**

Physical
Locked rooms
Cameras
Biometric (fingerprint, iris scanners, etc.)
Logical
Firewalls
Passwords
User IDs
Up-to-date software
Education of users

**Understand the advantages and disadvantages of networking computers**

Advantages
  Work sharing
  Resource sharing
  Centralised control/back-up
  Hot-desking
  Uniformity of machines

Disadvantages

    Reliance on centralised components

    Increased costs

    Increased technical support

    Slow down of network due to other users

## Explain why standards are required and discuss the impact of different standards

Standards required to communicate

Examples of standards include protocols

Two systems on different protocols have problems communicating

## Describe a range of health and safety problems related to working with ICT and measures for avoiding them

Health hazards

    Deep vein thrombosis (DVT)

    Repetitive strain injury (RSI)

    Carpal tunnel syndrome

    Ulnar neuritis

    Eye strain

    Back pain/ache

Safety hazards

    Trailing wires

    Fire

    Electric shock

    Unstable surfaces and chairs

    Food and drink

## Discuss the implications and consequences of ICT

Positive and negative factors

Reasoned conclusion

## Test 1

Answer the following in the context of a cinema that has created a membership scheme for its regular customers.

1. The cinema needs to register with the Data Protection Act (1998). One of the principles of the Act is that the data must be kept safe from unauthorised access. Identify **four** other principles of the Act. [4]

2. The cinema must make sure that the data is secure. Describe **two** methods the cinema can implement to ensure that the data is not accessible to unauthorised users. [4]

3. The cinema has networked its box office and main office computers. Describe **two** advantages to the cinema management of networking the computers. [4]

4. The cinema broadcasts a copyright notice at the beginning of each film. Describe the main aspects of the Copyright, Designs and Patents Act (1988). [4]

5. The cinema transfers data to national agencies who monitor numbers of viewers for each film. Both organisations use the same data transfer standard. Explain why both organisations need to have the same data transfer standard. [4]

6   Identify **two** safety hazards associated with working with computers in the cinema.   [2]

7   There are many health hazards associated with working with computers. Two of these are ulnar neuritis and deep vein thrombosis. Describe these **two** health problems.   [4]

8   Discuss the impact of ICT on cinemas.   [7]

## Test 2

Mrs Phipps works for a large insurance company. She is nervous about the amount of information about her that is stored by the company.

1   Describe **three** of the legal rights Mrs Phipps has under the Data Protection Act (1998).   [6]

2   Describe the impact of the Regulation of Investigatory Powers Act (2000) on Mrs Phipps.   [4]

3   The insurance company is concerned that employees copy software illegally. Describe **two** measures they could introduce to prevent employees copying software.   [4]

4   Describe **two** disadvantages of networking computers together.   [4]

5   The company is concerned about data security, so it has introduced passwords. Identify **two** methods that can be introduced to force the user to choose passwords that will be difficult to break. For each method, explain why it makes the password harder to break.   [4]

6   Explain, with examples, why ICT is not always the answer to every problem.   [5]

7   Mrs Phipps is currently looking at increasing the amount of work she does from home. Discuss the effect that ICT has had on teleworking.   [7]

# Examination technique

## Introduction

> **After reading this chapter you will be able to:**
>
> ■ understand how to learn the material
> ■ understand the requirements of a question
> ■ be familiar with the examination papers.

## The examination papers

There are two modules making up the AS award. The grade you are awarded depends on a combination of your mark for the structured tasks and your examination result. The technical phrase is 'aggregation'. You can take your time over completing the structured tasks but you will have just two hours to do yourself justice in the written paper.

The examiners looking at your paper will have a set of acceptable answers, called 'marking points', and you need to provide sufficient evidence in your answers to be awarded the allocated marks. You need to focus on hitting the requisite number of marking points in each of your answers.

Here are some general points for you to bear in mind in examinations.

### Handwriting
Make it neat to ensure the examiner can read your handwriting. Only use black or blue ink. Other colours cause confusion or are difficult to read.

### Essay questions
Answers must be in continuous prose. Avoid using bullet points. You may limit your marks if you do.

### Doodling
This gives a bad impression, so if you have time to spare, spend it going back over the paper to add more detail.

### Crossing out your answers
Use a single line through what you want to cross out. Do not obliterate it because you could still get some marks if it is actually correct and you have not written a new answer. Think carefully before you cross out a large section of text – is it really wrong or are you starting to panic and not think clearly?

**Marks for written content**

There are marks for the quality of written communication in your answers. These marks will be awarded for the essay type answers. Make sure, therefore, that you use punctuation and capital letters where necessary and that you spell the technical terms correctly, especially those that are given in the question.

## ■ The examination

This will probably be your first AS ICT examination, you will not have a previous grade to worry you, but it will still be a trial. It will look similar to some of the GCSE papers you will have taken. Do not be fooled into expecting the AS paper to be as easy.

This paper may have between 10 and 15 questions for you to answer to the best of your ability, and they will use a context to help you write suitable answers. The paper covers a lot of material and you need to prepare thoroughly for it – using this book is a good start!

Here are some reasons for poor performance.

**The shock of an AS paper**

You need to realise that AS is harder than GCSE.

**Candidates are not prepared**

Too many written answers show the candidate does not know the topic in the question. You will not have this problem, will you?

**Failing to answer adequately**

Some answers require a higher level of response: not just a list of points. Later we will discuss the types of questions set.

## ■ Answering the questions

The question paper has lines for you to write your answers. You may find that you can write a good answer, in your view, in half the space. If this is so, do not worry. The papers are designed to allow plenty of space for your answers but do not feel that you have to fill the lines, as some candidates do, usually by repeating an answer.

This paper requires a lot of technical knowledge in the seven areas set out in Chapters 1 to 7 of this book.

If you need to plan your answer then please do use a list of points, a diagram or any other device.

BUT do not use any colour ink other than blue or black – this is important.

You will be asked questions on very different points. Do not assume that one question leads into the next. In this module, all the questions are separate. A difficult consideration is just how much detail you need to go into in your answers. Do think about this and match your response to the marks allocated: a two-paragraph essay for two marks is not sensible. If you do this sort of thing you will leave yourself short of time at the end.

When you have finished a question, look carefully through your answer, while it is fresh in your mind. Ask yourself these questions:

- Does the answer make sense as you read it?
- Have you repeated an answer?
- Can you understand what you have written? Is it what you meant to write?
- Have you identified an item and then described or explained it when asked to do so?
- Have you given enough marking points for the marks available?
- Can your handwriting be read?

Now move on to the next question.

### < Activity >

Be prepared.

1 Obtain a copy of the syllabus (online at www.ocr.org.uk) and find ICT A/AS level.

2 Highlight the topics that you don't understand. Ask for help.

3 Look at past papers and identify which topics have appeared previously.

4 Find an essay question and plan an answer. Discuss your answer with others in your group.

# Developing an understanding of the required material

Before you can be successful in an examination you must understand the theory (or those topics set out in the syllabus). There are various ways of doing this, which we will look at now.

## Making notes

Some students find it difficult, or feel it is pointless, to make notes in their lessons. Please avoid this attitude. The act of writing notes helps your brain to remember the facts your teacher or the text book is making. Try to find useful models for difficult topics. For example, use lists with points and explanations in a table. Use diagrams if they help you understand. Drawing a similar diagram in the examination may also be a useful prompt to help you answer a question.

## Looking over notes

Now that you have some notes you must use them, for example:

- the night after the lesson to make sure you understand them
- when friends ask you questions
- when revising.

## Asking questions in lessons

This is a personal matter. Some students like to hide in a class to avoid being asked questions. Don't be shy. Ask if you do not understand. In this way you will gain confidence in providing answers. Examiners appreciate a candidate who exhibits confidence in their answers. It takes time and effort to become confident in a topic, but the effort is worthwhile. However, there is also the converse of being over-confident and going over the top in your answers.

## Try explaining queries to friends

This is a great way of making sure you know the topics. You will have to think of different ways of answering if your friend does not understand. If you do not know the answer then it is better to find out now rather than in the examination room.

## Try practice questions

Write many answers to questions and have them checked against the marking scheme.

Collect a group of friends.

1 Take your copy of the syllabus for the theory module and work through section 1.2 making sure that everyone knows what is meant by each section. For example, can you all 'describe common storage devices, indicating typical uses'?

2 Highlight the topics that you don't understand.

3 Ask for help.

# How you react to examination papers

This is something that needs careful consideration before you, the candidate, go into the examination. Either you can cope with examinations or you cannot, though some fall in between these extremes. The better you are prepared the more likely you are to be in the former group. Take your time in the examination room. The questions have been tested to ensure that most candidates will have sufficient time to complete all of the paper in the time allowed. Read the question paper through first, planning how you will answer each question. Do not worry that you have not been taught a particular scenario, look for the understanding required in each question then picture your answer. Try not to leave any questions unanswered.

You must read the question carefully and make sure that what you think the question is asking is accurate. It is a good idea to read the question twice. Recognise, from your knowledge and recall, what is being asked from the syllabus. Use your knowledge and the structure of the marks allocated to put together a set of information that you think will meet the needs of the question. This is the basis of your mental answer. You now have the task of setting this out clearly in words. Some candidates find this quite difficult so make sure you have plenty of practice.

One common error is to rephrase the same answer and imagine it is a second response. Examiners recognise this and will not award marks. You need to give different answers to earn more than one marking point.

# Types of examination questions and how to answer them

If you look at some past exam papers, you will see that the questions all include a keyword such as 'identify' or 'describe'. You must recognise these and respond correctly. These words determine what you are required to do to be awarded the allocated marks.

The keywords used are listed below.

### State or identify
Here, you have to write a single word or phrase.

**< Example >**

*A database package holds data in fields. For example, names would be stored as text.*

*State **three** data types, other than text, commonly used in databases. [3]*

The answer should be three from: Boolean, numeric, date, memo, object (such as a photograph or sound).

Note how the word 'three' is in bold font to make you aware of how many answers are required.

A single word from this list is all that is required. Other correct answers are possible and you would gain marks from these.

### Give
The candidate has to provide the examiner with more information than a single word statement.

**< Example >**

*The owner of a shop is worried about unauthorised users accessing his computer database if he goes online.*

*Give **two** examples of illegal actions using ICT. [2]*

Your answers should include two phrases from:

- Illegal use of data.
- Copying data.
- Hacking into restricted files.
- Intercepting credit card details.

Here you need to use a phrase. A single word such as 'hacking' (seen too frequently) will not be given marks. Make sure you provide enough detail. For example 'hacking into confidential data' is a much better answer and will be awarded marks.

### Describe

This is moving to a higher level of difficulty. These answers offer you the chance to earn usually two marks but sometimes more. You need to provide an answer that matches the question asked using the given context. As a rule of thumb, always give an example of use related to the scenario for describe answers. Remember a good description might earn extra marks in some questions. Take your time in thinking about these questions and preparing what you will write.

< Example >

*Spreadsheets are used for modelling situations. Describe the features of spreadsheet applications which enable them to be used just for modelling.*

Your answers should include a description such as, 'how variables can be changed [1] and the application automatically re-calculates values [1]'. Other features, such as formatting column widths, will not earn marks, as they do not relate specifically to modelling.

< Example >

*A word-processing package is used by both an engineering manager and the office secretary. The manager uses it to produce engineering reports, the secretary for letters.*

*(a) Describe **two** features of the word-processing package that would be important to the manager but not necessarily to the secretary. [4]*

*(b) Describe **two** features of the word-processing package that would be important to the secretary but not necessarily to the manager. [4]*

The answers to part (a) should include any two of:

- a thesaurus
- special symbols
- technical dictionary
- page numbering
- automatic formatting for subheadings.

For part (b) the answers could include any two of:

- mail merge
- standard letter templates
- images.

You would be awarded marks for stating what the feature is (e.g. thesaurus) and for describing what it was used for (e.g. looking up synonyms of words).

There is a range of possible answers here. Try to work out some more.

## Explain

This type of question usually requires you to provide both advantages and disadvantages to show each aspect in the context and to provide reasons for these being valid. There are questions that ask for just one side, so be very careful reading the questions. Your answers must be continuous prose. Using a list will only score low marks. These are fine for planning the structure of a short essay but are not at the same high level as prose.

---

**< Example >**

*The branch of a video rental shop has at least two electronic tills, including a processor and file storage, linked to a local file server in the shop. Whenever prices change or offers occur, updates are made on the local server, which then sends data to the tills. Only the manager of the shop is allowed to update the prices, not the sales assistants. Every few minutes the tills send data to the local server giving details of the sales.*

*Explain the advantages and disadvantages of each electronic till having its own processor and backing store. [4]*

Answers should include:

Advantages:
• Faster access to data.
• Individual record at each till in event of failure.

Disadvantages:
• More expensive hardware.
• Server does not always have totally up-to-date data.

You should provide both sides of the situation. Note you must not just state quicker, cheaper or easier. These must be qualified, for example, 'It is quicker to access data using an intelligent till.' You must also use different points in the advantages and disadvantages. Repeating the same point will earn no further marks.

---

**< Example >**

*Explain the advantages and disadvantages of wizards in applications [4].*

Advantage: easier [no marks so far] for a novice user to [1] quickly produce a result [1].

Disadvantage: The end result may not be [1] exactly what the user required [1].

There are a number of other answers, try to build up a list.

A similar question might be worded as: *Explain the advantages to the company of operatives using wizards to create database reports. [4]*

To be more effective in these higher level questions, first identify the item you will use and then write its description and, if required, the reason why it is appropriate.

## Discuss

This is an explanation that requires you to reach a conclusion.

< Example >

*Many readers of newspapers have access to the Internet. This allows them to read a wide range of online newspapers and magazines. Discuss the increasing availability of online newspapers and magazines. [8]*

The answers expected include a discussion of both the advantages and disadvantages. Items for discussion are:

- up-to-date news
- global news not just national news
- less chance of bias, e.g. state control of media
- legal considerations
- less capital tied up in printing
- variety of reading
- greater access to marketplace
- copyright of images/texts harder to police
- multimedia and other HTML features
- cannot be read as easily on the move
- effects on newsagent
- customised newspapers.

You **must** give a statement in conclusion that gives your view.

There are other sensible answers that would be accepted. Note the emphasis on reaching a conclusion. This can be for or against the point made in the question, depending on your evidence. It would be silly to write that something is a good idea if all of the items you have identified and explained are negative ones.

Do make sure you include a specific conclusion at the end of the answer. Examples of good starting words are: 'In conclusion…', 'Overall…', 'On balance…'.

## Compare

Here you will need to write about two ways of dealing with a situation. You will need to identify the good and bad features of the alternatives and describe them.

< Example >

*Compare the use of a spreadsheet and a database application for holding data on customers for a garage. [3]*

Your answer will need to identify a feature/item and give an explanation of how each application would cope. One method you can use to help you is a writing frame as shown here.

| Item/feature | Spreadsheet | Database |
|---|---|---|
| Search for a customer. | Can use a filter. | Can use parameter queries. |
| Sort records. | Can sort only a single column or all the columns. | Can only sort all of the columns. |
| Create a file for mail merge of selected customers. | Need to ensure comparability with program being used. May need to export to CSV format. | Can use built-in features and mail merge from within database. |
| Create a report on selected customers. | May need to export the data to create a functional report. | Can create and store reports internally. |
| Carry out and save queries. | Can carry out a query but cannot store them. | Built-in feature. |

You then need to write your answer in continuous prose. Make sure it is clear that you have made comparisons. Use words such as: 'whereas', 'and', 'but'.

< Activity >

1 Look through past papers and find questions using 'compare' and 'explain' as keywords. Produce writing frames to structure your answer.

2 Now write answers in continuous prose.

3 Do a number of these because they are where you can gain a good number of marks.

# How to practise answering questions

You really must spend time working on questions.

## At the end of a topic
Here you will have the opportunity to find out what you have learned in the topic. Your teachers may well give you tests at this point.

## Before school tests
It makes sense to do well in school tests. Your applications for further education are based on the outcomes of these tests. It is another opportunity to measure your knowledge and understanding under examination conditions.

### According to your revision plan
You will draw up a schedule for revision! Then over this period you should answer questions to ensure you know the style to use and the subject matter.

### Past papers
Use them. They are the best guide to the style of question to be set. Your centre will have copies. They are not available online. Do be aware that each examination board uses the same subject material in their syllabuses but expects different marking points in the answers to their AS examinations. That is why you need specialist books like this one.

### Identify likely topics
You should have built up a table of the topics in questions from over the past few years of papers and looked for a pattern. The syllabus uses letters of the alphabet as code to identify each section.

### In the examination
This is the end point that all the preparation has been leading up to. You really do need to be prepared. You then stand much more chance of giving answers that will be awarded marks. There are some techniques that you could use in the examination room that might help you do the best you can.

- Focus on the question you are answering – Forget the last question and the next section. Concentrate on reading the current question and structuring the best answer you can to match the key word and the marking scheme. Some candidates go wrong in a question and this disturbs their concentration for several more questions. Try to focus and forget!
- One mark per minute – If a question is worth two marks then do not spend more than two minutes writing the answer. Sometimes candidates' essay answers are too long and detailed. This means that later answers are rushed and marks are lost because time has been wasted.
- Find a relax point – During the examination you will need to give your brain, back and eyes a brief rest. Look at the clock or a point at some distance just to relax for 30 seconds or so. Do not look around the room, as this may distract others. It will also interrupt your thought processes. Take two different pens with different shapes to help rest your hand when you write for a sustained period.
- No crossing out – If you do need to cross out anything, then be organised. Use a single line and then calmly write a second answer.

- Always read carefully what you have written – Is it exactly what you need to say? The words used and their order can make a difference, so take care. You need every mark.
- Just a bit extra – Just add one more example in your response if it is appropriate. Just take that bit of extra time to think about your answer before you start to write. Take care reading your answer.
- Last few words – Remember that examiners really would like to give you the marks, but they need to see that you can write a clear answer to the question set. Examiners are nice people, but they cannot read your mind! As you write your answers, think about what the examiners will read from your response.

# 9 Introduction to coursework

Figure 9.1 System development work flow

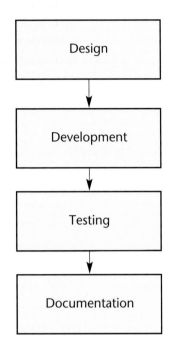

## Introduction

The coursework for OCR AS ICT is worth 40% of the whole AS-level. It is therefore a very important part of the qualification and enables students who are more practically minded to gain some good marks in addition to the marks gained in the examinations.

Each year a new piece of coursework is set by OCR that is called *Structured ICT Tasks* unit code G062. The *Structured ICT Tasks* require you to carry out a set of tasks and provide evidence of what you have done. Each year a different scenario will be used, for example the tasks could be about a local gymnastics club or a children's hospital. When you complete the tasks, you will need to show evidence of the following skills:

- Design
- Development
- Testing
- Documentation

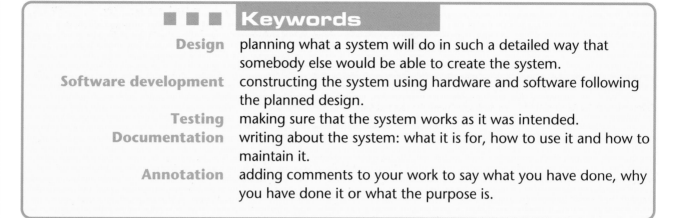

■ ■ ■ **Keywords**

| | |
|---|---|
| Design | planning what a system will do in such a detailed way that somebody else would be able to create the system. |
| Software development | constructing the system using hardware and software following the planned design. |
| Testing | making sure that the system works as it was intended. |
| Documentation | writing about the system: what it is for, how to use it and how to maintain it. |
| Annotation | adding comments to your work to say what you have done, why you have done it or what the purpose is. |

# Choosing the correct software

When you approach the tasks, you need to decide from the beginning what software you are going to use for each task. Sometimes, the task will tell you what software you should use, which makes this decision simple. Often, the tasks will tell you what needs to be done, but will not actually specify the software to use.

A common problem is when students look at part (a) of the task and choose their software straight away. When they get to a later part (e.g. part (d)) of the task they then discover that the software they started with will not complete the job.

< Example >

**(a) Produce a business card that can be used by Frank.**

This could be done using several pieces of software. Let's assume that presentation software is chosen to produce the business card.

**(d) All the employees are to have business cards. Using mail merge, produce a business card for each employee.**

This is now a problem because presentation software is not designed to be used with mail merge. In this case, the whole task would need to be started again.

# Which bits can you do?

When you read each task, you should try to do as much as possible. Sometimes, part of a task may be beyond your capability. If this is the case, then leave it until later and concentrate on the other tasks that will get you marks.

Sometimes, even a single question might seem too difficult, but if you break it down into what is needed to be done then you will usually find that you can at least complete part of it. Do this even if it is as simple as putting a title on a form with a couple of buttons, because, for example, you may not know how to make a sub-form and so may at least gain the marks for the title and buttons.

**Show evidence of the formulae and functions used.**

You must show the row and column headings (e.g. 1, 2, 3; A, B, C).

Some of the functions that are required might be quite complex, such as LOOKUP functions or IF functions with lots of routes. However, there may be some simpler formulae that perform straightforward calculations. These might include multiplying a value by the VAT rate or multiplying the quantity by the price. Some simple functions that you could attempt might include a SUM function to add up all the prices or a MAX function to determine the highest value.

So don't be put off by a question that on the surface appears to be too difficult. Instead, look to see what you could do to get at least some marks.

# Annotation

Some questions will specifically ask you to annotate your work. If you are asked to annotate your work then you will only get marks if you do so. Sometimes you will be told what the annotation should be. It will usually involve one of the following:

- describing what you have done to achieve a printout/screenshot
- describing the purpose of a printout or screenshot
- giving reasons for choices that you have made
- identifying input and output data values.

Annotation can be done by handwriting directly on to the work. Some students prefer to use the text box and arrow features available in a word processor. Some prefer to 'number' each part of a printout or screenshot and then write their annotation on a separate page with reference to the numbers.

In the chapters that follow, you will see different methods of annotation. It is usually better to use a word processor's text box and arrow features, as these are less likely to get lost than handwritten annotation on a separate piece of paper.

# Quality

You should ensure that the work you produce is of a high quality, as it will be assessed by your teacher and may be sent to an external moderator for further scrutiny.

| Do | Do not |
|---|---|
| Include a cover page that has your name, centre name, centre number and candidate number on. | Assume that your teacher will provide a cover sheet for you. |
| Number each page so that your teacher can make reference to the pages when marking the work and just in case your work gets split up. | Use plastic wallets for each section. These are very annoying as teachers and moderators have to remove them and they are likely to discard them. |
| Put your name and candidate number on every page in case the pages get split up. | Print everything in colour just for the sake of it. It will waste ink. |
| Present your work in a flat file or use treasury tags. | Present your work in a bulky ring binder. |
| Print pages in colour if colour is relevant. | |
| Separate each main task by using a cover sheet or coloured piece of paper. | |
| Write the task number (e.g. 2bii) on each page to identify the evidence you are producing. | |
| Put all of your work into order. | |

# Design

## Introduction

Design is the process of planning what a system will do and what it will look like. It is not about producing the system. The elements that you will be asked to design will depend upon the type of task and the software that will be used.

In this chapter you will find out how to produce designs for:

- Design layouts
- Screen connectivity
- Design specifications
- Databases
- Spreadsheets
- Routines
- Flow charts

**Figure 10.1** Traditional design

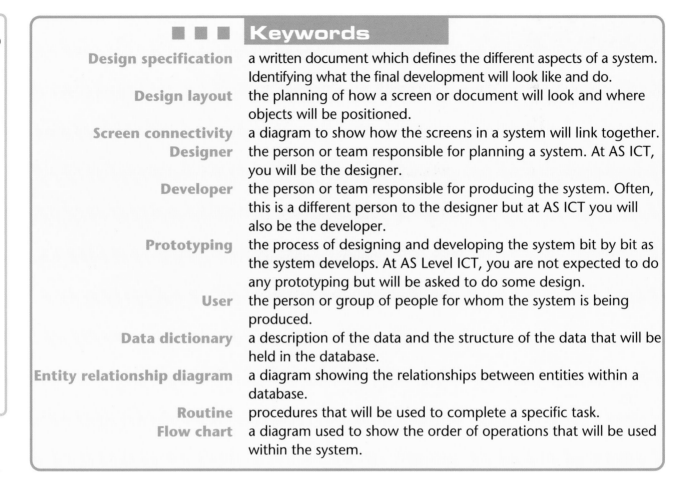

# Design the layout of data capture forms, screen layouts, report layouts and/or other forms of output (for example audio output)

## ■ Screen layouts

When designing the layout, it is important to remember that you are producing a 'sketch' of what you want the final developed version to look like. There is no need for fancy artwork or detailed sets of data. However, the design must be clear enough for the developer to know what they are supposed to produce.

Remember that in industry, the designer and developer are usually different people. For example, the design layout on page 207 is for a data entry screen in a database for entering details of a new product. Notice that, as well as showing the position of objects, it is also necessary to explain what each object will do. Colours, fonts, sizes, etc. are usually found in the design specification (see pages 211–14) although it is acceptable to annotate these on the layout as well. It is not necessary to colour in a design layout.

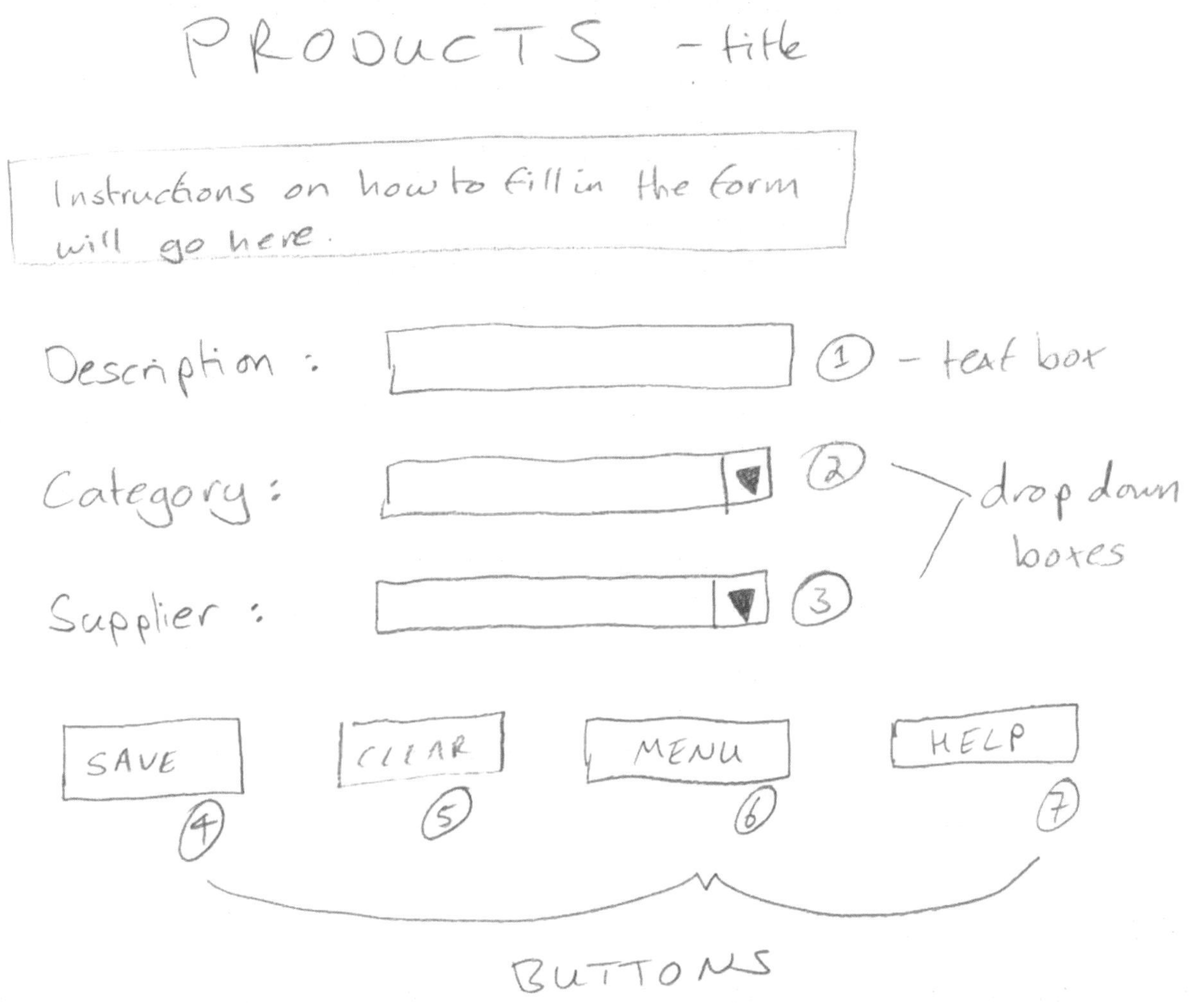

< **Example** >

**Figure 10.2** Example of draft design layout

**1** Text box for description should allow up to 30 characters to be entered.
**2** Drop-down box for category will show the categories listed in the table called CATEGORY. Only those categories can be selected.
**3** Drop-down box for supplier will show the ID, Name, and postcode of the data in the SUPPLIER table. Only those suppliers can be selected.
**4** The Save button will save the data on the screen into the PRODUCTS table.
**5** The Clear button will clear all the input data on the screen without saving it.
**6** The Menu button will close the products form and open the menu. If data hasn't been saved, then the user should be prompted to save it first.
**7** The Help button will go to a help screen to explain what all the options on the data entry screen mean.

Design the layout of data capture forms, screen layouts, report layouts and/or other forms of output (for example audio output)

# Dos and do nots

| Do | Do not |
|---|---|
| Separate forenames and surnames. | Use a single name. |
| Separate address lines and the postcode. | Use a single box for the whole address. |
| Use controls that allow selection of data (e.g. drop-down box, list box, radio buttons, tick boxes). | Produce a piece of artwork. |
| Include space for instructions for the user. | Colour everything in using the final colours. |
| Use buttons/hyperlinks with clear labels. | Assume somebody else will know what you intend. |
| Research other types of screens and outputs to see what they look like. | Produce the final developed version. |
| Read the question carefully so that you include everything asked for. | Use a computer if the task tells you not to. |
| Annotate your work to explain what each item is or will do. | |

**< Activity >**

Design the layout of a screen that will be used for inputting details of the computers at your school.

# Report layouts

A report layout is different to most screen layouts as it does not require any input. It is an output only and is usually designed for the printer.

**< Example >**

This example shows a report for listing all the products available. It is not sufficient on its own as it also needs a design specification (see pages 211–14).

1 The description, category and supplier data will be repeated for each record in the PRODUCTS table.
2 n = page number, nn = total number of pages.
3 ## = total number of products in PRODUCTS table.

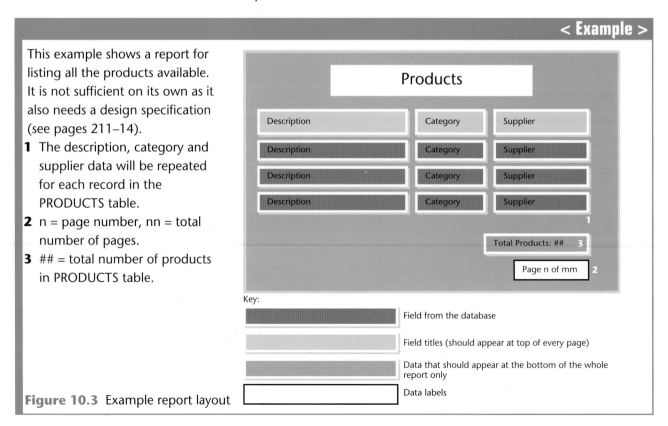

Key:

Field from the database

Field titles (should appear at top of every page)

Data that should appear at the bottom of the whole report only

Data labels

**Figure 10.3** Example report layout

Design the layout of a report that will show a list of all the students in your class including their dates of birth and contact details.

## Audio output

If the final development is going to include audio (sound), then you will need to design what that sound will be. You do not need to create the sound at this stage. Sound is usually used for multimedia presentations and web pages but it can be used for other applications too.

< Example >

This example is a design of the audio that will be used for a quiz created in a spreadsheet.

| Action | Sound to play | Duration |
|---|---|---|
| User opens the quiz | 'Let's play' | 1 second |
| Correct answer given | Applause | 3 seconds |
| Wrong answer given | 'Uh oh' | 1 second |
| User clicks 'Score my quiz' | 'You got $n$ out of $nn$ questions correct', where $n$ = number correct and $nn$ = total number of questions. | 4 seconds |

< Activity >

Design the sound that will be used in a presentation to eight-year-old children about the different types of dinosaur.

## Video output

If the final development is going to include video (or animation), then you will need to design what it will do. Video is usually used for multimedia presentations and web pages but it can be used for other applications too. The best way to do this is using a story board.

< Example >

The short example below is a design of the video that will be used to show the inside of a computer.

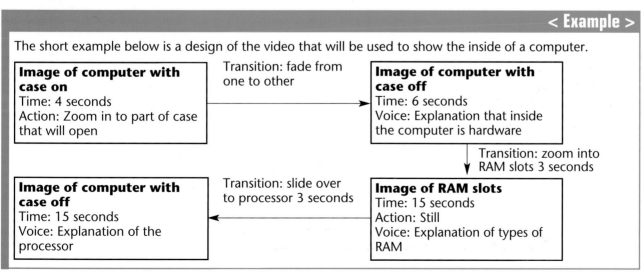

**Figure 10.4** Example video storyboard

Design the layout of data capture forms, screen layouts, report layouts and/or other forms of output (for example audio output)

# Design how input screens and outputs link together as part of the interface

Many applications have several screens and outputs that will link together through hyperlinks and buttons. You will need to specify how these screens and outputs link together. Some links will be bi-directional (two-way) while others will only go in one direction (uni-directional).

**Figure 10.5** Example of screen connectivity diagram

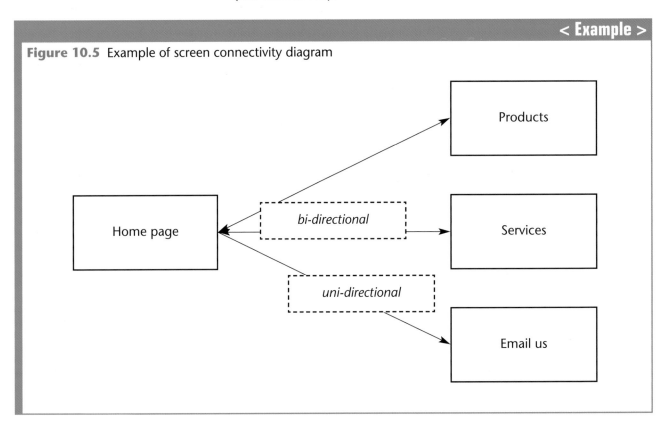

In this simple example, there are three hyperlinks on the home page. One goes to 'Products', another to 'Services' and another to 'Email us'. On the Products page, there is a hyperlink to return to the Home page: that is why it is bi-directional. Similarly, on the Services page, there is a hyperlink to return to the Home page and so the link between Services and the Home page is also bi-directional. However, when the user clicks the link to 'Email us', it opens the user's email client software and there is no option there to return to the Home page so the link is one-way.

Often links are much more complex and so a screen connectivity diagram is needed to show the full set of links. This is a series of lines. Each line represents a screen. Each arrow represents a link. There should always be an exit route.

< Example >

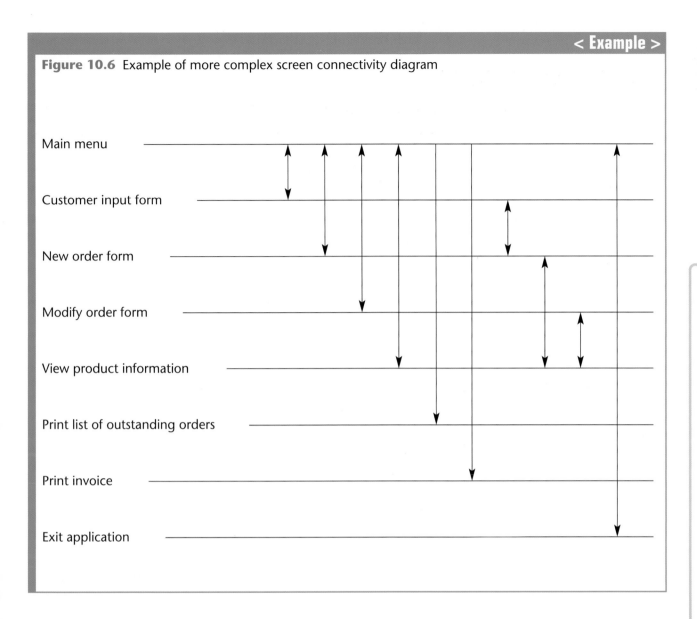

**Figure 10.6** Example of more complex screen connectivity diagram

# Produce written design specifications

In a design specification, you need to 'specify' what the final development will look like and what it will do. This is best achieved by bullet point lists and tables. It can also be done by annotating a design layout.

## General specifications

For any screen or output, you should consider:

- fonts
  - size
  - style
  - colour
  - main text
  - titles
  - sub-titles
- other colours
  - background
  - shading
  - borders
  - images/logos
- positioning of objects (where they will be located)
- sizes
  - screen
  - paper
  - images
- orientation (landscape/portrait)
- what instructions may be necessary.

## Mail merge

For mail merge documents, you should consider which data will be:

- merge fields
- calculated fields
- the same for all documents/letters.

### < Activity >

Mrs Smith is the Head of ICT at a secondary school. She needs to send a letter to all parents informing them of the Key Stage 3 SATS results for Maths, Science and English for every child in Year 9. The letters must be addressed personally to each parent and have the results (a number between 1 and 8) for each subject clearly identified. Produce a design specification for a mail merge document that will do this.

# Multimedia

For multimedia presentations, you should consider:

- animations and their timings for all objects
- transitions and their timings for all objects
- whether the presentation will be automatic, controlled using buttons or manually operated
- what each button will do
- what will happen at the end of the presentation
- what will go on the master slide
- how sounds will operate
- how videos will operate.

**< Example >**

Here is an example of a design specification for a multimedia presentation.

**Objects**

| Object | Size | Colour | Style | Other |
|---|---|---|---|---|
| Main title on slides | 36 pt | Dark blue | Bold, Arial | Centred at top, not animated |
| Sub-title on slides | 28 pt | Light blue | Bold, Arial, italic | Centred under main title, not animated |
| Main text on slides | 20 pt | Purple | Bullet points, Arial | Each bullet to appear one at a time upon clicking of mouse |
| Text in footer | 14 pt | Light blue | Arial | To be always on the screen |
| Logo in footer | 100 × 100 pixels | Company logo colours | Embossed | To be always on the screen |
| Background | | White | Plain | |
| Buttons | 16 pt | White text, dark blue button | Arial | |

**Processes**

- Animation will simply 'appear' for all objects upon the click of a mouse. All objects except the main bullet point text should be on the screen already. There will be no animation sounds.
- Transitions will be for each slide to 'dissolve' into the next upon the click of a mouse. There will be no transition sounds.
- The presentation will be run manually, but buttons will be available to go to the 'next' slide, the 'previous' slide and the 'home' slide.
- At the end of the presentation, a blank black screen should be shown.
- The master slide will include:
  - the white background
  - the company logo in the bottom right-hand corner
  - the name of the presenter and company in the bottom left-hand corner.
- There will be a short 20-second sound clip of a train arriving at a station (on slide 2). This will be shown as a sound icon that the presenter can click to activate.
- There will be a short 10-second clip of a train passing a level crossing (on slide 5). This will appear automatically when the slide is opened.

## Websites

For websites, you should consider:

- what each hyperlink/button will do
- the style of hyperlinks and buttons
- what information will be on every page
- what file structure will be used
- what naming conventions will be used
- whether style sheets or frames will be used.

## Spreadsheets

For spreadsheets, you should consider:

- what routines (macros) may be required
- what buttons will be used and their process
- what calculations will be required
- how input areas will be highlighted
- how outputs will be highlighted.

## On-screen forms

For an on-screen form (e.g. on a website, database, spreadsheet), you should consider:

- what instructions will be necessary
- what types of input will be used:
  - text boxes
  - list boxes
  - drop-down boxes
  - option buttons
  - tick boxes
- buttons that should be used (e.g. submit, clear, cancel).

### < Activity >

A local doctor's surgery would like an online form to be produced for its website that will allow patients to order repeat prescriptions. Produce a design specification for the online form.

# Design the data structures/models necessary to solve a given problem

When designing a database, you are effectively producing a data dictionary. You will be asked to produce certain aspects of the data dictionary in any given task. You do not need to do more than is asked of you.

## ■ Entity relationship diagrams (ERDs)

You may be asked to design an entity relationship diagram for a given scenario. Always use pen and paper for this as it will clearly distinguish between design and development. However, beware that if you are asked to produce, rather than design, an entity relationship diagram, then you should use database software.

Firstly identify all of the entities that you will need. Then identify the relationships that exist between the entities. If you have any many-to-many relationships then create a link entity between the two.

Here is an example of a many-to-many relationship being broken down.

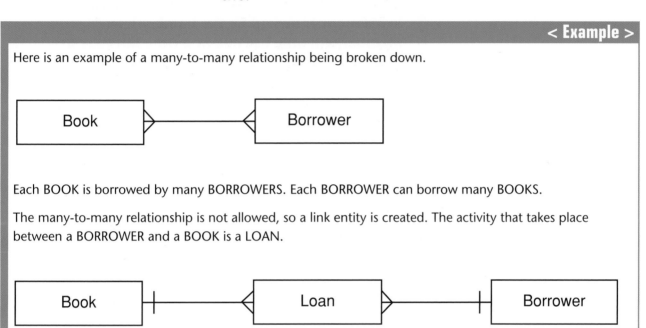

Each BOOK is borrowed by many BORROWERS. Each BORROWER can borrow many BOOKS.

The many-to-many relationship is not allowed, so a link entity is created. The activity that takes place between a BORROWER and a BOOK is a LOAN.

The LOAN entity must contain a foreign key for each entity that it now links to. Sometimes this is all that is needed, but in this case there are other data that can be stored about the loan, for example Date Taken, Date Due, Fine.

Ensure that you include the degree of the relationship (e.g. one-to-many, one-to-one). Then ensure that you have no circular relationships (i.e. relationships that create a 'loop' between entities).

< Activity >

Design an entity relationship diagram for the following scenario:

**A marching band keeps records about its members, the instruments that each member borrows and the events that take place. Each instrument is owned by the band and each member will only use one at a time but may use different instruments over a period of time. The band also needs to know which members attended each event.**

## ■ Entity structures

You could be asked to identify the fields, primary keys and foreign keys that would be used within each entity (table). The standard database notation most commonly used for this is:

ENTITY-NAME(<u>Primary Key</u>, Foreign Key 1, Foreign Key 2, Attribute 1, Attribute 2, Attribute 3)

The ENTITY-NAME should always be in capitals and, although not essential, it is good practice to use singular rather than plural (e.g. CUSTOMER not CUSTOMERS).

The primary key should always be underlined. Although you may have been taught about composite primary keys (i.e. a primary key that is made from two or more fields), when creating a database, always use a single primary key as this will make development much easier. If you are unsure what to use as a primary key, then create an ID field (e.g. CustomerID). You can then be sure that this will be unique to each record. However, if there is an obvious primary key such as NI (National Insurance) number, or VIN (Vehicle Identification Number) then use this as the primary key.

The foreign keys should always be overlined. There is no pre-defined method to do this within a word processor so just draw a line. The foreign key must **always** be spelt exactly the same as the primary key that it relates to. **Remember that there is always one foreign key for every 'many' side of a relationship**. This means that an entity may have more than one foreign key if there is more than one relationship for that entity.

Remember the rules of normalisation. Apply these when creating a table. In particular, ensure that all data is in 1NF (first normal form) by making sure that all data is atomic. For example, always use forename and surname rather than fullname; break down the address into different components.

Here is an example of an entity structure design for an order processing system.

CUSTOMER(<u>CustomerID</u>, Title, Forename, Surname, Telephone, HouseNo, Street, District, Town, County, Postcode)

PRODUCT(<u>ProductCode</u>, Description, Price, Quantity_in_Stock)

ORDER(<u>OrderCode</u>, CustomerID, Date)

ORDERLINE(<u>OrderLineID</u>, ProductCode, OrderCode, Quantity_Purchased)

1  Identify **all** the errors in the following entity structures.

　　a)　VEHICLES(<u>VIN</u>, Reg_No, Make, Model, Engine Size)

　　b)　VET(<u>Surname</u>, Forename, Specialism, DoB)

　　c)　STUDENT(<u>StudentID</u>, Surname, Forename)

　　　　TUTORGROUP(<u>TGID</u>, Name, Student, Tutor)

　　　　TUTOR(Surname, Forename)

　　d)　DOCTOR(<u>DoctorID</u>, Surname, Forename)

　　　　PATIENTS(<u>PatientID</u>, Surname, Forename, DoB)

　　　　APPOINTMENT(<u>Doctor</u>, <u>PatientID</u>, <u>Date</u>, Time)

2  Design the entity structure for the following scenario.

**A tool hire company loans out its specialist power tools to customers. It only has one of each tool. The company need to know who has hired the tool, where they live and how to contact them. For each tool, they need to know its name, a brief description, its category and its value. Each time a tool is hired, they need to know the date and time it was taken out and the date and time it is due back.**

Design the data structures/models necessary to solve a given problem

## Data types

An important part of a data dictionary is to know the type of data that will be stored for each attribute and the length and/or format of that data. You might be asked to show data types in a number of different ways. Sometimes you will be asked to identify the attributes as well as the data types, and sometimes you will be given the attributes and asked to identify the data types.

### < Example >

Here is an example of one method of showing the data types, sizes and formats for a customer table.

**Entity = CUSTOMER**

| Attribute | Data type | Length/size | Format |
|---|---|---|---|
| CustomerID | Integer | 5 digits | 99999 |
| Surname | Text | 20 characters | xxxxxxxxxxxxxxxxxxxx |
| Forename | Text | 20 characters | xxxxxxxxxxxxxxxxxxxx |
| DateofBirth | Date | 8 | DD/MM/YYYY |
| Telephone | Text | 13 characters | 0000000000000 |
| Photograph | Picture | 11 kB | JPG |
| MailingList | Boolean | 1 | Tick box |

### < Activity >

Produce a data dictionary to show the design of data types, lengths and formats for the entity PRODUCT.

**Entity = PRODUCT**

| Attribute | Data type | Length/size | Format |
|---|---|---|---|
| ProductCode | | | |
| Description | | | |
| QuantityinStock | | | |
| ReorderLevel | | | |
| ReorderAmount | | | |
| Category | | | |
| Picture | | | |

## Validation

Often validation will be asked for as part of the data dictionary, but sometimes you will be asked to design it separately.

When designing validation, it is important to identify the type of validation (e.g. length, data type, range, format/picture, lookup, presence). You may be expected to follow this up by creating customised validation error messages. Therefore, if you are given a choice of which attributes to create the validation on, you should consider how you will customise the validation error message later on. For example, if you are using Microsoft Access, it is not possible to create data type checks that give customised error messages.

You will also need to identify the validation rule, and the error message that will appear if the rule is violated. Rules should always be positive (i.e. they should tell the user what to do, rather than simply telling them what was wrong).

< Example >

Here is an example of one method of showing the data types, sizes and formats for a customer table.

**Entity = EMPLOYEE**

| Attribute | Validation type | Rule | Error message |
| --- | --- | --- | --- |
| EmployeeID | Length | Length must be exactly five letters. | "Please enter an Employee ID that is five characters long using letters only." |
| Gender | Lookup in list | Must be either 'M' or 'F'. | "Only enter M for Male or F for Female." |
| Email | Format | Must include text before '@' and text after '@'. | "Enter an email address that includes the @ symbol with the address before and domain after." |
| DateofBirth | Range | Must be at least 18 years old. | "Enter a date of birth that is at least 18 years before today" |
| Surname | Presence | Must be present. | "Please enter a surname – do not leave it blank." |
| National Insurance | Format | Must be of format two letters, six numbers, one letter from A–D. | "Please enter two letters, then six numbers, then one letter from A to D – do not use any spaces." |

**Design the data structures/models necessary to solve a given problem**

< Activity >

Design part of a data dictionary to show the type of validation, validation rule and customised error messages for the following scenario.

**Products have codes that are made up using three numbers, one letter and one number, for example 123B2. A description must always be given and the date it was first produced must always be before today's date. Each product is either 'In stock' or 'Out of stock'. The cost of buying the product must be under £100 and the price of selling the product must be at least 10 per cent above the cost.**

Entity = PRODUCT

| Attribute | Validation type | Rule | Error message |
|---|---|---|---|
| ProductCode | | | |
| Description | | | |
| DateProduced | | | |
| Stock | | | |
| Cost | | | |
| Price | | | |

## Other data dictionary designs

Sometimes you might be asked to design a combination of data dictionary items.

< Example >

Here is an example of one method from a question paper from May 2008.

Entity = HIRE

| Attribute | Data type | Key | Validation |
|---|---|---|---|
| HireID | Integer | Primary | |
| BookingID | Integer | Foreign to BOOKING | Must exist in BookingID in BOOKING table. |
| CategoryCode | Text (3) | Foreign to CATEGORY | Must exist in CategoryCode in CATEGORY table. |
| Quantity | Integer | | Must not be higher than the number of available bikes for this category. |

If you are asked to design a spreadsheet, you are likely to be asked to design the layout and the calculations that will be used. When designing a layout, you should bear in mind the principles for screen layouts on pages 206–8 and design specifications on pages 211–14. You do not need to identify the cell which data will be stored in as this will be decided upon during the development stage.

For calculations, this will often be part of a screen layout design, but the main principle is to identify the calculation that will need to take place. For example Profit = Selling Price − Cost. It is not necessary to use cell references at this stage as the exact cells will not be known until the development stage.

Note: *This example includes part of a design specification as annotation.*

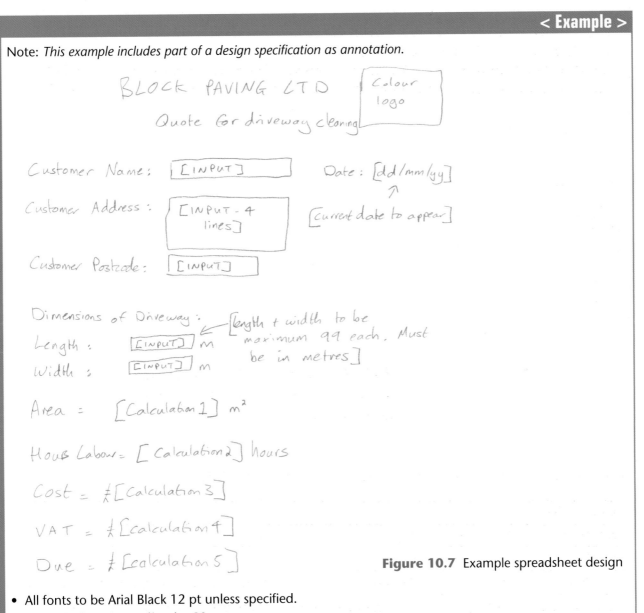

**Figure 10.7** Example spreadsheet design

- All fonts to be Arial Black 12 pt unless specified.
- Title 'Block Paving Ltd' to be 20 pt.
- 'Quote for driveway cleaning' to be 14 pt.
- Prompts (those with colons) to be in bold.
- Input boxes to be yellow.
- Amount 'due' to be in bold.
- Prices to have two decimal places.
- Calculation 1 = length × width.
- Calculation 2 = area ÷ 15, rounded up to next hour.
- Calculation 3 = hours labour × 25.
- Calculation 4 = cost × 0.175.
- Calculation 5 = cost + VAT.

# Specify any routines using methods such as flow charts

A routine is a procedure that takes place. For example, you might be asked to describe the routines that take place for each button that is pressed. You must be specific when describing the routines and say exactly what should happen. For example, writing 'Open form' is not specific enough, but 'Open customer input form with no records showing' would be better.

< Example >

| Button | Routine |
| --- | --- |
| Exit | Prompt the user by asking if they are sure they want to exit. If they click 'Yes', then exit the application, if they click 'No', then return to the main menu screen. |
| Data entry | Open the 'data entry menu' screen. |
| Show all nurses on each ward | Open the report called 'Nurses on wards'. |
| Print medication list | Print the report called 'Daily medication list'. |
| Help | Open the document which contains the instructions for this application. |
| NHS website | Open the NHS website in a separate window. |

As part of designing a routine, you might be asked to produce a flow chart to show the procedures that will need to take place. Although it is not essential to use these symbols, the symbols below are the standard symbols used in flow charts.

Terminator

Used for beginning and end (e.g 'Click submit button').

Process

Used to show each process that takes place (e.g. 'Display confirmation message').

Connector

Used to join together terminators, processes and decisions.

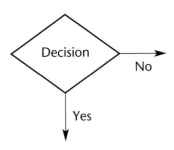

Used when a decision needs to be made (e.g. 'Does the email address include an "@" symbol?') – there will be two possible routes: yes and no.

A flow chart can be used to show the process that a user must follow or the process that a computer will follow. It may include a mixture of both.

The important principles to remember are listed in the next table.

| Principle | Good example | Poor example |
| --- | --- | --- |
| Always start and finish with a terminator. | Start with a terminator even if it is as simple as 'Start'. | Start with a process or a decision. |
| Be specific with decisions. | Use 'Is temperature above 25°C?' | Use 'Is it too hot?' |
| Be specific with processes. | Use 'Display confirmation message'. | Use 'Display message'. |
| Ensure all decisions have two routes. | Use a 'Yes' route AND a 'No' route. | Miss out a route – there must always be two for each decision. |
| Connect all processes. | Each process has a connector going to it and a connector coming from it. | A process is left with only a connector from it, but doesn't have one going to it. |

This example shows how the validation takes place after a web form has been completed.

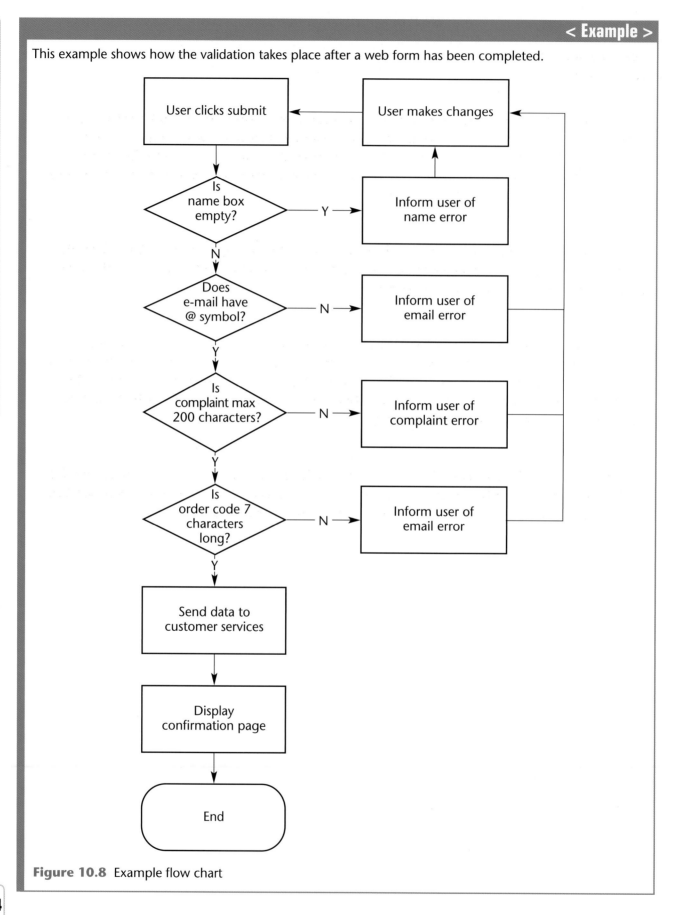

**Figure 10.8** Example flow chart

< Example >

< Activity >

Design a flow chart that will show how Peter will be expected to enter data into the data entry screen described below.

The data entry screen is to record a new loan for a book. Peter will first need to select the borrower from the list of borrowers. If the borrower exists then he can click the borrower's name, if the borrower does not exist in the list then he will need to enter the details of a new borrower. Once he has entered the details for a new borrower, he can continue.

Peter will then need to select the book. He will do this by scanning the barcode. If the barcode is recognised then he can move on to the next stage, if not then he will need to re-scan the barcode.

He will then need to decide the date the book must be returned. He will be presented with a date that shows him a default date of one month in advance. If he wants to accept this then he clicks 'Accept date'. If he wants a different date, then he must click 'Change date' and then enter the new date by selecting from an on-screen calendar, then clicking OK.

Finally, Peter will be asked by the computer if the book should be loaned out. He will be prompted with 'Yes' or 'No'. If he clicks 'Yes', then the loan is recorded in the database. If he clicks 'No' then the loan will be cleared.

# 11 Software development

## Introduction

**Figure 11.1**

Software development is the process of following a design to produce an application. The application can be part of a bigger piece of software. For example, you might be asked to create an application that manages the data for a library – you would most likely use a database to do this. The purpose of this chapter is to explain how to produce the necessary evidence in order to answer questions. There are lots of online resources that show how to solve specific problems such as creating a combo box, and so this book does not show step-by-step how to solve problems.

A big time saver is to read the question carefully. Plan ahead by looking at what will be required later on in the question. Choose your software carefully. Only show the evidence that you have been asked for – there is no point doing anything extra as you won't get any extra marks. It is also not necessary to show how you did everything stage by stage (your teacher does not need to know which menus you have used). Usually only the outcomes need to be shown. If you are required to show stage-by-stage evidence then the question will ask for it.

In this chapter you will find out how to produce evidence for:

- data structures
- user interfaces
- customised routines
- word-processing tasks
- desktop publishing tasks
- spreadsheet tasks
- graphics tasks
- website tasks
- multimedia tasks
- database tasks
- incorporating different types of media
- customised outputs
- security methods.

| | |
|---|---|
| **Interface** | the method used for communication between the user and the computer: usually a screen or sound. |
| **Customising** | adapting the way a feature works so that it has a 'personal' feel. This involves changing the properties of a feature. |
| **Evidence** | proof that you have created what was asked for, usually by means of a printout or an annotated screenshot. |
| **Annotation** | a description of what you have done, or why you have done it, usually accompanying a screenshot or printed evidence. |
| **Screenshot** | a picture of the screen. If created using the 'PrtScr' button, the picture is copied to the clipboard so that it can be pasted into a document. |
| **Multimedia** | a combination of any text, images, animation, sound and video in a single document. |

# Create data structures using appropriate software tools

Following from the design section of the coursework, you may be asked to show evidence of data structures. This usually focuses on databases. You are likely to be asked to produce evidence of:

- entity relationship diagrams
- data types
- data formats
- data lengths
- primary keys
- foreign keys.

It is **not** advisable to use the documenter feature in Microsoft Access as this produces lots of pages that are very difficult to follow and often misses out crucial evidence.

## Entity relationship diagrams

When producing evidence for an entity relationship diagram, ensure that you show the **degree** of the relationship. This means the type of relationship, for example one-to-one, one-to-many. Remember that many-to-many relationships are not allowed. Also include **all** tables. If you have been unable to create all the relationships then at least show the ones you have been able to do.

< Example >

This example uses the number '1' to indicate the **one** side of a relationship and the infinity symbol ∞ to indicate the **many** side of a relationship.

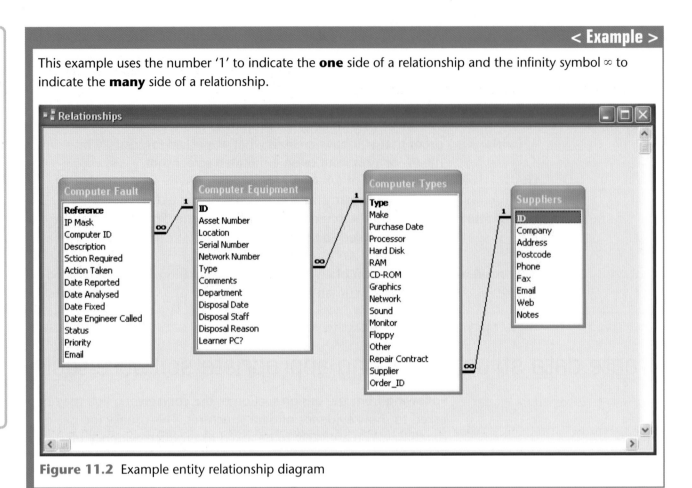

**Figure 11.2** Example entity relationship diagram

Common problems with creating relationships can be due to **not** using the same data types for a foreign key and a primary key or having data in the 'foreign'/'many' table that does not exist in the 'primary'/'one' table. It is better to create relationships **before** you enter any data into the tables.

## ◼ Data types

When producing evidence for data types, ensure that **all** the attributes (fields) are showing. A common error is to give a telephone number a 'Number' data type. This is incorrect because numbers cannot begin with zero. Also, a telephone is a string of numbers/digits – it is not a number that can be used in a calculation. Look at what happens if a telephone number is set as a number:

| Customer : Table | |
| --- | --- |
| Customer | Telephone Number |
| 1 | 1215551111 |
| 2 | 2085552222 |

**Figure 11.3**

Data types can be set for several applications including databases, spreadsheets and web forms, among others.

< Example >

Example for a database

This screenshot shows all the field names (attributes) together with the data types for a database table (entity) called COMPUTER TYPES.

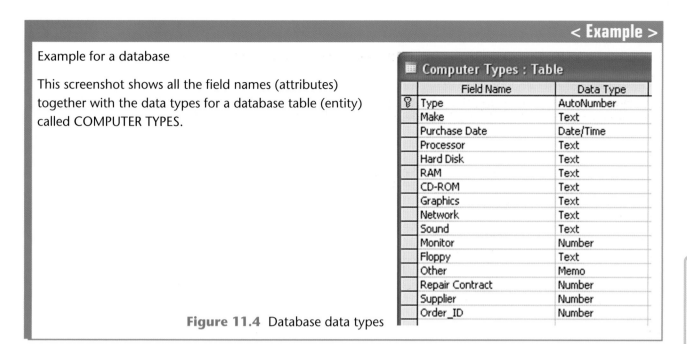

| Field Name | Data Type |
|---|---|
| Type | AutoNumber |
| Make | Text |
| Purchase Date | Date/Time |
| Processor | Text |
| Hard Disk | Text |
| RAM | Text |
| CD-ROM | Text |
| Graphics | Text |
| Network | Text |
| Sound | Text |
| Monitor | Number |
| Floppy | Text |
| Other | Memo |
| Repair Contract | Number |
| Supplier | Number |
| Order_ID | Number |

**Figure 11.4** Database data types

< Example >

Example for a spreadsheet

Notice how in this example, some annotation is necessary to identify which cell the data type evidence is referring to. This same screenshot and annotation could be used for showing the data format, which is two decimal places.

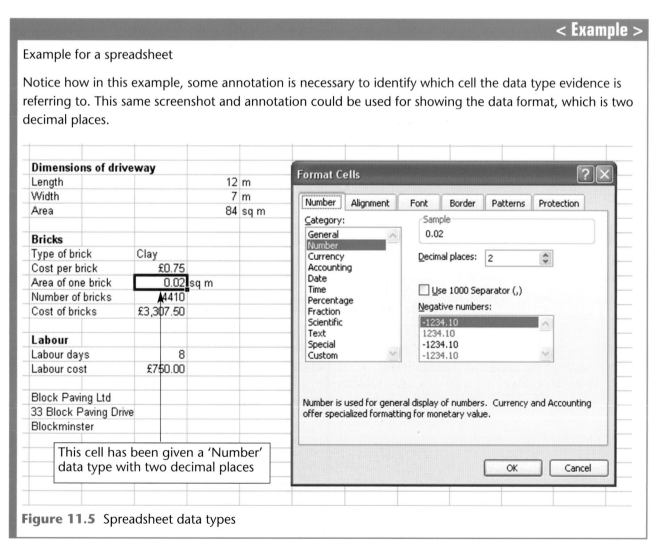

This cell has been given a 'Number' data type with two decimal places

**Figure 11.5** Spreadsheet data types

Create data structures using appropriate software tools

< Example >

Example for a web page form

This screenshot also requires some annotation to clarify which field is being used. It's important here not to get mixed up with the terms 'data format' and 'data validation'. By selecting 'Integer', only integers will be allowed, which is also a type of validation. An example of data format would be setting the data to display using a comma for separating thousands.

The data type has been set to integer

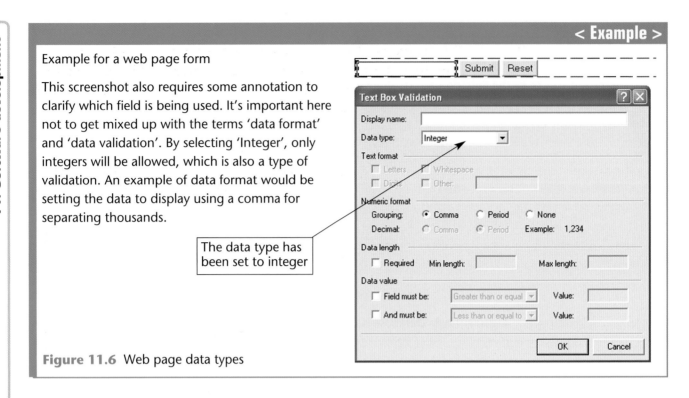

**Figure 11.6** Web page data types

## Data formats

This has been briefly covered in the previous section on data types for spreadsheets and web page forms. However, in databases, some extra work is required to show evidence of the data formats used. In Microsoft Access, it is necessary to show each field individually. Therefore only show this evidence if it is specifically asked for.

< Example >

Although it's not essential, the annotation helps to clarify what has been done. Input masks are sometimes classed as Formats, however they are really a method of validation and so will be covered later.

I have set the format of 'Purchase Date' to be 'Short Date'

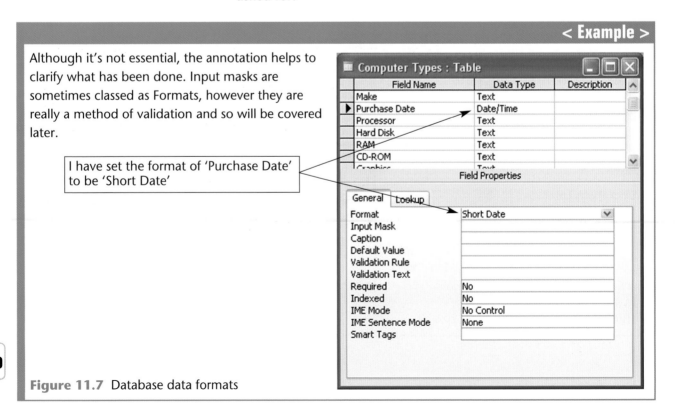

**Figure 11.7** Database data formats

## Data lengths

This requires the same evidence within a database as for data formats. It is rarely asked for as it is so simple, but if it is asked for, only show the evidence required. Do not show every single field if only one field is asked for.

< Example >

As with data formats, annotation is not essential, but it does help to clarify what has been done. This maximum length can also be a method of validation, but beware that it is unable to produce a customised error message and therefore might not answer some questions about validation.

I have set the length of the 'Make' field to 15 characters

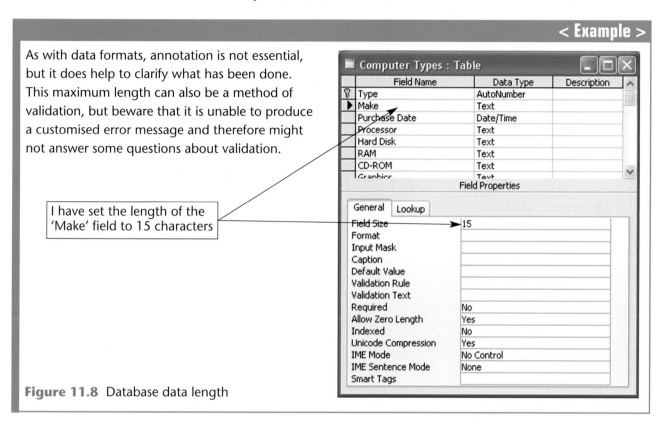

**Figure 11.8** Database data length

## Primary keys

Evidence that a primary key has been set up is often required. It cannot be assumed that the first field listed is a primary key. Evidence must be shown to indicate that it has been set up as a primary key. One way might be to show the table in design view. Another might be to show that it is the bold field in an entity relationship diagram. If you are asked to show evidence of a composite key, then you must show that more than two fields have been used as a primary key. However, remember that it is always good practice to use a single field for a primary key unless specifically asked to do otherwise.

< Example >

**Figure 11.9** Example of a single field primary key

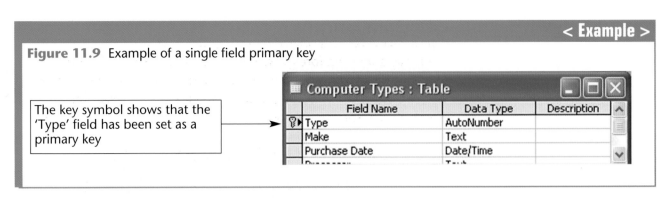

The key symbol shows that the 'Type' field has been set as a primary key

< Example >

**Figure 11.10** Example of a composite field primary key

The key symbols show that the 'BookID', 'BorrowerID' and 'DateTaken' fields have been set as a compostire (multiple) primary key. The combination of the data in all three of these fields for each record is unique

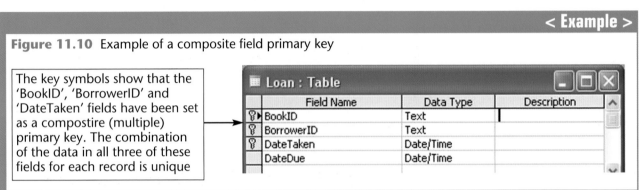

## ▇ Foreign keys

Showing evidence of foreign keys depends very much upon the software being used. One method is to show how a relationship has been set up on the field to make it a foreign key.

< Example >

**Figure 11.11** Example of an entity relationship diagram illustrating foreign keys

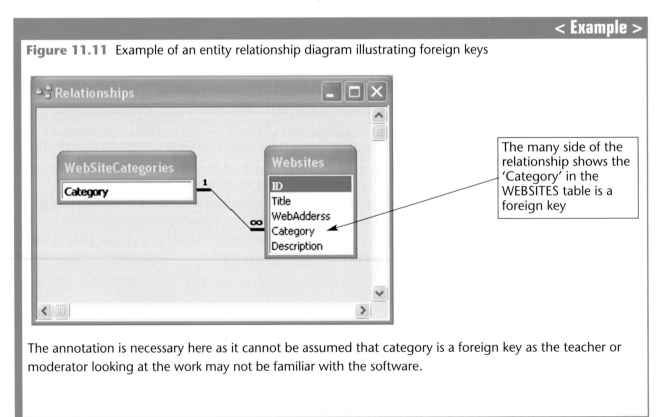

The many side of the relationship shows the 'Category' in the WEBSITES table is a foreign key

The annotation is necessary here as it cannot be assumed that category is a foreign key as the teacher or moderator looking at the work may not be familiar with the software.

It is tempting to expand the related data in the primary table view, however this only shows the primary key and does not actually show the foreign key. In the next screenshot, the primary key is shown for the 'WebSiteCategories' table, but no foreign key is shown for the 'Websites' table. Therefore do not use this method for showing foreign keys.

WebSiteCategories : Table

| Category |
|---|
| - A-level ICT |

| Title | WebAddress |
|---|---|
| ICSTIS | www.icstis.org.uk |
| Map Zone | www.mapzone.co.uk |
| Alice Bot | www.alicebot.org |
| * | |

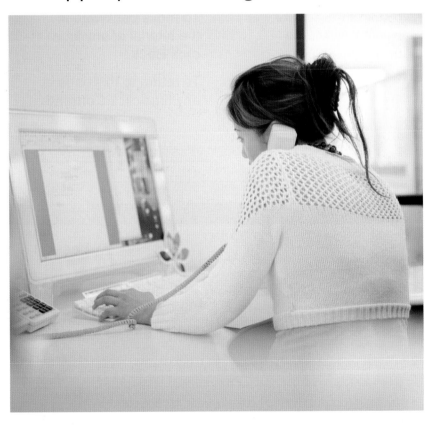

**Figure 11.12** Foreign keys in a database table

# Create user interfaces appropriate to a given audience

**Figure 11.13**

An interface is the method used for communication between the user and the computer, and usually uses screens or sounds. An interface could be used within a spreadsheet to ask the user to enter some data, or it could be a menu within a slideshow where clicking buttons takes the user to different slides. Instructions could be given visually or verbally.

If you have produced or have been given a design layout for a user interface, then it is essential that you follow that design when creating the user interface in software. Whether you have a design or not, it is critical that you follow the 'Dos and Do Nots' on page 208 about designing interfaces.

If you have access to a colour printer, then print the interface in colour. If you only have access to a monochrome printer, then annotate your work to show the colours you have used.

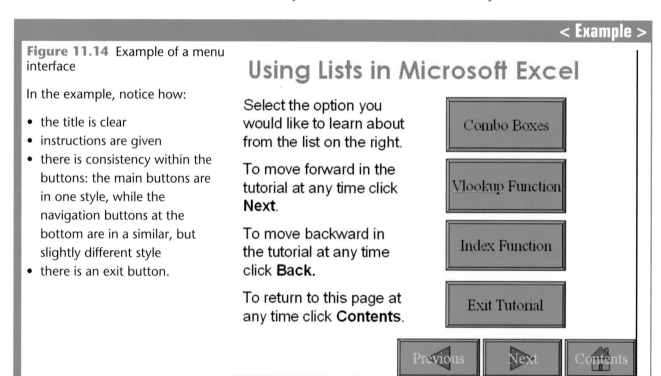

**Figure 11.14** Example of a menu interface

In the example, notice how:

- the title is clear
- instructions are given
- there is consistency within the buttons: the main buttons are in one style, while the navigation buttons at the bottom are in a similar, but slightly different style
- there is an exit button.

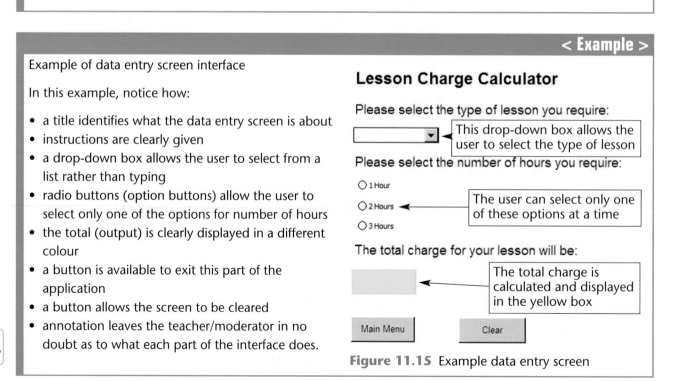

Example of data entry screen interface

In this example, notice how:

- a title identifies what the data entry screen is about
- instructions are clearly given
- a drop-down box allows the user to select from a list rather than typing
- radio buttons (option buttons) allow the user to select only one of the options for number of hours
- the total (output) is clearly displayed in a different colour
- a button is available to exit this part of the application
- a button allows the screen to be cleared
- annotation leaves the teacher/moderator in no doubt as to what each part of the interface does.

**Figure 11.15** Example data entry screen

## ▉ The audience

When producing an interface, it is very important to consider the intended audience. All audiences will require instructions, but an experienced audience will require less detailed instructions than an inexperienced audience.

**Figure 11.16**

Young children will require:

- larger fonts (14–16 pt)
- lots of colour (although consistent)
- pictures to help understanding
- more selection and less typing
- sound to read out instructions
- lots of feedback.

**Figure 11.17**

An adult audience is more likely to require:

- average size font (12 pt)
- limited use of colour so their focus is on the content
- pictures only if they are informative
- options to enter more data if required
- instructions on the screen, but subtle
- feedback that helps, but doesn't slow them down.

Examples of designing for an audience might be if you are producing an interface for an army cadet corps, then you might want to consider using khaki-based colours and images of tanks, whereas if you are producing an interface for a beauty parlour, then you may want to consider pink-based colours and images of finger nails.

# Create customised routines using methods such as validation, macros and wizards

A 'customised' routine means that it is not something that the software automatically does. It is something that you have tailored the software to do. For example, you could create a button that moves from one worksheet to another in a spreadsheet or you might have created a macro that will clear the screen.

## ◼ Validation

Most of the time, you will be asked to produce some evidence of customised validation methods. This would normally be part of a database, spreadsheet or web page form. You will be told what type of evidence you need to produce. One type of evidence is to show how you set up the validation rule. Another type of evidence is to show the customised error message that appears when you enter invalid data into the input area.

Often you will be asked to produce different types of validation. This includes length, data type, range, format/picture, lookup and presence checks. The table on page 237 shows how each of these can be achieved in databases, spreadsheets and web page forms. If you are asked for customised error messages, then use the options below that only allow customised error messages. Do **not** use the options that do **not** allow customised error messages.

| Validation | Database | Spreadsheet | Web page form |
|---|---|---|---|
| Length | The standard length of a field does not give a customised error message. Therefore try using the LIKE command, e.g: LIKE "?????" means five characters must be used. | Select the text length option for validation. Alternatively, use the LEN function that checks the length and displays a message if an error is made. | You can select the minimum required length and the maximum required length. If you want an exact length, then set these to be the same. |
| Data type | Very difficult if you need a customised error message, so avoid this. | You can usually choose integers, reals, dates and times. | Data types can usually be set to integers or numbers. Setting it to text does not validate the data as it will allow anything. However, the text format options allow you to specify whether letters or digits are allowed. |
| Range | Use a rule such as ">date()" (which means after today) or similar using >, <, >= or <=. | Numbers, dates and times can be set up with a minimum and maximum required value. | You can choose how to compare your data and with what values. |
| Format/picture | An input mask does not give a customised error message. Therefore try using the LIKE command, e.g: LIKE"[A-Z][A-Z][0-9]" requires two letters followed by a single digit. | This is very difficult to achieve but could be accomplished with a series of IF functions comparing each character of the cell. | This is not normally possible, although some software may provide the option. |
| Lookup in list | Use a rule such as ="Male" or "Female". | You can either type in the list in the validation option, or select a range of cells that contains the list. | This would be achieved using a drop-down list (combo box). |
| Presence | Use a rule such as "IS NOT NULL". Using the "Required" function does not give a customised error message. | Use an IF function to compare the value of the cell with "" and display an error message if it is blank. | This can be achieved by setting the 'required' option. |

Each of the examples that follow show how you should produce the evidence for both setting up the validation and seeing the customised error message. It is essential that, when you show the customised error message, you also annotate the input data that you have used.

< Example >

Example of validation using a database

The first screenshot shows how the validation was set up.

Notice how all of the following have been shown in this example:

- The field the validation has been set up on.
- The validation rule.
- The customised error message.
- Annotation to confirm each stage.

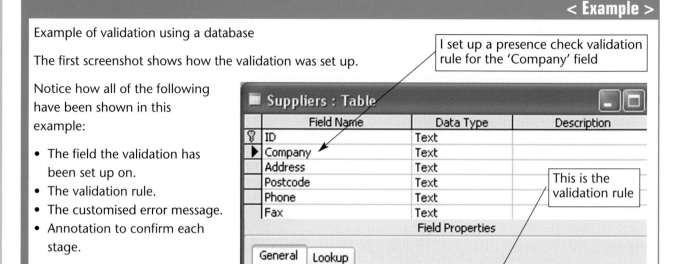

I set up a presence check validation rule for the 'Company' field

This is the validation rule

This is the customised error message that will appear if no data is entered

**Figure 11.18** Setting validation in a database

The second screenshot shows how the validation rule generates a customised error message when invalid data is entered.

Notice how:

- the input is clearly shown (this is very important)
- the annotation explains how and why the error message appeared
- the screenshot shows the title of the field (Company) so that it is clear that this field was used
- the error message matches the error message set up as Validation Text in the first screenshot.

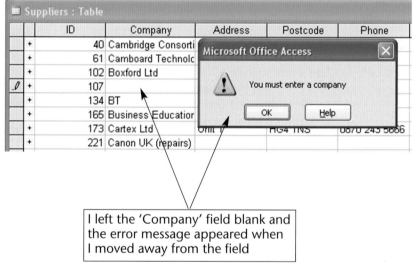

I left the 'Company' field blank and the error message appeared when I moved away from the field

**Figure 11.19** Validation error message

< Example >

Example of validation using a spreadsheet

The first screenshot shows how the validation was set up.

Notice how all of the following have been shown in this example:

- The cell the validation has been set up on.
- The validation rule.
- Annotation to confirm each stage.

This means that only whole numbers are allowed (data type check)

This is the cell which is validated

This is where I specified the minimum and maximum values

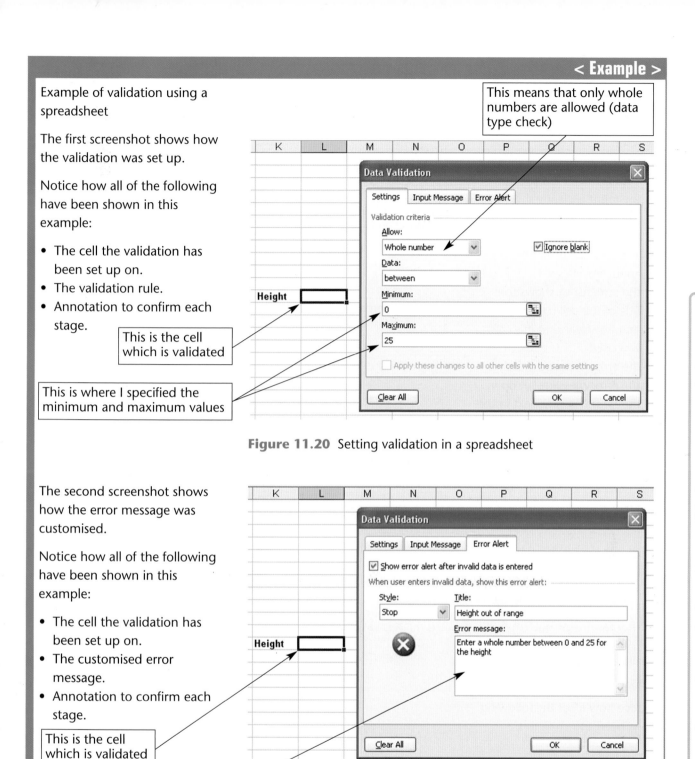

**Figure 11.20** Setting validation in a spreadsheet

The second screenshot shows how the error message was customised.

Notice how all of the following have been shown in this example:

- The cell the validation has been set up on.
- The customised error message.
- Annotation to confirm each stage.

This is the cell which is validated

This is the customised error message that I set for the cell

**Figure 11.21** Setting validation error message

Create customised routines using methods such as validation, macros and wizards

The third screenshot shows how the validation rule generates a customised error message when invalid data is entered.

Notice how:

- the input is clearly shown (this is very important)
- the annotation explains how and why the error message appeared
- the screenshot shows the title of the cell (Height) so that it is clear that this cell was used
- the error message matches the error message set up in the Error Message text in the second screenshot.

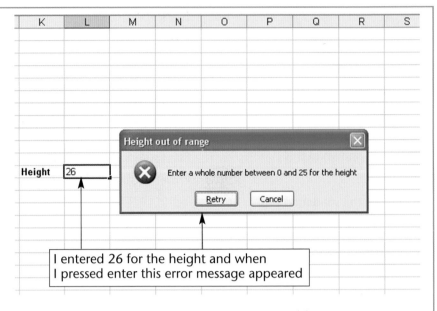

Height 26

**Height out of range**

Enter a whole number between 0 and 25 for the height

Retry    Cancel

I entered 26 for the height and when I pressed enter this error message appeared

**Figure 11.22** Validation error message in spreadsheet

< Example >

**Figure 11.23** Example of validation using a web page form

Only one screenshot is used here. The reason for this is that to show a validation rule working, a website has to be hosted correctly, and this is not something that can usually be achieved in schools and colleges.

Notice how all of the following have been shown in this example:

- The field the validation has been set up on (Customer Code).
- The validation rule.
- Annotation to confirm each stage.

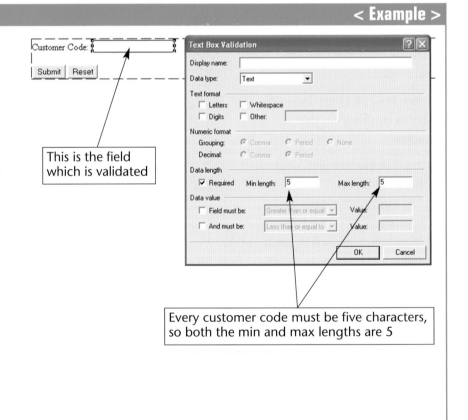

Customer Code:

Submit    Reset

This is the field which is validated

**Text Box Validation**

Display name:

Data type:  Text

Text format
 Letters   Whitespace
 Digits    Other:

Numeric format
 Grouping:  Comma   Period   None
 Decimal:   Comma   Period

Data length
 Required   Min length: 5   Max length: 5

Data value
 Field must be:  Greater than or equal   Value:
 And must be:    Less than or equal to   Value:

OK    Cancel

Every customer code must be five characters, so both the min and max lengths are 5

## Macros

A macro is usually used to perform a set (group) of instructions one after another automatically, rather than the user performing them each manually.

There are usually two elements of evidence that you will need to show for macros. Firstly you will need to show the steps that you went through to create a macro. Secondly you will need to show the code that has been generated. Both elements of evidence will need annotating. Although you do **not** have to write the code, you may be expected to identify what each section of code does by annotating it.

< Example >

The commentary below shows how a student might present evidence for creating a macro that carries out a simple sorting procedure. A button is ready for the macro, but will not be used in this example.

I gave the macro the name 'SortList' then started to record

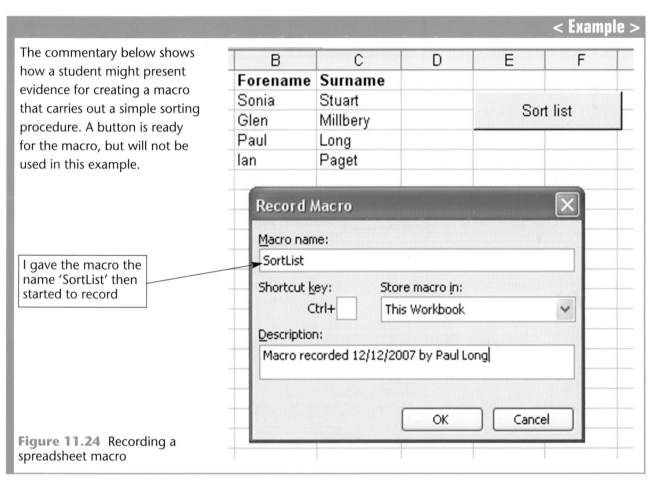

**Figure 11.24** Recording a spreadsheet macro

Create customised routines using methods such as validation, macros and wizards

**241**

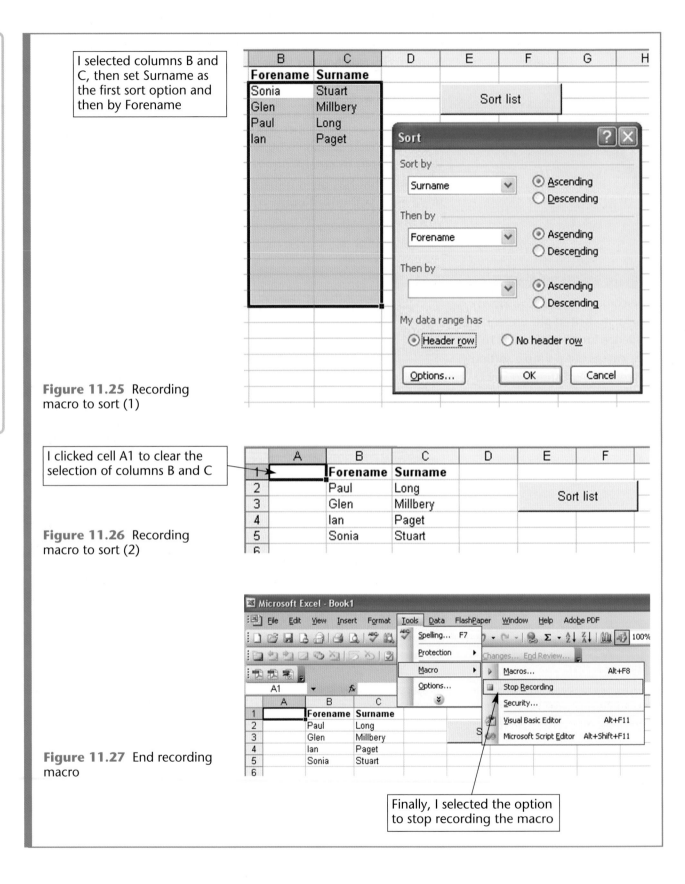

I selected columns B and C, then set Surname as the first sort option and then by Forename

**Figure 11.25** Recording macro to sort (1)

I clicked cell A1 to clear the selection of columns B and C

**Figure 11.26** Recording macro to sort (2)

**Figure 11.27** End recording macro

Finally, I selected the option to stop recording the macro

The student has also been asked to show evidence of the macro code that has been produced and to annotate it to show what each section does:

```
Sub SortList()
'
' SortList Macro
' Macro recorded 12/12/2007 by Paul Long
'

' The row below shows that columns B and C were selected.
    Columns("B:C").Select

' The section below shows how the sort was first set to be ascending on column C (Surname),followed by ascending on column B (Forename).
    Selection.Sort Key1:=Range("C2"), Order1:=xlAscending, Key2:=Range("B2") _
        , Order2:=xlAscending, Header:=xlGuess, OrderCustom:=1, MatchCase:= _
        False, Orientation:=xlTopToBottom, DataOption1:=xlSortNormal, DataOption2 _
        :=xlSortNormal

' The lines below shows how cell A1 was selected and the macro assigned to the button at the end.
    Range("A1").Select
        ActiveSheet.Shapes("Button 3").Select
        Selection.OnAction = "SortList"
End Sub
```

**Figure 11.28** Example code for macro

Notice how the student has used apostrophes in the code to put in comments (annotation): these automatically turn to green. This could also have been done using text boxes and arrows after taking the screenshot.

You might also be asked to show how you have linked the macro to a button, toolbar or key press. The same principles as all evidence apply: show annotated screenshot evidence of how you have achieved each step. The question will usually tell you what evidence is required.

## Wizards

Wizards allow you to create a feature quickly by answering a set of questions. The feature will then be created. An example is creating a combo box (drop-down list) in a database. Usually the question will only ask you to show evidence of the final result rather than the step-by-step stages that you went through. Read the question carefully to see what is required.

< Example >

Show evidence of the drop-down list that you have produced for the category field. Ensure your evidence shows the options that can be selected.

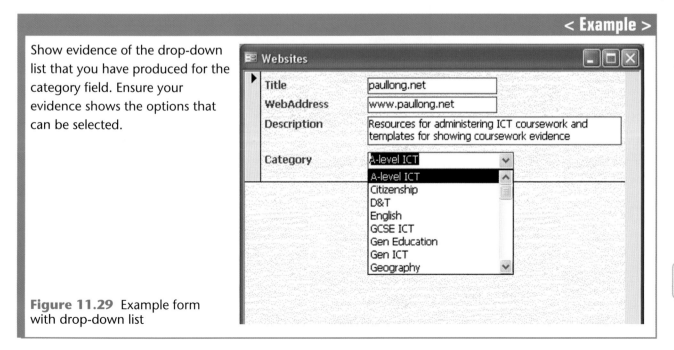

**Figure 11.29** Example form with drop-down list

243

# Use word-processing software to create and edit documents – in particular candidates will be expected to use mail merge

There are many tasks that word processors can be used for. It's not possible to cover them all in this book, but some of the more common ones that OCR will test are covered below. Other skills are likely to be required in the structured tasks, but it is the principle of producing the evidence that is most important. As long as you know how to produce the evidence, you can apply this to any skill.

## Templates

Templates are the layout of standard documents. A template can be used many times to create new documents with the same layout.

You will usually be required to show evidence of how you have saved a document as a template and then to show how this template has been used to create a new document.

**< Example >**

Show evidence of how you saved the template for the school.

Notice how:

- the screenshot is annotated to clarify what has been done

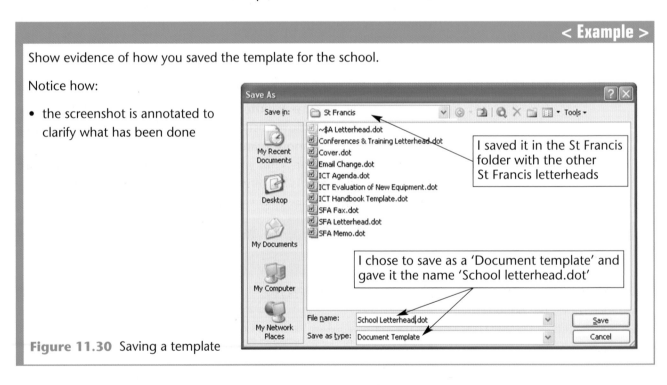

I saved it in the St Francis folder with the other St Francis letterheads

I chose to save as a 'Document template' and gave it the name 'School letterhead.dot'

**Figure 11.30** Saving a template

< Example >

Show evidence of how you used the template to create a new letter to parents.

The annotation isn't essential, but it helps to clarify what has been done.

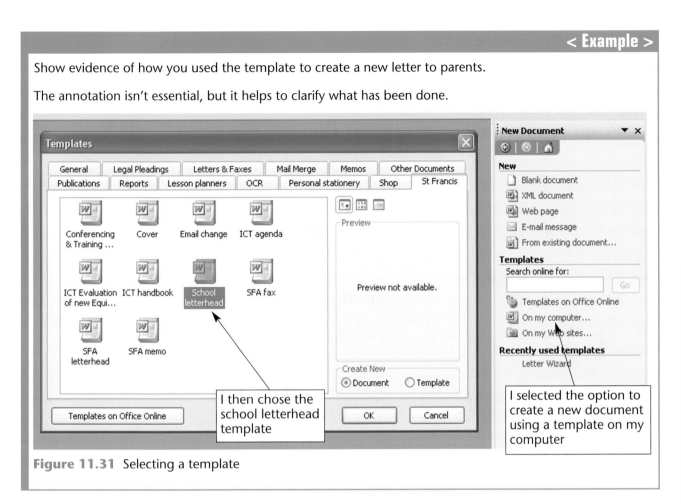

**Figure 11.31** Selecting a template

## Data capture forms

A data capture form is a form used to collect data. It is not an online/on-screen form. It is a printed form. For example, it could be a questionnaire about reading habits or an application form to join a health club. When you create a data capture form you need to make it as easy to complete as possible. You also need to consider how the data will be stored at a later stage.

< Example >

### What is your favourite type of film?
### Tick one only.

❑ Horror          ❑ Comedy          ❑ Action

❑ Thriller          ❑ Romantic          ❑ Other _____

**Figure 11.32** Good example of a form

Notice how an instruction has been given. Notice also how tick boxes are used and each option is clearly separated from the other. An option to give another type of film is also given (although this might not always be appropriate).

Use word-processing software to create and edit documents – in particular candidates will be expected to use mail merge

The data captured can now be used in a database. A field called 'TypeofFilm' can be created and the responses recorded.

The example below is **not** a good one.

## What is your favourite type of film? _____

**Figure 11.33** Bad example of a form

This makes the question very difficult to answer. The person filling in the form may not know what is meant by 'type' of film. This means that you won't get the answers you are looking for.

| Do | Do not |
|---|---|
| Separate forenames and surnames. | Use a single name. |
| Separate address lines and the postcode. | Use a single box for the whole address. |
| Use tick boxes that allow the person filling in the form to select from a list. | Have all open questions as this makes it difficult to store the data at a later stage. |
| Include instructions on how to fill in the form and what to do with it when it's completed. | Use lots of different fonts. |
| Research other types of screens and outputs to see what they look like. | Use colour as it makes printing lots of copies very expensive. |
| Read the question carefully so that you include everything asked for. | Use large fonts that mean the data capture form uses lots of pages. |
| Include a title. | |
| Try to keep the data capture form to one page (one or two sides) maximum. | |
| Include units (e.g. m for metres, £, etc.) so the user doesn't have to write them in themselves. | |
| Use a spell checker and then check the spelling yourself. | |

## ■ Mail merge

Mail merge is the process of using data (from a data source) within a main document (e.g. letter) to produce several copies of the document in the same format but with different data. For example, you may be asked to produce a business card for all the employees within a company. The data source will be the names, email addresses and telephone numbers of the employees; the main document will be the layout of the business card and will include everything that is common to the company (i.e. logo, company name, address, etc.) and fields from the data source.

You are likely to be asked to produce the following evidence:

- merge field codes
- data source
- merged data.

When producing the evidence for merge field codes, it is important to ensure that they are clearly marked (usually by << and >>). You must also ensure that the merge field codes you use are only for data that will change. For example, the address of the company on a business card will not change and so this should be normal text, whereas the name of the employee will change each time so this should be a merge field.

< Example >

# «Forename» «Surname»
## Driving Instructor

Mobile: «Mobile»  E-mail: «EMail»@ekltd.com

EK Ltd, 5 Lichfield Road, Aldridge, Walsall, WS9 0PQ
Tel: 01922 555 555    www.ekltd.com

**Figure 11.34** Using mail merge to make business cards

Notice the following:

- Merge field codes are clearly separated using << and >>.
- Merge field codes are **only** for data about the individual instructor.
- Any data about the driving school is **not** a merge field code.
- <<Next Record>> is used so that more than one instructor can be printed on the same page, (however the question may not ask for this).

The data source is where the actual data will come from. In the example of business cards, it will include the forename and surname, mobile number and email address of the employees. The data source can either be a database table/query, a spreadsheet or a word-processed table. It could also be a contact list in email software, but this is unlikely to be asked for.

Use word-processing software to create and edit documents – in particular candidates will be expected to use mail merge

< Example >

### Instructor : Table

| | InstructorID | Forename | Surname | Mobile | Email | Level | Gender |
|---|---|---|---|---|---|---|---|
| | 1 | Angela | Keepax | 0777 111 333 | angela | Senior | F |
| | 2 | Jean | Uxpern | 0777 111 334 | jean | Senior | F |
| | 3 | Danny | Sampson | 0777 111 335 | danny | Junior | M |
| | 4 | Jane | Caston | 0777 111 336 | jane | Junior | F |
| | 5 | Jock | Smith | 0777 111 337 | jock | Senior | M |
| | 6 | Sulim | Khan | 0777 111 338 | sulim | Junior | M |
| | 7 | Sam | Carlton | 0777 111 339 | sam2 | Senior | M |
| | 8 | Peggy | Walters | 0777 111 340 | peggy | Junior | F |
| | 9 | Fiona | Gilbert | 0777 111 341 | fiona | Senior | F |
| | 10 | Wendy | Saxby | 0777 111 342 | wendy | Junior | F |
| | 11 | Serena | Riaz | 0777 111 343 | serena | Senior | F |
| ▶ | (AutoNumber) | | | | | | |

**Figure 11.35** Database table for mail merge

Notice the following:

- Only the data about each instructor is stored in the data source. No data about the driving school is needed as this would be redundant.
- In this case, a database table has been used as the data source.

You may be asked to show how you connected the main document to the data source. This evidence should show the filename of the data source.

< Example >

This screenshot shows that the process is to 'Select Data Source' and the file name of the actual data source used.

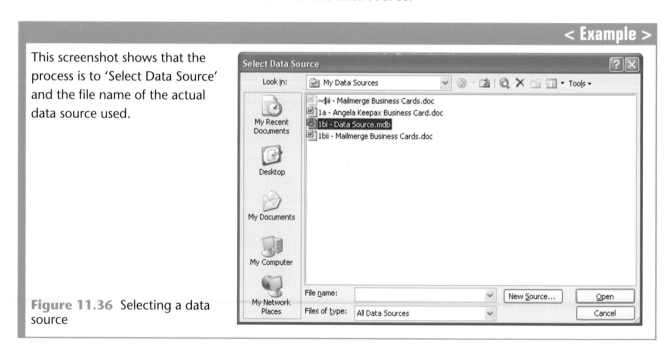

**Figure 11.36** Selecting a data source

To produce evidence of the merged data, you should merge the data source with the main document. In this example, it will produce a set of business cards with about eight on each page. If it will produce letters, there needs to be a separate page for each letter. This evidence will usually be printed rather than providing screenshots. Ensure that you include the number of merged documents asked for in the question.

Sometimes, you will be asked to include only some records. For example, you may be asked to produce business cards only for the senior female instructors or you may be asked to produce letters to customers who are willing to be on a mailing list and in a particular age range. There are two main methods of achieving this:

- Use a query instead of a table in a database.
- Use the filter feature in the mail merge main document.

You will need to show clear evidence that only the data required has been used. You will need evidence of the criteria used for the query and that the query has been applied/used.

< Example >

This example is for senior female driving instructors. It is using a query in a database. The first screenshot shows the criteria used.

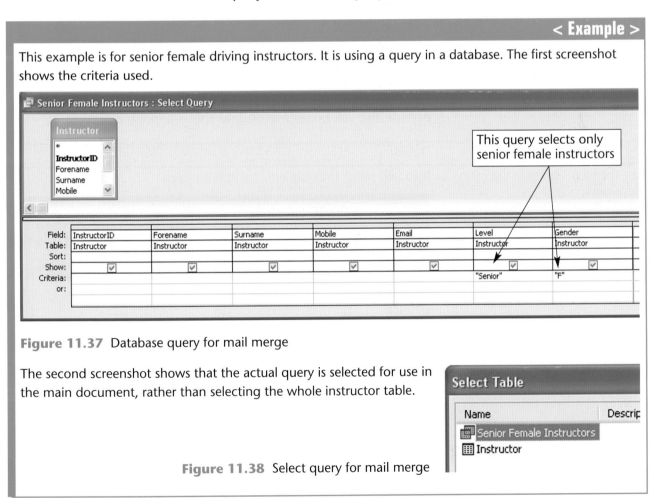

This query selects only senior female instructors

**Figure 11.37** Database query for mail merge

The second screenshot shows that the actual query is selected for use in the main document, rather than selecting the whole instructor table.

**Figure 11.38** Select query for mail merge

Use word-processing software to create and edit documents – in particular candidates will be expected to use mail merge

The third screenshot confirms that only female senior instructors have been used.

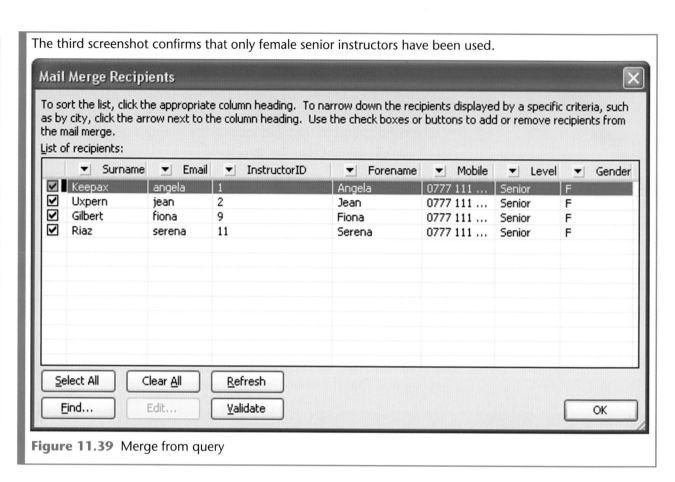

**Figure 11.39** Merge from query

If you are using the filter feature in the main document then do not use the tick boxes method, as this is a manual process.

| Do | Do not |
|---|---|
| Use the filter feature in the main document. | Manually select the recipients using tick boxes. |

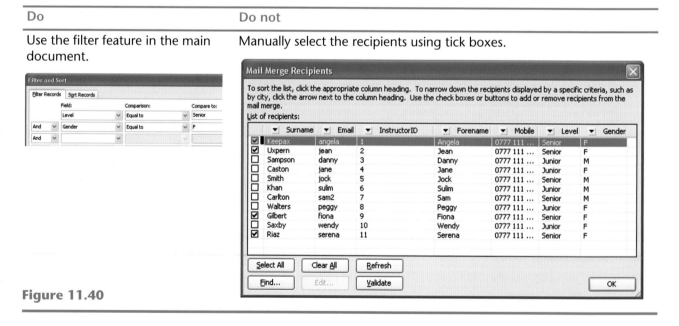

**Figure 11.40**

Sometimes you will be asked to use **word fields**. These are fields within the word processor that carry out a particular function at the time of the merge process. One example is <<Next Record>> which will move on to the next record. Another is the <<IF>>

field. This can be used to compare data from the data source with pre-defined values and then give an output. When producing evidence, provide what the question has asked for. You are most likely to be asked to show evidence of:

- setting up the word field
- the word field being used or its syntax
- the output of the word field.

< Example >

Produce business cards for all the instructors in the driving school. If the instructor is a senior instructor, then display the word 'Senior' before 'Driving Instructor' on the business card. If the instructor is a junior instructor, then do not display anything before 'Driving Instructor'.

The screenshot to the right shows how the IF word field was inserted. The screenshot below has been generated by clicking Shift+F9 and displays the full syntax of the IF word field.

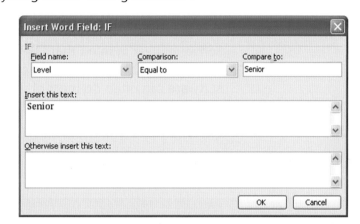

**«Forename» «Surname»**
{ IF Senior = "Senior" "Senior" "" } Driving Instructor

**Figure 11.41** Merging with a condition

The final screenshot below shows the output of the IF word field by showing how the senior instructors have the word 'Senior' displayed, but the junior instructors do not have anything displayed.

**Figure 11.42** Result of merging with a condition

Use word-processing software to create and edit documents – in particular candidates will be expected to use mail merge

The example that has been used in this book has been for people, which is a very common type of data to use for mail merge. However, it could be about objects or events. For example, you could be asked to produce a set of property information sheets about houses for sale.

# Use desktop publishing software to create and edit documents

Before deciding to use desktop publishing (DTP) software, make sure that it is the appropriate software to use. If you need word-processing features such as a contents page or footnotes/endnotes later on in the task, then avoid using DTP software. Bear in mind that DTP software is used where lots of work is required on the layout of the document. Word-processing software can often do most of what DTP software can do, although it can be a bit more fiddly.

Like word-processing software, DTP software can be used for mail merge. The same type of evidence as word-processing software is required.

**< Example >**

Produce a CD cover for the New Wine conference photos that will be given to each of the delegates from St John's Church in Walmley. Each cover should be personalised so that it has the name of the delegate included.

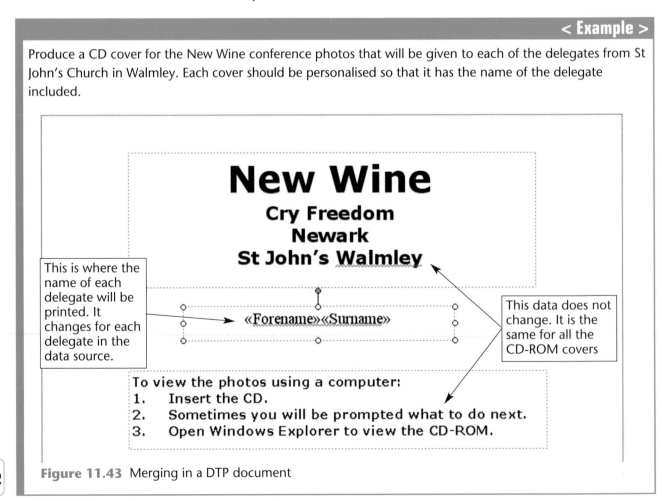

**Figure 11.43** Merging in a DTP document

# Use functions and formulae to solve a problem

Spreadsheets should be used to solve numerical problems or problems where lots of decision making is required. If you are required to produce an interface, then you should follow the guidance on page 208 as well as any specific advice given in this section.

## Row/column headings

When you provide printouts of your work, ensure that you include the row and column headings (i.e. 1, 2, 3 (rows) and A, B, C (columns)). This is so that any formulae and functions that you create can be checked. Without row and column headings, you are not likely to get the marks for formulae and functions.

If you have more than one worksheet, then ensure all worksheets have row and column headings. If you need extra printouts or screenshots because the spreadsheet is large, then ensure that these printouts/screenshots also have row and column headings.

< Example >

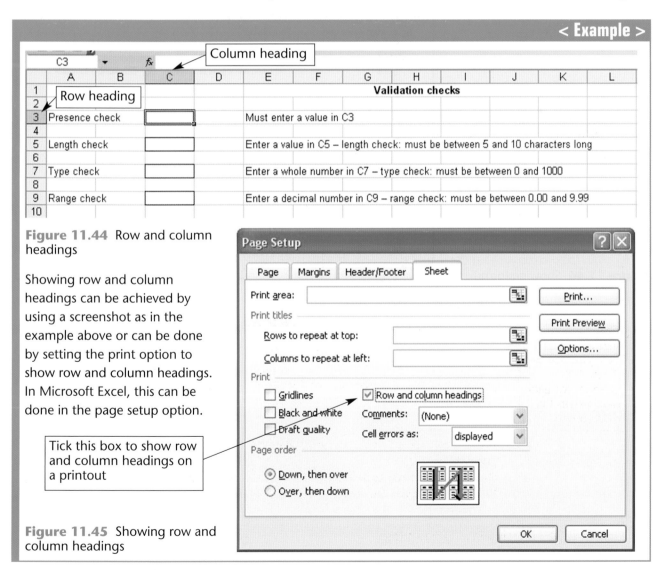

**Figure 11.44** Row and column headings

Showing row and column headings can be achieved by using a screenshot as in the example above or can be done by setting the print option to show row and column headings. In Microsoft Excel, this can be done in the page setup option.

Tick this box to show row and column headings on a printout

**Figure 11.45** Showing row and column headings

# Formulae and functions

You are very likely to be asked to show evidence of formulae and functions. You should ensure that you do all of the following when showing formulae and functions:

- Show row and column headings.
- Show the whole formula/function. This may mean showing it in the formula bar or extending the size of the column.
- Annotate each formula/function. It is not necessary to repeat the annotation for replicated formulae/functions.
- Show evidence of any other cells and worksheets that are referenced by the formulae/functions.

The easiest way to show evidence of formulae and functions is to select the option to display them in Tools > Options.

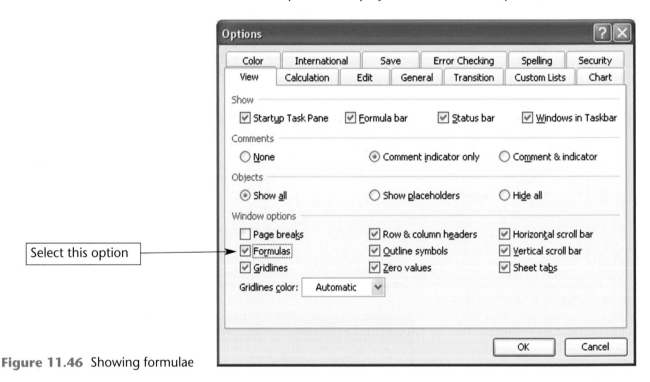

**Figure 11.46** Showing formulae

< Example >

| | A | B | C | D |
|---|---|---|---|---|
| 1 | | | | |
| 2 | | | | |
| 3 | | | | |
| 4 | | | | |
| 5 | | Customer Name: | ='Input Screen'!F20 | |
| 6 | | | | |
| 7 | | Customer Address: | ='Input Screen'!F22 | |
| 8 | | | ='Input Screen'!F23 | |
| 9 | | | ='Input Screen'!F24 | |
| 10 | | | ='Input Screen'!F25 | |
| 11 | | | | |
| 12 | | **Dimensions of driveway** | | |
| 13 | | Length | ='Input Screen'!H14 | m |
| 14 | | Width | ='Input Screen'!H16 | m |
| 15 | | Area | =C13*C14 | sq m |
| 16 | | | | |
| 17 | | **Bricks** | | |
| 18 | | Type of brick | =INDEX('Brick Types'!A2:D9,'Input Screen'!L1,2) | |
| 19 | | Cost per brick | =INDEX('Brick Types'!A3:D9,'Input Screen'!L1,4) | |
| 20 | | Area of one brick | =INDEX('Brick Types'!A4:D9,'Input Screen'!L1,3) | sq m |
| 21 | | Number of bricks | =(C15/C20)+(0.05*C15/C20) | |
| 22 | | Cost of bricks | =C21*C19 | |
| 23 | | | | |

These formulae pick up the name and address from the 'Input Screen' worksheet

**Figure 11.47** Displayed formulae

**=C14*13**
This formula multiplies the length of the driveway by the width of the driveway.

**=INDEX('Brick Types'!A2:D9, 'Input Screen'!L1,2)**
This function looks up the number of the type of brick selected from L1 on the input screen and returns the type of brick from column 2 in the A2:A9 range of the 'Brick Types' worksheet.

**=INDEX('Brick Types'!A2:D9, 'Input Screen'!L1,4)**
This function looks up the number of the type of brick selected from L1 on the input screen and returns the cost per brick from column 4 in the A2:A9 range of the 'Brick Types' worksheet.

**=INDEX('Brick Types'!A2:D9, 'Input Screen'!L1,3)**
This function looks up the number of the type of brick selected from L1 on the input screen and returns the area of the brick from column 3 in the A2:A9 range of the 'Brick Types' worksheet.

**=(C15/C20)+(0.05*C15/20)**
This formula divides the area of the driveway by the area of each brick to determine the number of bricks required. It then adds another 5% (0.05) of bricks.

**=C21*C19**
This formula multiplies the number of bricks required by the cost of each brick to determine the total cost of the bricks that will be required.

The 'Input Screen' worksheet that some of the formulae/functions make reference to is shown to the right.

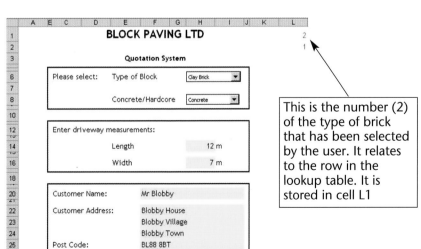

**Figure 11.48** Input screen for Figure 11.47

This is the number (2) of the type of brick that has been selected by the user. It relates to the row in the lookup table. It is stored in cell L1

**Use functions and formulae to solve a problem**

**255**

The screenshot on the right shows the 'Brick Types' lookup table that the LOOKUP functions make reference to.

|   | A | B | C | D |
|---|---|---|---|---|
| 1 |   | Brick | Area | Cost |
| 2 | 1 | Natural brick | 0.02 | £0.50 |
| 3 | 2 | Clay brick | 0.02 | £0.75 |
| 4 | 3 | Yorkshire cobble | 0.08 | £0.75 |
| 5 | 4 | Natural granite cobble | 0.08 | £0.75 |
| 6 | 5 | Concrete block | 0.01 | £0.40 |
| 7 | 6 | Natural slabs | 0.36 | £5.50 |
| 8 | 7 | Clay slabs | 0.36 | £7.50 |
| 9 | 8 | Yorkshire slabs | 0.36 | £7.50 |

**Figure 11.49** Example LOOKUP table

< Activity >

Look at the extract below of a spreadsheet that is used to calculate fees.

|   | G | H | I | J | K |
|---|---|---|---|---|---|
| 1 |   |   | Deadline | 01/04/2004 |   |
| 2 |   |   |   |   |   |
| 3 | Date of application | Payment category | Fee | Discount | Fee payable |
| 4 | 30/04/2004 | Adult | £12.00 | £0.00 | £12.00 |
| 5 | 28/03/2004 | U12 | £5.00 | £1.00 | £4.00 |
| 6 | 02/04/2004 | 12–15 | £7.00 | £0.00 | £7.00 |
| 7 | 01/04/2004 | Stu/OAP | £9.00 | £0.00 | £9.00 |

**Figure 11.50** Fees spreadsheet

Annotate the formulae/functions shown below. Annotation should explain what each formula/function does and what result it produces.

|   | G | H | I | J | K |
|---|---|---|---|---|---|
| 1 |   |   | Deadline |   |   |
| 2 |   |   |   | 38078 |   |
| 3 | Date of application | Payment category | Fee |   |   |
| 4 | 38107 | Adult | =IF(H4="Adult",12,IF(H4="U12",5,IF(H4="12–15", 7,IF(H4="Stu/OAP",9,"invalid category")))) | Discount | Fee payable |
| 5 | 38074 | U12 | =IF(H5="Adult",12,IF(H5="U12",5,IF(H5="12–15", 7,IF(H5="Stu/OAP",9,"invalid category")))) | =IF(G4<$J$1,1,0) | =I4-J4 |
| 6 | 38079 | 12–15 | =IF(H6="Adult",12,IF(H6="U12",5,IF(H6="12–15", 7,IF(H6="Stu/OAP",9,"invalid category")))) | =IF(G5<$J$1,1,0) | =I5-J5 |
| 7 | 38078 | Stu/OAP | =IF(H7="Adult",12,IF(H7="U12",5,IF(H7="12–15", 7,IF(H7="Stu/OAP",9,"invalid category")))) | =IF(G6<$J$1,1,0) | =I6-J6 |
|   |   |   |   | =IF(G7<$J$1,1,0) | =I7-J7 |

**Figure 11.51** Formulae for Figure 11.50

a) =IF(H4="Adult",12,IF(H4="U12",5,IF(H4="12–15",7,IF(H4="Stu/OAP",9,"Invalid Category"))))

b) =IF(G4<$J$1,1,0)

c) =I4-J4

## ◼ Conditional formatting

If you use conditional formatting then you are likely to need to show evidence of how you set up the conditional formatting, and the results of the conditional formatting. You should ensure that your evidence includes:

- reference to any colours if a monochrome printer is used
- output for all possible routes of the conditional format (i.e. the result of condition 1, condition 2 and condition 3 if appropriate)
- input for all possible routes of the conditional format
- output shown with the input.

< Example >

If an answer is given correctly then 'Well done!' will be displayed. If an answer is given incorrectly then 'Try again!' will be displayed. When 'Well done!' is displayed, it should have a green background, whereas 'Try again!' should have a red background. Show evidence of setting up a method of achieving this and what happens when each message is displayed.

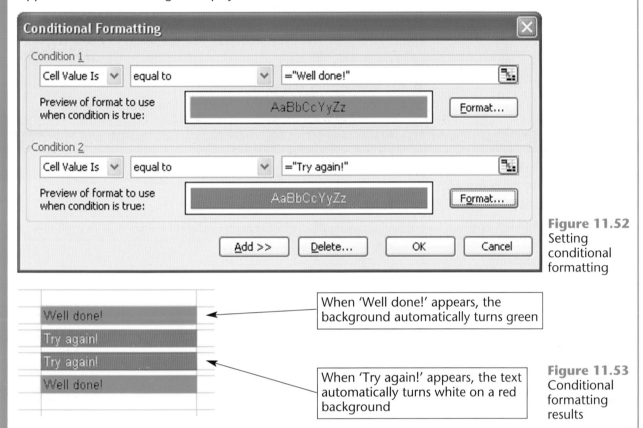

**Figure 11.52** Setting conditional formatting

When 'Well done!' appears, the background automatically turns green

When 'Try again!' appears, the text automatically turns white on a red background

**Figure 11.53** Conditional formatting results

## ■ Charts

If you are asked to produce a chart, then you should follow the guidelines given below.

| Do | Do not |
|---|---|
| Include an appropriate title. It should be:<br>■ short enough to be a title<br>■ descriptive enough to make sense.<br>For example, 'Percentage of customers purchasing each product' | Highlight more data than is required as this will give strange charts. |
| Show values on both the x- and y- (sometimes z-) axes. | Include the total with the data that makes up the total because the total will produce a really high bar or will take up 50% of a pie chart. |
| Include axes labels. | Use 'fancy' charts such as 'Area' and '3-D' charts that are very difficult to interpret. |
| Include a legend if different colours or shadings are used. | Include a legend if only one colour or shading is used. |

Use functions and formulae to solve a problem

# Use graphics software to create and edit graphical images

As graphics is quite a specialised area, you are unlikely to be asked to carry out anything very complicated. You might be asked to change the quality of a picture by sharpening it, or by increasing the brightness. The evidence that you are likely to need will be:

- the image before it was improved
- the image after it was improved
- a screenshot of the feature used for the improvement.

< Example >

The Hodder '100 years' logo has been scanned into the computer and is currently shades of pale blue that look more like cyan. Improve the logo so that the darker blues are showing correctly. As evidence, show the original logo, the improved logo and an annotated screenshot of how you improved it.

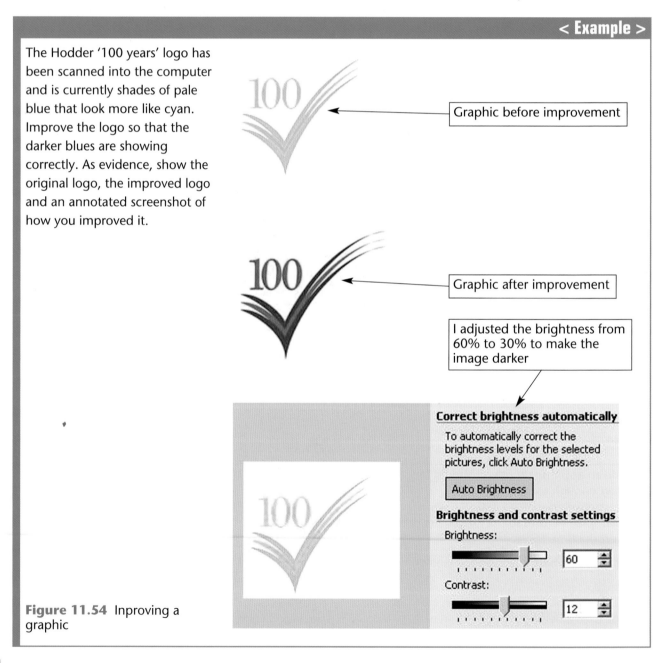

Graphic before improvement

Graphic after improvement

I adjusted the brightness from 60% to 30% to make the image darker

**Correct brightness automatically**

To automatically correct the brightness levels for the selected pictures, click Auto Brightness.

Auto Brightness

**Brightness and contrast settings**

Brightness:

60

Contrast:

12

**Figure 11.54** Inproving a graphic

# Use web design software to create and edit web pages

Website tasks will usually require you to create some web pages, often including a web page form. You will also need to show the structure of your website, including how the pages link together and the file structures used.

## Web pages

Web pages are similar to any document produced in that the audience must be considered and the same principles for thinking about the layout and avoiding clashing colours should be applied. However, there are a few other considerations that need to be made. Web pages also include:

- online forms
- a file structure that needs to be properly managed
- hyperlinks to other web pages
- images that need to be downloaded when the page is viewed
- features that require specialist web design software to create and edit.

## Online forms

An online form is a method of collecting data from users on the World Wide Web. As an online form is also an interface, you need to follow the advice about interfaces on pages 233–6 of the development section and page 208 of the design section about designing screen layouts. In particular, you should consider the following:

| Do | Do not |
|---|---|
| Separate forenames and surnames. | Use a single name. |
| Separate address lines and the postcode. | Use a single box for the whole address. |
| Use controls that allow selection of data (e.g. drop-down box, list box, radio buttons, tick boxes). | Have all open questions as this makes it difficult to store the data at a later stage. |
| Include instructions on how to fill in the form and what to do with it when it's completed. | Use large fonts that mean lots of scrolling has to be done to get through the form. |
| Use buttons/hyperlinks with clear labels and annotate them to identify their target locations. | Assume that because you have shown a printout that includes a list of the target page names that these are hyperlinks. |
| Research other online forms to see what they look like. | Use lots of different fonts. |
| Read the question carefully so that you include everything asked for. | Miss out anything that has been asked for. |
| Annotate your work to explain what each item is or will do. | Assume that what you have printed is enough evidence without explanation. |
| Include a title. | Use clashing colours or lots of colours as this will put the user off. |
| Include units after or before input boxes (e.g. m for metres, £, etc.) so the user doesn't have to write them in themselves. | Have input fields too close to each other. |
| Use a spell checker and then check the spelling yourself. | |
| Use contrasting colours for text and background. White or very pale backgrounds are advisable. | |
| Include a confirmation (submit) button and a cancel (clear) button. | |

< Activity >

Considering the principles you have learned above, what could be done to improve the following online form?

Parent / Guardian Details:

Title:

Forename:

Surname:

E-Mail:

Child Details:

Forename:                Surname:

Class:        ○ 1    ○ 2    ○ 3    ○ 4    ○ 5    ○ 6    ○ Reception

Submit

Figure 11.55 A web form

## ██ File structures

When you create your pages, you should carefully plan how you intend to save your files. Look at the advice given below.

| Do | Do not |
|---|---|
| Use sensible file names such as 'index.html' or 'contactus.html'. | Use default file names such as 'page1.html', 'page2.html'. |
| Use a separate folder for each page and the files that will be associated with that page. | Use one single folder with all the files in that folder. |
| Either put images in the folder for the page they belong to or use a separate folder called 'images' or similar. | Use several copies of the same image (e.g. the company logo) as this wastes space. |
| Use lowercase letters for all file names. | Use capital letters, spaces or other special characters in file names. |

| Do | Do not |
|---|---|
| Use compressed file formats for pictures such as JPEG or GIF. | Use large file formats such as BMP or formats that are not recognised by all computers such as PSP. |

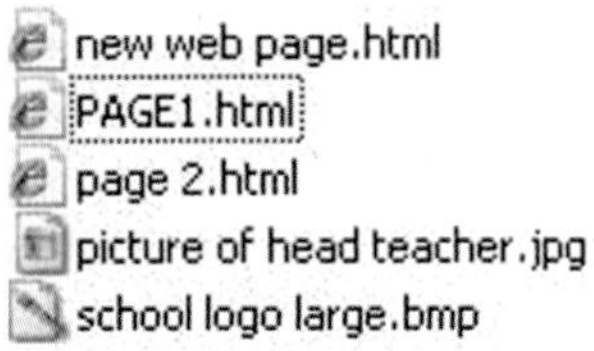

Figure 11.57  Poor file structure

**Figure 11.56**  Good file structure

## ██ Links

In order for your end users to be able to navigate around the website, you will need to create hyperlinks (or buttons) that when clicked will move to each page. When creating hyperlinks, you should do the following:

- ██ Ensure that every page has a link back to the home page.
- ██ Ensure that every page can be navigated to.
- ██ Start all external links with **http://** (e.g. **http://www.ocr.org.uk**).
- ██ Use **relative** links, not **absolute** links (see example).
- ██ Show evidence of each hyperlink you have created by:
    - printing the HTML code and highlighting each link, or
    - printing a diagram produced by web design software.

| Do | Do not |
|---|---|
| Use relative links. | Use absolute links. |

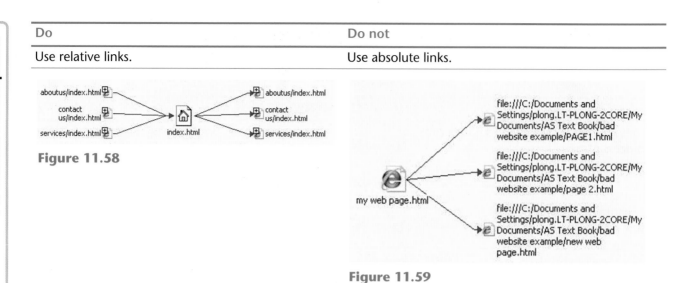

Figure 11.58

Figure 11.59

These links will work in any folder, including if they are uploaded to the Web because the file references are 'relative' to their starting location.

These links will not work on a different computer as they will be looking for the files in a specific location that will not exist.

## Images

Images can be included on web pages directly or they can be downloaded when following a link. The most important thing to consider with images is that they can take a long time to download. The bigger the file size (not physical size) of an image, the longer it takes to download. If there are lots of pictures on a page then the website will take a long time to download.

Therefore, consider the following when including images:

- Reduce the file size of an image so that it is no more than it needs to be (do not simply change its physical size on the screen).
- Only include a few (a maximum of about five) images on a screen at a time.
- If large images are needed, use a thumbnail or hyperlink to access the larger image.

## Web design tools

It is very important that you choose the right software tool for the job. While a word processor or desktop publisher can create basic web pages, it often doesn't include the tools that manage the links correctly or the file structures. However, a web design tool such as Adobe Dreamweaver or Microsoft FrontPage will have extra features that help to create a website, including the ability to manage links and file structures correctly.

# Use multimedia software to create and edit presentations, sounds, animations and videos

The most common multimedia tasks you will be asked to create will be presentation slide shows. However, it is also possible that you might be asked to edit sounds, animations or videos. Whichever of these you are required to do, the most important thing as always is to read the question carefully and provide the evidence that is being asked for.

## Consistency

When producing any document, consistency is always important. If it's a video, then it's important to use consistent methods of on-screen titles and consistent transitions. If it's a multimedia presentation then you should think about keeping the following consistent:

- title font styles
- main text font styles
- text colours
- background colours
- position of text.

Consistency doesn't necessarily mean exactly the same, although it often helps. As most of your evidence will be printed, white backgrounds are always a good idea. However, you might decide, when producing a presentation for children, to use a range of pastel colours for the background of each slide – although the colours are different, they are consistently pastel.

The simplest way to maintain consistency is to use a master slide. The fonts styles, sizes and colours that are allocated to a master slide are then used for every slide within the presentation, as long as you do not alter them manually. Similarly, any images, buttons or text that you include on a master slide will be repeated on each slide. For example, you could include on a master slide:

- a company name
- a company logo
- a slide number (it changes automatically)
- a button to return to the menu screen.

< Example >

Figure 11.60 Example of master slide

In this master slide, the following have been customised so that every slide has:

- pink title text in Arial font
- a slide number
- the author's name
- the Microsoft Excel logo
- buttons to go to the previous, the next and the contents slides.

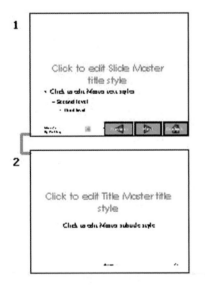

Figure 11.61 Using two master slides

Sometimes, you will not want the master slide to be included on a particular slide. For example, this might be because you do not need the logo, author and contents buttons on the contents slide. One way of achieving this is to use a separate title master and slide master. The title master can then be used for title slides such as contents slides.

Another method is to omit the background graphics from the master slide for the current slide only.

Figure 11.62 Omitting background from master slide

## Buttons

If you are producing a 'kiosk' presentation or one that will be controlled by the use of buttons, then you will need to provide evidence of the actions of the buttons. These actions could include opening:

- another specific slide
- the first, last, previous, next or last viewed slide
- another presentation
- a file from another application.

Read the question carefully and provide evidence of each button that you have been asked to show evidence for. Make sure that you also make it clear which button you are showing evidence for.

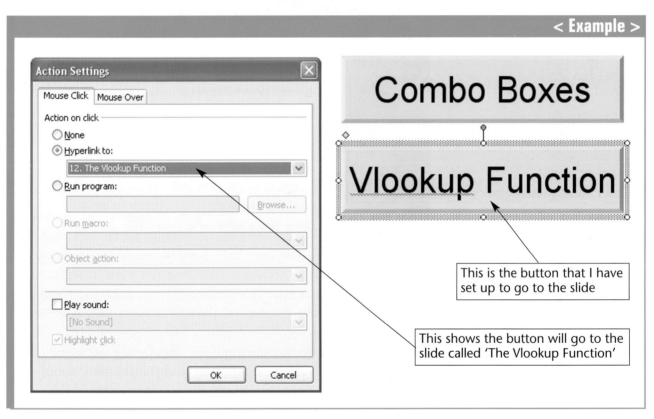

**Figure 11.63** Annotating evidence

## Automatic transitions

If you need a presentation that will run without user intervention (automatically) then you are likely to need to show two pieces of evidence:

- evidence of the automatic transitions
- evidence of what happens at the end.

Always make sure that you include part of your slide with the screenshot so that it is clear you have applied the skill to the slide show you have been asked to create.

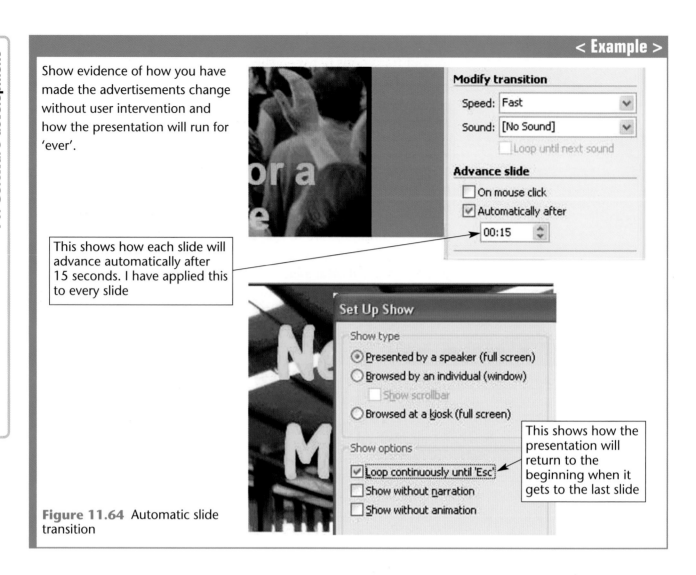

Show evidence of how you have made the advertisements change without user intervention and how the presentation will run for 'ever'.

This shows how each slide will advance automatically after 15 seconds. I have applied this to every slide

This shows how the presentation will return to the beginning when it gets to the last slide

**Figure 11.64** Automatic slide transition

## Audience

When you produce your presentation, always consider the audience that you are producing it for. The same rules as for desktop publishing apply. In addition, you should think about whether it is really necessary to use sound, animations and transitions as these can be very distracting. If you are producing a music quiz, then you are obviously going to have music on slides, but if you are producing a presentation for a salesperson to give, then they are not going to want sounds of dogs barking as each slide changes, or applause as each piece of text appears. Similarly they are not going to want to see text spinning around the screen.

## Video

You may be asked to create a short video clip or to edit an existing video clip. You can usually do this with a web cam (it is not necessary to use expensive camcorders). You might be asked to:

- add titles to clips
- put transitions between clips
- change the appearance of clips
- cut down an existing clip
- join a few clips together to make a single video
- save the video in an appropriate format.

If you are using Microsoft Windows, then Windows Movie Maker is a free piece of software that will achieve all of these things.

The evidence required will depend on the question, so read it carefully and ensure you provide the evidence necessary.

< Example >

Edit the video of somebody changing gear to include text that identifies each gear that is being used. Show evidence of the text you have added and how you saved the final movie.

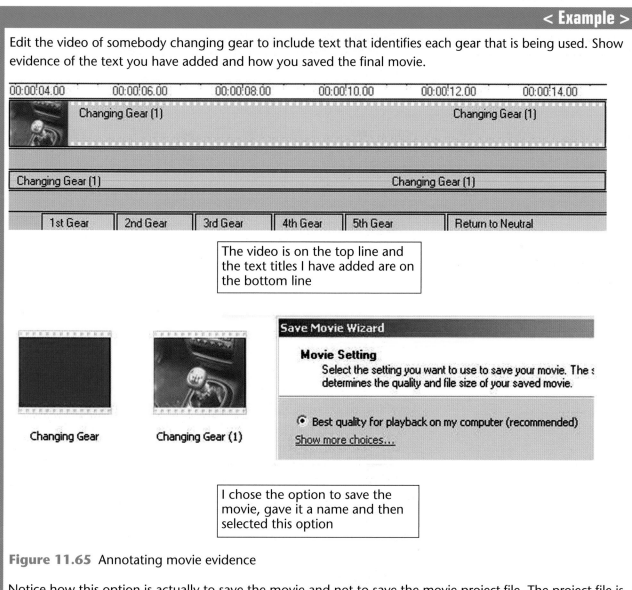

The video is on the top line and the text titles I have added are on the bottom line

I chose the option to save the movie, gave it a name and then selected this option

**Figure 11.65** Annotating movie evidence

Notice how this option is actually to save the movie and not to save the movie project file. The project file is for the purposes of editing the video but does not contain the final output. Therefore, this shows the correct method of saving the actual movie.

## Sound

It's very difficult to show evidence of exactly how you have edited a sound file, but you may be asked to do some simple editing of sound such as:

- cutting a sound clip down
- stitching sounds together
- adding an echo to some sound.

Sound editing software is widely available, but one that is common and used by many schools is called Audacity.

**< Example >**

Edit the sound 'come.mp3' so that the music between 30 seconds and 45 seconds fades away and then returns directly to normal at 45 seconds.

I highlighted the music between 30 seconds and 45 seconds and then selected the 'Fade Out' option

You can see by the shape of the sound that it fades out towards the end of the time period and then gets loud again at 45 seconds

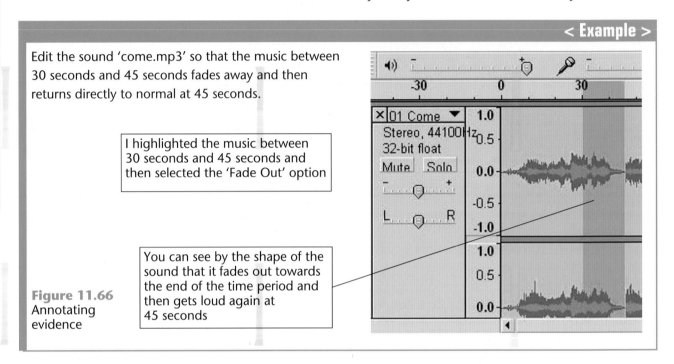

**Figure 11.66**
Annotating evidence

# Use database software to solve problems

Anything to do with data structures for databases has already been covered in the 'data structures' section of this chapter. However, there are some types of evidence that are specific to databases alone. Something really important to bear in mind is that the database task is usually the last task and thus the hardest one. However, there will always be aspects of the task that are approachable by all and, even if you can not answer every part of the task, you should at least try what you can so that you can get some marks.

## Queries

You will almost always be asked to provide evidence of a query. This could be an ordinary 'Select' query, or it could be an 'Update', 'Delete' or 'Append' query. It could also be a 'Cross-tab' or 'Count' query. There is not enough space to cover all of these in this book, but you will find plenty of instructions freely available on websites on how to do these. You will also only need to learn how to do the ones that are required for the tasks, although you should have an awareness of what the different types of query do.

When producing evidence of your query, you should ensure that you include:

- all the fields and tables that data is needed from (but do not include extra tables)
- the full set of criteria – do not miss any out
- evidence of the type of query (e.g. Update, Delete, etc.)
- any expressions that you have created.

< Example >

Produce a query that will show all the orders that have not been invoiced during the 2006–7 financial year and for each order line show the total price, the order number and the supplier.

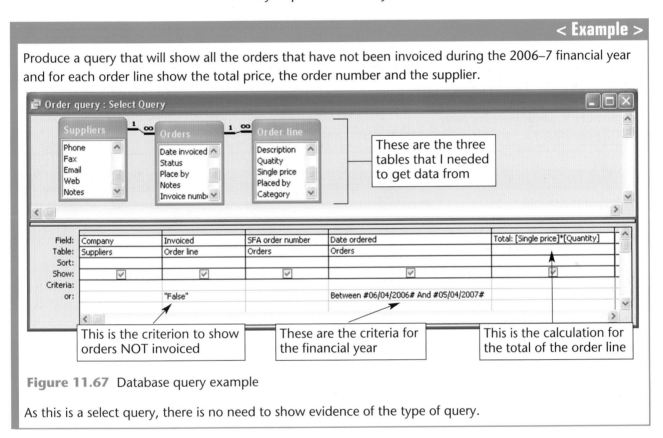

Figure 11.67 Database query example

As this is a select query, there is no need to show evidence of the type of query.

## Forms

The same principles apply as to online forms and user interfaces. A lot of forms and sub-forms can be created using wizards based on one or more tables. Always delete any fields that are duplicated (e.g. where a foreign key is shown, it is not necessary to show the related primary key as well). Think about common buttons such as:

- save
- delete
- cancel
- close.

You can also display calculations in forms. These can be included by creating a new text box and then putting the calculation in there. When you create a calculation that adds up data from all the records or counts all the records, then it should go in the **form footer**, **not** the page footer. There is a strange aspect to Microsoft Access that you should be aware of. If you want to add up data, you cannot directly add up a set of fields. You have to add up a calculation of those fields.

< Example >

Show how you have displayed the total value of the order.

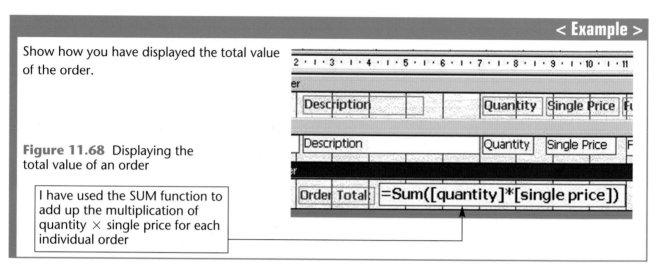

**Figure 11.68** Displaying the total value of an order

I have used the SUM function to add up the multiplication of quantity × single price for each individual order

< Activity >

Identify at least eight improvements that could be made to this form.

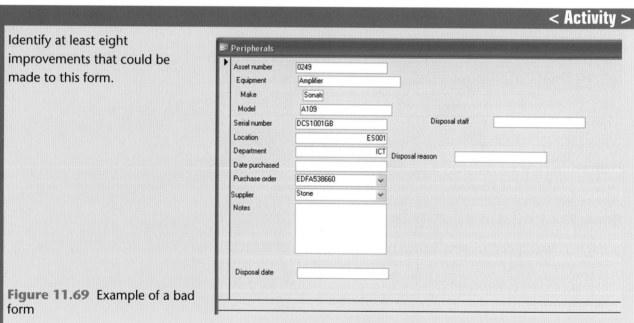

**Figure 11.69** Example of a bad form

## Reports

A report is a method of presenting a list or summary of data from one or more tables within a database. When showing evidence of a report, you should ensure that:

- a sensible title is used and is fully visible
- any sub-titles are used for grouped data
- if separate pages are required for different groups of data then this is done
- any calculations are visible
- data from all required tables is shown

- all fields asked for are shown
- information is displayed (e.g. forename and surname, rather than just ID)
- data is laid out neatly in columns, aligned properly and fully visible.

The same principle as forms applies when you create a calculation that adds up data from all the records or counts all the records – the calculation should go in the **report footer** (or if appropriate, the **group footer**), **not** the page footer. Putting the calculation in the report footer will perform the calculation once for the whole report (e.g. it will count all the customers on the whole report). Putting the calculation in the group footer will count all the customers within each group (e.g. it will count all the customers in each town).

Reports can also include labels or charts. Labels/business cards/envelopes can be used to organise the data in a format that is suitable to print onto those media. Charts can be used to show summaries of data.

## ▉ Macros

Macros within databases are quite simple. When you create a new macro, you will simply fill in a 'form' for each of the actions you want to complete.

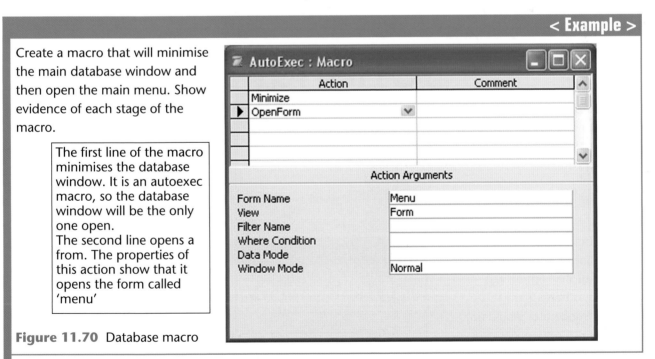

**< Example >**

Create a macro that will minimise the main database window and then open the main menu. Show evidence of each stage of the macro.

> The first line of the macro minimises the database window. It is an autoexec macro, so the database window will be the only one open.
> The second line opens a from. The properties of this action show that it opens the form called 'menu'

**Figure 11.70** Database macro

The macro in this example was very simple. However, if it had several lines, you may need to create a separate screenshot for each line to show the properties in the lower pane of the window. You may also only run some actions if a particular 'condition' is met. You would need to show this evidence too.

# Incorporate various types of data (such as text, images, sound, video, animation) into a single document

This is mainly going to take place in multimedia presentations and on websites. However, it might be that images are used within a database (e.g. a picture of each person) or that a spreadsheet is used as a quiz and it includes sounds and videos. Sound might be used for instructions. Usually the evidence that will be required will be to show that the text, image, sound, video or animation has been imported into the main document. Therefore it will be necessary to ensure that your evidence includes:

- part of the main document
- the process for importing (e.g. insert, picture from file)
- the full filename of the file being imported.

If you are importing sound, video or animation into a presentation, you may need to set it up so that it plays automatically. For example, if the presentation is one which must run without user intervention and it has to include a video, then you should show evidence of how you set the video to run automatically without the user having to click something.

---

**< Example >**

Import a video of somebody changing gear into the presentation. The user would like the video to play as soon as the slide appears. Show evidence of how this was done.

Notice how part of the slide has been included in the screenshot so it is clear that the movie is being imported into this particular slide and not just any document.

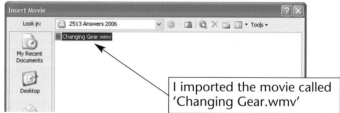

I imported the movie called 'Changing Gear.wmv'

Notice how this screenshot needs annotating to confirm that the 'Automatically' option was selected, otherwise the teacher/moderator would not know which option was chosen.

I then selected the option to make it play automatically

**Figure 11.71** Importing video

# Create customised outputs

Most software will give default outputs using wizards or basic tools such as tables, queries, charts and labels. However, in order to meet the requirements of the user and to ensure that the needs of the audience have been accounted for, it is necessary to customise an output.

This is a label that has been created by a wizard. It is used to stick onto the folder that contains the licence paperwork for each piece of software in a school. However, to the uninformed, the second and third lines don't make much sense.

It is an output, but only contains data. It needs customising in order to turn it into information.

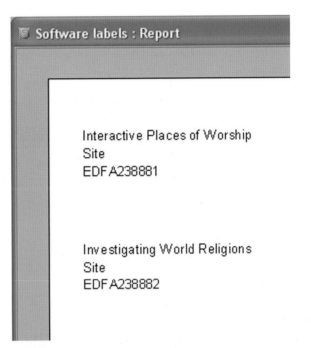

**Figure 11.72** Example report

This version has now been customised by adding some titles, making the main information bold, and making the title larger. So instead of simply using a wizard, the output generated by the wizard has been customised to meet the needs of the audience.

**Figure 11.73** Customised report

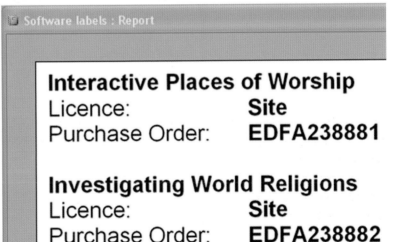

# Set up appropriate security methods

Security is not just about stopping hackers. It's also about keeping data safe from accidental damage. Therefore security could include making parts of a document read-only. It could also involve hiding parts of a document which are confidential or do not need to be seen by other users.

## Word processor

It's possible in a word processor to do the following:

- Make reading of the document password protected.
- Have a different password if changes need to be made.
- Protect a form so that only the inputs can be selected.
- Protect a document so that only reviews (e.g. comments) can take place.

Evidence would need to include a screenshot to show that the security has been applied.

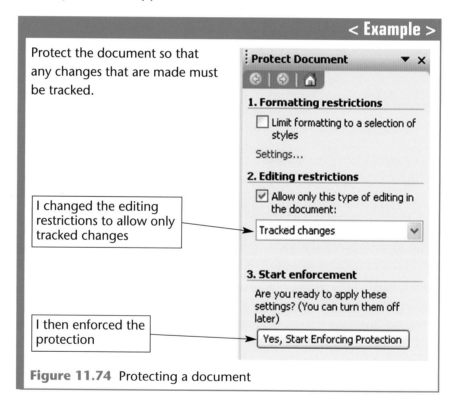

Protect the document so that any changes that are made must be tracked.

I changed the editing restrictions to allow only tracked changes

I then enforced the protection

**Figure 11.74** Protecting a document

## Spreadsheet

There are lots of security methods in spreadsheet software. Some of these include:

- make the document password protected to read
- have a different password if changes need to be made
- protect a worksheet so that only input cells can be changed
- hide columns
- hide worksheets.

As with the word processor, evidence would need to include a screenshot to show that the security has been applied.

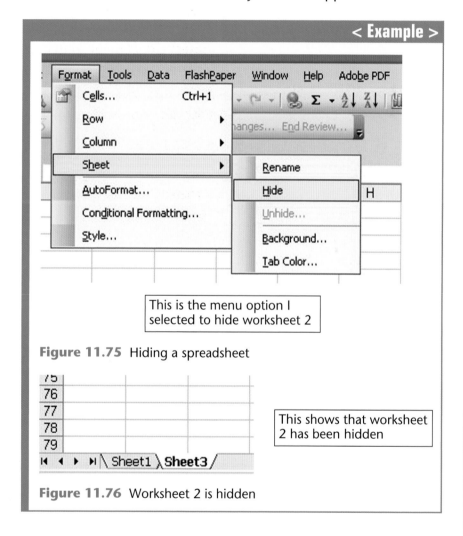

**< Example >**

This is the menu option I selected to hide worksheet 2

**Figure 11.75** Hiding a spreadsheet

This shows that worksheet 2 has been hidden

**Figure 11.76** Worksheet 2 is hidden

## Database

There are many security methods in database software. Some of these include:

- set a password for the database
- set up users and user groups
- assign different rights to different groups of users
- set text boxes and other inputs to be read only.

< Example >

The user is concerned that the supplier's details on the order form may get changed accidentally. Show evidence of how you have set up the data for the supplier so that it cannot be changed, but so the data about the order can still be edited.

I changed the properties of the 'Supplier' fields (e.g. address) so that each of the supplier fields was 'locked'

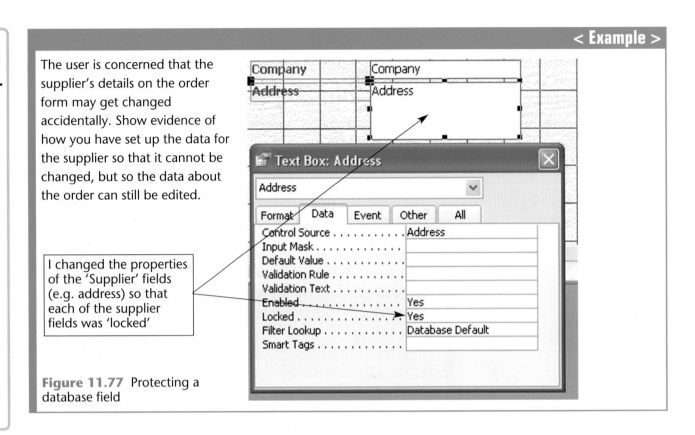

**Figure 11.77** Protecting a database field

## Introduction

Testing is the process of trying to discover errors within a software solution. It is impossible to say with 100 per cent certainty that a software solution has no errors, as some may not be found. But if a lot of effort has been put in to finding errors then, once all are corrected and no further errors found, it can be assumed that the solution is working well.

In order to test a software solution thoroughly, the tester will want to try their hardest to find errors. Therefore, in order to put a software solution through its paces, as many aspects of the system as possible must be tested. If you had just built a bridge, you wouldn't just test it by driving a couple of cars over it, you would also test it by driving a hundred lorries over it all at the same time to test it to extremes. Similarly, with software, it is necessary to test it to its extremes in case it cannot cope.

In this section you will find out how to produce evidence for:

- test data
- test plans
- software testing

**Figure 12.1**

| ■ ■ ■ ■ | **Keywords** |
| --- | --- |
| Test data | data that has been chosen specifically for the purpose of testing a software solution. |
| Test plan | a detailed plan that identifies exactly what must be done in order to test a software solution. |
| Valid | a value which is acceptable/sensible (i.e. it fits within the rules). |
| Invalid | a value which is not acceptable (i.e. it does not fit within the rules). |
| Extreme | an acceptable value which is at the boundary of the rule. |
| Validation rule | a rule which determines the values that are allowed to be input. |
| Navigational paths | different methods of moving around a document, usually by hyperlinks and buttons. |

# Select suitable test data that could be used to test a given problem, including normal, invalid and extreme data where appropriate

## ▉ Testing inputs

This mainly relates to testing validation rules. The purpose is to see if valid data will be accepted and if invalid data will be rejected.

In order to ensure that each validation rule is tested thoroughly, four different types of data should be used:

- valid (normal) data
- extreme valid data
- invalid (erroneous) data
- extreme invalid data.

You will usually be asked to give reasons for your choice of data. This should focus on the type of validation and an explanation of why you believe the data you have chosen is relevant.

When choosing data, give exact values: do not just give a range. For example, if you are testing the validation rule '>50', then choose an invalid data item such as '35'. Do not just say 'a number between 0 and 50': you need to be specific. If you are told to give five items of test data, then give at least eight so that you have some spare. However, if you are told that only your first five will be marked, then ensure you choose five good ones to start with.

You should always try to give a range of types of data (see above) but sometimes there won't be extremes available because the validation rule will be a presence check or a format (picture) check.

### < Example >

Range check

Give **four** different items of test data that could be used to test the validation rule '<=25'. For each item of test data, give a reason why it has been chosen. Only your first four items of test data will be marked.

| Test data | Reason |
|-----------|--------|
| 5 | This is valid data as it is lower than 25. |
| 32 | This is invalid data as it is higher than 25. |
| 25 | This is extreme valid data as it is the highest value that will be accepted. |
| 26 | This is extreme invalid data as it is the lowest value that will not be accepted. |

< Example >

Format (picture) check

Give **three** different items of test data that could be used to test the validation rule for a National Insurance number. For each item of test data, give a reason why it has been chosen.

| Test data | Reason |
|---|---|
| JA 44 80 52 B | This is valid data as it matches the pattern two letters, six numbers, one letter between A and D. |
| JA 44 8C 52 D | This is invalid data because it includes a letter (C) where there should be a number. |
| JA 44 80 522 B | This is invalid data because it has 10 characters instead of nine. |
| JA 44 80 5 B | This is invalid data because it has eight characters instead of nine. |
| JA 44 80 52 E | This is invalid because the last character is supposed to be between A and D; E is outside this range. |

< Example >

Look up in list check

Give **three** different items of test data that could be used to test the validation rule for gender. For each item of test data, give a reason why it has been chosen.

| Test data | Reason |
|---|---|
| Male | This is an item in the list and so it should be acceptable (valid). |
| Female | This is a different item in the list and so it should be acceptable (valid). |
| Mail | This is not an item in the list and so it is invalid and should not be accepted. |

< Activity >

1 Give **four** different items of test data that could be used to test the validation rule for <1000. For each item of test data, give a reason why it has been chosen. Only your first four items of test data will be marked.

2 Give **three** different items of test data that could be used to test the validation rule for ="Mr" or "Mrs" or "Miss". For each item of test data, give a reason why it has been chosen.

3 Give **three** different items of test data that could be used to test the validation rule for Product Code (two numbers, three letters, one number). For each item of test data, give a reason why it has been chosen.

4 Give **six** different items of test data that could be used to test the validation rule for >=1000 AND <=2000. For each item of test data, give a reason why it has been chosen. Only your first six items of test data will be marked.

Select suitable test data that could be used to test a given problem, including normal, invalid and extreme data where appropriate

## ■ Testing outputs (formulae/functions)

When testing outputs, this usually concerns the result of a formula/function, a macro or a query/report. There are other examples, but these are the main ones that this text book will focus on.

Some formulae are very simple to test. These might be like =A1+B1. All you have to do here is choose a data value for A1 and a data value for B1. These are so simple that you are unlikely to be asked to provide just test data.

Some functions require quite a few inputs and therefore your ability to identify all the inputs might be tested. This could be =SUM(A1:A5). The common error here would be to answer the question by saying 'choose a different value for each of A1 to A5'. However, this is not test **data**: it is just a description. Test data would be something like 'A1 = 3, A2 = 25, A3 = 42, A4 = 3, A5 = 199.

Some functions are a bit more complex. The IF function is an example of this. An IF function will look at the data input, compare it with different values, and then give a different output depending on its input value. There may be several routes of an IF function. In this case, every route should be tested.

**< Example >**

If an answer is correct, then 'Well done!' should be displayed. If an answer is incorrect, then 'Try again!' should be displayed. If an answer is not given, then nothing should be displayed. Give **three** items of test data with reasons that could be used to test the question 'What does UK stand for?'

| Test data | Reason |
| --- | --- |
| United Kingdom | This is the correct answer, therefore it will test the 'Well done!' route of the IF function. |
| United Kings | This is an incorrect answer, therefore it will test the 'Try again!' route of the IF function. |
| Null response (leave cell blank) | This means the question hasn't been answered so it tests the 'nothing should be displayed' route of the IF function. |

Do **not** give answers such as:

■ 'the correct answer'
■ 'an incorrect answer'

as these are **not** data items. They are descriptions.

< Activity >

The closing date for entering a competition is 1 May 2009. If an entry is received at least two months before the closing date, then a £10 discount will be given. If an entry is received at least one month before the closing date then a £5 discount will be given. Any entries received in the fortnight before the closing date will not receive a discount. Give **six** items of test data, with reasons, that could be used to test the discount that should be given. Only your first six items of test data will be marked.

< Tip >

When answering this question, remember that there are some extremes involved too – each discount date.

## ■ Testing outputs (queries/reports)

When testing a query, it is necessary to select data that:

- meets the conditions of the query
- does not meet the conditions of the query
- meets some, but not all, of the conditions of the query
- if numerical values are involved, includes extreme values.

The data will be in the form of records. If there is a query to list all the female customers, then it is necessary to have both female and male customer records. If there is a query to list all the female customers in London, then it is necessary to have records which include:

- female customers in London
- male customers in Leeds (or any other city)
- female customers in Birmingham (or any other city)
- male customers in London.

If there is a query to list all customers born before 1 January 2010, then it is necessary to have records which include:

- customers born before 1 January 2010 (e.g. 1 February 2009)
- customers born after 1 January 2010 (e.g. 5 May 2010)
- customers born on 1 January 2010 (i.e. extreme, but not matching)
- customers born on 31 December 2009 (i.e. extreme and matching).

Select suitable test data that could be used to test a given problem, including normal, invalid and extreme data where appropriate

< Example >

Give **five** records that could be used to test the query for Junior Members with more than three awards. Give a reason for your choice of each record.

| Surname | Forename | Type | Awards | Reason |
|---------|----------|------|--------|--------|
| Cox | Jane | Junior | 5 | Will meet both criteria. |
| Dawson | Andrew | Senior | 2 | Will not meet either criteria. |
| Johnson | Edith | Junior | 1 | Only meets the Junior criterion. |
| Jones | Andrea | Senior | 5 | Only meets the awards criterion. |
| Probert | Peter | Junior | 3 | Only just doesn't meet the awards criterion. |
| Mullins | Petra | Junior | 4 | Only just meets the awards criterion. |

< Activity >

1 Give **four** records that could be used to test the query for computers with at least 512 MB of RAM. Give a reason for your choice of each record.

2 Give **four** records that could be used to test the query for concerts that take place at the NEC and are sold out.

3 Give **six** records that could be used to test the query for computers with at least a 120 GB hard disk and an Intel® Centrino® processor.

## ■ Testing relationships

When testing a database, part of the testing should involve testing that the relationships work. In order to do this, enough records need to be chosen to check the one-to-many and one-to-one relationships work correctly.

< Example >

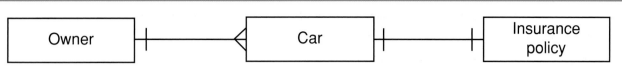

In this scenario, you would need to select records that will test each of the two relationships.

**One OWNER has many CARS**

A record for OWNER that has only one CAR.

A record for OWNER that has no CAR.

Two CAR records that have the same OWNER.

This ensures all the possibilities of the one-to-many relationship work.

**One CAR has one INSURANCE POLICY (foreign key is in CAR)**

A record for CAR that has one INSURANCE POLICY.

A record for CAR that has no INSURANCE POLICY.

Try and enter a record for CAR with the same INSURANCE POLICY as another record for CAR. This should not be allowed to happen.

This ensures all the possibilities of the one-to-one relationship work and that MANY will not be allowed.

# Produce a test plan that could be used to test a solution

A detailed test plan identifies exactly what must be done in order to test a software solution. In the real world, the person who creates the test plan is usually different to the person who carries out the testing. Therefore, the tester needs to be given enough information to know how to carry out a test. The tester must be told in the plan exactly which data to use, for precisely which inputs and must know exactly what to expect as the result of the test.

Data that is used in a test plan must be specific. In the sections below, you will be given examples of good test plans, but you will also be shown examples of bad test plans where you will need to identify the pitfalls.

## ■ Navigational paths

Navigation can appear in lots of software. Although its main use is in slide shows and web pages, there may also be buttons within a spreadsheet or database, or hyperlinks within a word-processed document. Each method of navigation (e.g. hyperlink, hotspot and button) needs to be tested to ensure that it goes to the correct location.

The test plan will need to identify each navigation item in turn. For each navigation item, it will need to identify what needs to be done to test that navigation item and what the expected result will be. It must be obvious to the tester which navigation item is being referred to.

**< Example >**

| Number | Item to test | How to test it | Expected result |
|---|---|---|---|
| 1 | 'Reports' button on main menu. | Click once on the 'Reports' button. | Reports menu will open. |
| 2 | 'Charts' button on main menu. | Click once on the 'Charts' button. | Charts menu will open. |
| 3 | 'Exit' button (yes route) on main menu. | Click once on the 'Exit' button, then when prompted, click 'Yes'. | A prompt will appear asking if you are sure you want to exit. On clicking 'Yes', the application will close. |
| 4 | 'Exit' button (no route) on main menu. | Click once on the 'Exit' button, then when prompted, click 'No'. | A prompt will appear asking if you are sure you want to exit. On clicking 'No', the prompt will disappear and the main menu will be showing. |
| 5 | 'Return to menu button' on Reports menu. | Click once on the 'Return to menu button'. | Reports menu will close and main menu will be showing. |

This is only part of a full testing plan for the navigational paths. There are likely to be other buttons that will need testing. However, you will usually be asked to test different types of feature and therefore it will only be necessary to test one button.

< Activity >

What is missing from the following test plan and why? There are six errors.

| Number | Item to test | How to test it | Expected result |
|---|---|---|---|
| 1 | 'Home' hyperlink | Click the 'Home' hyperlink | Home page will appear. |
| 2 | Button | Click the button. | Confirmation page will appear. |
| 3 | 'Birmingham' hotspot on the map on the locations page | Click the hotspot. | Appropriate page will appear. |

## ■ Validation rules

When testing validation rules, it is necessary to identify the input data values to use, the type of input data value (valid, invalid, extreme) and the expected result. Common mistakes are to:

- not put an exact value for the input (e.g. to say 'enter a name not in the list') – *which name should the tester enter?*
- not clearly identify where to input the data (e.g. to say 'test for correct answers') – *which answer is the tester testing?*
- not put an exact error message for expected result (e.g. to say 'error message will appear') – *which error message will this be?*

< Example >

| Number | Description | Input value | Type | Expected result |
|---|---|---|---|---|
| 1 | Check letters cannot be entered in the mileage input. | 'a' | Invalid | 'Only enter numeric values for mileage' |
| 2 | Check numbers can be entered in the mileage input. | 5 | Valid | Data is accepted. |
| 3 | Check a maximum of seven passengers can be entered. | 7 | Valid extreme | Data is accepted. |
| 4 | Check less than seven passengers can be entered. | 4 | Valid | Data is accepted. |
| 5 | Check a maximum of seven passengers cannot be exceeded. | 9 | Invalid | 'Only enter up to seven passengers' |
| 6 | Check a maximum of seven passengers cannot be exceeded. | 8 | Invalid extreme | 'Only enter up to seven passengers' |

Produce a test plan that could be used to test a solution

< Activity >

What is missing from the following test plan and why? There are nine errors.

| Number | Description | Input value | Type | Expected result |
|---|---|---|---|---|
| 1 | Check validation message works. | 5 | Invalid | Error message appears. |
| 2 | Check maximum of eight works. | 8 | Valid | Data is accepted. |
| 3 | Check quantity is between 0 and 20. | A number above 20 | Valid | Data is accepted. |
| 4 | Check 'Male' works for gender. | Male | Invalid | Data is accepted. |
| 5 | Check 'Female' works. | Female | Valid | Data is accepted. |
| 6 | Check only 'Male' or 'Female' can be entered for gender. | Something other than male or female | Invalid | #Value |
| 7 | Check data is present for surname. | Enter a surname | Valid | Data is accepted. |

## Calculations

Testing calculations is very similar to testing validation except that all the types of test data will be valid as the purpose is to find out if the calculation works or not. The common mistakes are also similar. They include:

- not putting an exact value for the input (e.g. to say 'enter a number for the quantity') – *which number should the tester enter?*
- not clearly identifying where to input the data (e.g. to say 'enter 5') – *where should the tester input the number 5?* (A location such as 'enter 5 for the quantity' or 'enter 5 in B7' should be given)
- not putting an exact answer for the expected result (e.g. to say 'calculation works correctly') – *how will the tester know if it works correctly?*

< Example >

| Number | Description | Input value | Expected result |
|---|---|---|---|
| 1 | VAT formula works correctly. | Price = '10' | Price including VAT = £11.75 |
| 2 | Hours labour formula works correctly. | Length = '5' Width = '20' | Hours labour = '5' |
| 3 | Hourly wage 'look up' works correctly. | Scale = 'Junior' | Hourly wage = £6.50 |

< Activity >

What is wrong with following test plan and why?

| Number | Description | Input value | Expected result |
|--------|-------------|-------------|-----------------|
| 1 | Formula works correctly. | Length = '3'<br>Width = '3' | Area = '9' |
| 2 | Check the salary function works. | A number less than 10 | Salary is correct |
| 3 | Check total miles works correctly. | Start mileage = '23,302' | Total miles = 125 |

## ■ Queries

When testing if a query works, you will need to visually look at the test data (records) that you have and see which ones you expect will be listed when the query is run. This list should then be compared with the expected results when the test is run.

< Example >

**1** Query: All 17" flat screen monitors.

   I would **expect** the following records to be listed:

   53–68, 70, 71 (Total: 18)

**2** Query: All laser printers faster than 16 ppm.

   I would expect the following records to be listed:

   PR25, PR36, PR42 (Total: 3)

## ■ Multimedia and web

The same principles for creating a test plan apply here in that the tester must know exactly what to do and exactly what to expect. There are extra aspects that need testing with multimedia presentations and websites, including whether the presentation or website will:

- work on different types of computer
- have correct/accurate content
- have correct spelling
- be consistent in layout
- be consistent in the use of colour and fonts
- have certain information on every slide/page
- open videos or sounds automatically
- show pictures correctly
- work on different browsers (web only)
- download in a reasonable time limit (web only)
- open if the URL is typed (web only)
- open if the icon for the presentation is clicked (presentation only).

**Produce a test plan that could be used to test a solution**

< Example >

| Number | Item to test | How to test it | Expected result |
|---|---|---|---|
| 1 | Works on different types of computers | Open home page on Apple Mac. | Home page can be viewed on Apple Mac. |
| 2 | Different browsers | Open home page in Firefox. | Home page can be viewed in Firefox and has the same layout as in Internet Explorer. |
| 3 | Consistency | Visually check every web page. | All text will be Arial. |
| 4 | Home page hyperlink | Click on the 'Home' hyperlink on the 'Contact us' page. | Home page opens. |
| 5 | Spelling of each specialist is spelt correctly | Visually check the 'specialists' page. | The specialists are spelt 'orthopaedic', 'gynaecology', 'obstetrician', 'cardiovascular', 'physiotherapy'. |
| 6 | Music plays on home page | Open home page. | Beethoven's 5th symphony plays in the background within five seconds of the page opening. |
| 7 | Download speed | Open website by typing www.kidshospice.biz into a browser connected to 2 Mbps broadband. | Home page appears with all pictures present within three seconds. |

These are only a few examples. If this was done for real, then there would be many more testing entries.

< Activity >

What is wrong with the following test plan?

| Number | Item to test | How to test it | Expected result |
|---|---|---|---|
| 1 | Works on different types of computers | Open home page on different computers. | Home page can be viewed on different computers. |
| 2 | Spelling is correct | Visually check the 'About us' page. | All words and names are spelt correctly. |
| 3 | Colour of snooker balls | Visually check the 'colours' page. | All the colours are correct. |
| 4 | Video appears | Watch video. | Video plays automatically when page is opened. |
| 5 | Consistency | Visually check all the pages. | All pages are consistent. |

## Differences

Questions will quite often ask you to plan tests for 'different' aspects or features. If you are asked to do this then you must not do two tests on the same formula/function or the same aspect of a presentation. This is particularly important if only the first five or six tests will be marked. If the question leaves it open, then you can, of course, do more tests and some could be on the same aspect. Same aspects might include:

- testing font consistency and then testing colour consistency
- testing an image appears on slide 1 and then on slide 5
- checking spelling on the home page and then on the contact page
- checking the colour of snooker balls and then the number of points for each ball (both are to do with accuracy)
- opening a web page on an Apple Mac and then another test to open it on a PC
- testing the 'contact us' hyperlink and then the 'about us' hyperlink (both are hyperlinks, but buttons can be separate, so can hotspots; external links are different to internal links).
- testing invalid input of 'Mail' for gender and then 'Feemale' for gender (both are invalid tests for the same input)
- testing a multiplication formula twice
- testing a formula that calculates VAT and then testing a replicated copy of that formula in the same column.

However, note that different routes of an IF function (i.e. the TRUE route and the FALSE route) are classed as different tests.

You can also plan valid, extreme and invalid tests on the same input cell as these are different tests.

# Test a solution, providing documented evidence that the solution has been tested

When a test plan has been created, the test plan is later followed by a tester to see if each test passes or fails. If the actual results (what happens) match the expected results (what was expected to happen) then the test passes. If not, the test fails.

You may be asked to follow a test plan or to carry out some testing without a plan. If you are asked to carry out some testing without a plan, then the question will tell you exactly what evidence to provide. For example, you may be asked to test a mail merge works by printing out the final set of mail-merged documents.

If you are asked to follow a test plan, then it is very important that you follow the plan precisely and do not deviate from it.

## Test numbers

A test plan will usually number each test that is to be carried out. Therefore, when producing evidence that a test has been carried out, you should include the test number.

## Annotation

For each test that you carry out, it is really important to identify the input data that was used (from the test plan) and the actual output. You should then compare the actual output with the expected result and annotate to say whether the test passed or failed. If it failed, this is OK (unless the question tells you the test must pass), but you should annotate to explain why the test failed.

If you do not annotate the input and output then you will probably not get any marks, as your teacher will not be able to identify the exact input data that you used.

**< Example >**

This is a bad example. It shows the problem of not annotating the input and output data. This test is to put in a date in the future to see if it generates the error message.

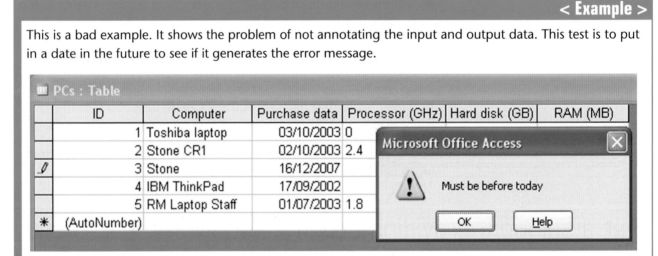

**Figure 12.2** Poor example of error message

An assumption could be made that 16/12/2007 was input to generate the error message, but we cannot be sure. It depends on which date this test was run: is 16/12/2007 in the future or the past? Therefore, it is important to annotate both the input data and the output data.

## Following the test plan

If you are given a test plan, then you must follow it precisely. If the test plan tells you to input '5' then you must use '5' and not choose another number. If the test plan is expecting an error message of 'Must be before today', then an error message of 'Date is too late' would mean the test had failed.

< Example >

The following examples of test runs follow the test plan below.

| Number | Description | Input value | Type | Expected result |
|---|---|---|---|---|
| 1 | Check letters cannot be entered in the start mileage input. | 'a' | Invalid | 'Only enter whole numbers between 0 and 999,999' |
| 2 | Test total mileage formula works correctly. | Start mileage = '10,230' End mileage = '10,345' | Valid | Total mileage = '115' |
| 3 | Check no data can be entered into the total mileage. | '15' | Invalid | Value cannot be entered |

**Test 1**

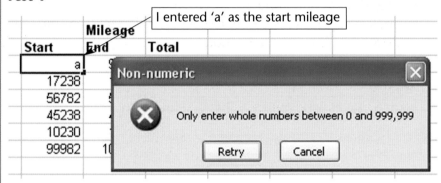

I entered 'a' as the start mileage

An error message has appeared. It matches the expected result, so the test has been passed

**Figure 12.3** Spreadsheet test 1

Notice how:

■ the exact same input as the test plan has been used

■ the output has been identified as the error message

■ the error message is exactly the same as expected

■ the test has been annotated to say that it passed.

**Test 2**

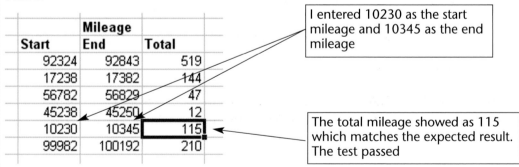

I entered 10230 as the start mileage and 10345 as the end mileage

The total mileage showed as 115 which matches the expected result. The test passed

**Figure 12.4** Spreadsheet test 2

Notice how:

■ the exact same numbers as the test plan have been used

■ both inputs have been annotated

■ the output has been identified as '115'

■ the test has been annotated to say that it passed.

Test a solution, providing documented evidence that the solution has been tested

**Test 3**

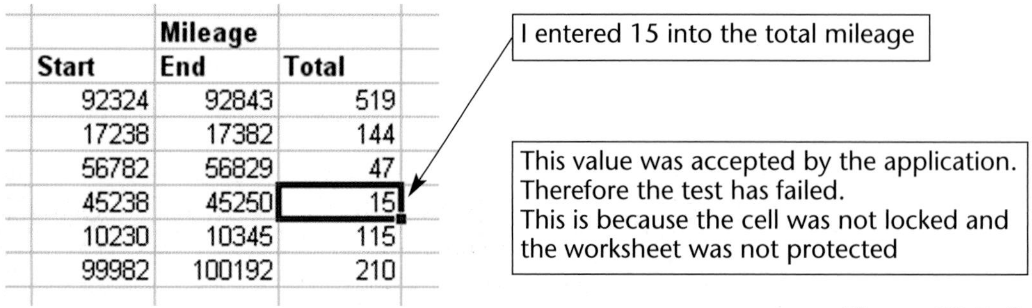

| | Mileage | | |
|---|---|---|---|
| **Start** | **End** | **Total** | |
| 92324 | 92843 | 519 | |
| 17238 | 17382 | 144 | |
| 56782 | 56829 | 47 | |
| 45238 | 45250 | 15 | |
| 10230 | 10345 | 115 | |
| 99982 | 100192 | 210 | |

I entered 15 into the total mileage

This value was accepted by the application.
Therefore the test has failed.
This is because the cell was not locked and
the worksheet was not protected

**Figure 12.5** Spreadsheet test 3

Notice how:

- the exact same number as the test plan has been used

- the input has been annotated

- the output has been identified as not appearing

- the test has been annotated to say that it failed

- a reason has been given to explain why the test failed.

## Introduction

**Figure 13.1**

Documentation is the process of producing documents that will support the application that has been created. The documentation could be targeted at the user to help them use the software or it could be targeted at a developer who may in the future make changes to the software or fix errors.

In this chapter you will find out how to produce evidence for:

- user documentation
- help sheets
- electronic documentation
- technical documentation

### ■ ■ ■ Keywords

| | |
|---|---|
| **User documentation** | documentation that will help a user to use an application. It should include a contents list, an introduction, the hardware requirements, the software requirements, instructions, a glossary and troubleshooting sections. |
| **Help sheet** | a small document that contains instructions on how to use an application or part of an application. |
| **Electronic documentation** | documentation that can be accessed directly from within an application without the need for paper instructions. |
| **Technical documentation** | documentation that is created for the purpose of future maintenance so that the application can be repaired or upgraded. |

## Prepare user documentation for a system to include contents, overview, hardware/software requirements, glossary of terms and troubleshooting

It is important to understand from the beginning that user documentation is about how to use an application that has already been created. It is not about showing somebody how to re-create an application. For example, if a mail merge has been created, then the user documentation would cover how to edit the recipients list, how to open the mail merge file, and how to print the mail merge documents. It would not be about showing the user how to link the mail merge master document with the data source, insert fields, etc. as this should already have been done.

User documentation must include all of the following sections:

- a contents list
- an introduction/overview
- the hardware requirements
- the software requirements
- instructions
- a glossary
- troubleshooting.

## Contents

Full user documentation should always include a contents page. It is important that the contents page includes the page numbers for each main section.

There is a way of generating an automatic contents page in Microsoft Word which involves the use of styles. If you set up your main headings to be in the style 'Heading 1' and sub-headings in the style 'Heading 2' and so on, then your contents page can be generated automatically.

< Example >

Assuming that the contents are on the first page, then this is page two.

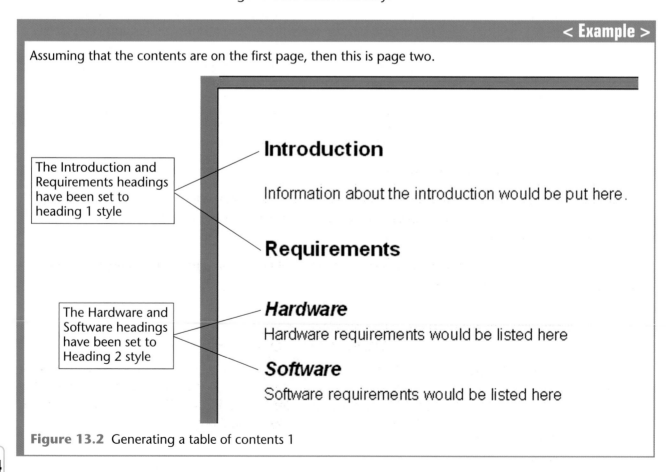

The Introduction and Requirements headings have been set to heading 1 style

### Introduction

Information about the introduction would be put here.

### Requirements

The Hardware and Software headings have been set to Heading 2 style

### Hardware

Hardware requirements would be listed here

### Software

Software requirements would be listed here

**Figure 13.2** Generating a table of contents 1

This is page three.

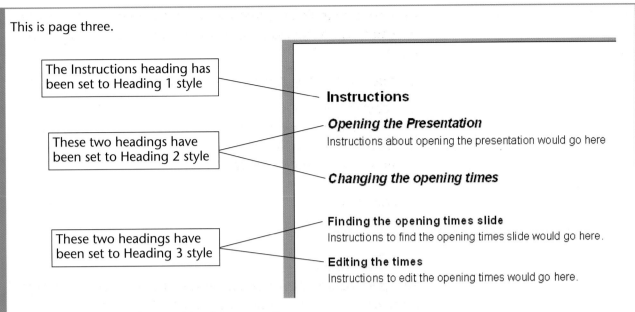

The Instructions heading has been set to Heading 1 style

**Instructions**

These two headings have been set to Heading 2 style

*Opening the Presentation*
Instructions about opening the presentation would go here

*Changing the opening times*

These two headings have been set to Heading 3 style

**Finding the opening times slide**
Instructions to find the opening times slide would go here.

**Editing the times**
Instructions to edit the opening times would go here.

**Figure 13.3** Generating a table of contents 2

This is the automatic contents page that has been created by clicking Insert > Reference > Index and Tables..., and then selecting the Contents tab.

**Figure 13.4** Generating a table of contents 3

Any text that has been set to a 'Heading' style has been included automatically in the contents page. Any other text is not included. The style of this particular type of contents page indents Level 2 headings once and Level 3 headings twice.

If you update your user documentation, then you must remember to update the contents page by right clicking it and selecting Update Field.

**< Example >**

This documentation will show you how to:

- open the quiz
- answer questions in the quiz
- check your score
- change answers that you have already given
- close the quiz.

## ▦ Introduction/overview

An introduction to the user documentation should be an overview of what it is about or its purpose. It only needs to be a paragraph of about three or four sentences. It gives the user an indication of what the user documentation will help them to do.

- 22" touch screen monitor
- 1024 × 768 graphical display
- Intel® Pentium® 1.2 GHz processor
- 512 MB RAM
- 10 MB spare disk space for the touch screen quiz
- 4 GB disk space for the main software

- Microsoft® Windows® XP
- Microsoft® PowerPoint® 2000 Viewer

## Hardware requirements

This is simply a list of the hardware that is required to use the application. It should not be a screenshot of requirements from the Microsoft website. It should be based on the application that has been created. For example, if the application that has been created is for use on a touch screen, then a touch screen would be part of the hardware requirements. The rest of the hardware should be based around what is needed as a minimum for the main software to run.

## Software requirements

This is simply a list of the software that is required to use the application. It will usually consist of an operating system and the software that the application was created in. Brand names should be used as this is not an examination paper and the user will need to know exactly which version of the software is required.

## Instructions

The instructions section will show the user how to use different aspects of the application. The principles to be followed here should be the same as for a help sheet. See page 298 for details on how to write instructions for a help sheet.

## Glossary

The glossary is a list of common words found within the documentation and their definitions. All words used should be related to the documentation, that is they should be words that have been used within the documentation. Using other words is going beyond the scope of the documentation.

A common error is for a glossary to contain definitions such as 'RAM – Random Access Memory', 'PPM – pages per minute'. While these are correct, they most likely have nothing to do with the application area that the user documentation has been written for.

If you are asked to provide a specific number of glossary terms, then try to do at least 1.5 times that many as this will allow you to make a couple of mistakes. If you are not asked for a specific number, include at least eight definitions.

< Example >

This documentation is about taking a photograph using a digital camera and importing it into a slide. Four definitions were asked for.

| Term | Definition |
| --- | --- |
| Slide | A screen in the presentation. |
| USB lead | A lead with a flat end that connects to the computer and a smaller connection that connects to the cradle. |
| USB port | A flat socket in the computer that is used for a USB lead to be connected to. |
| Cradle | The device that holds the digital camera, charges it, and connects it to the computer. |
| Button | An object on the screen that allows the user to click it to move from one screen to another. |
| Import | The process of transferring a picture from one application into another. |
| View finder | A small part of the camera that, when you look through it, will show you what you are taking a picture of. |

Notice how printer, mouse, keyboard, etc. are not included. The printer is not required for this task, and although the mouse and keyboard may have been referred to in the documentation, they are weak answers to give.

## Troubleshooting

This section is about producing a list of common errors that the user might find within an application and then giving solutions as to how these errors might be corrected. A good starting point is to include all the error messages that you have created for any validation rules.

It is very important that the common errors are related to the user documentation and not just general problems with a computer. If there is no need to print a document (e.g. a touch screen presentation) then to include printer problems such as paper jams is completely irrelevant.

A common error is to identify the problems and give reasons for the problems without providing a solution. The user needs a solution in order to know what to do to put it right.

If you are asked to provide a specific number of problems, then try to do at least twice that many, as this will allow you to make a couple of mistakes. If you are not asked for a specific number, include at least five problems.

This documentation is about taking a photograph using a digital camera and importing it into a slide. Two problems and solutions were asked for.

| Problem | Cause | Solution |
|---|---|---|
| Picture does not display on the camera LCD screen when trying to take a picture. | 1 Camera may be turned off.<br>2 Display is currently set to the view finder. | 1 Turn on the camera by pressing the power button.<br>2 Press the 'DISP' button. |
| When I put the camera in the cradle, I can't open the 'Removable disk' on the computer. | 1 The camera is not turned on.<br>2 The USB lead is not connected. | 1 Turn on the camera by pressing the power button.<br>2 Check the USB lead is firmly connected to both the cradle and the USB port at the back of the computer. |
| When I try to import the picture, I cannot see the list of photographs. | 1 You are not looking at the correct folder.<br>2 You have tried to import a video or sound or tried to open a new presentation. | 1 Change the 'Look in' drop-down option to be 'Removable disk'.<br>2 Click Insert > Picture > From File… . |
| The picture takes up more than the whole screen when it has been imported. | The picture is a large resolution. | Resize the image by clicking it once, then drag the handles at the corners of the image to make it smaller. |

# Prepare an instruction guide to show a user how to use part or all of a system

The guidance given for help sheets should also be used for the instructions part of user documentation on page 296.

A help sheet is a small document that contains instructions on how to use an application or part of an application. A help sheet may be a single-sided sheet of paper, it could be double-sided or a couple of pieces of paper attached together. The term help sheet is used to separate it from full user documentation as a help sheet does not require contents pages, hardware/software requirements, glossary or troubleshooting sections. It is simply a set of instructions.

## Which instructions should be included?

The best way to decide on what instructions to include on a help sheet is to carry the task out yourself. For example, if you are asked to write a help sheet about how to take and import photographs from a digital camera into a particular presentation, then you should carry out the following steps:

1 Turn the computer on and log on to give a starting point.
2 Ensure the camera is turned off.
3 Ensure there are no leads connected from the camera to the computer.
4 Take a photograph.
5 Write down everything you have to do.
6 Import the photograph.
7 Write down everything you have to do.

Precision is very important so that the user is left in no doubt as to what to do. For example, its not good to give an instruction like 'add some text to the slide'. A better instruction is 'Click Insert > Text box, and then draw a box where you want the text to appear. Now type the text into the text box.'

## Associated tasks

As you write things down, you will notice things that you may not have thought about if you had tried to write the instructions from memory. For example, during the task of importing the photograph, you would have noticed that you need to open the presentation before you can import the photograph. While taking the photograph you may have noticed that you have to set the camera to photo-taking mode before you can take the photograph.

When you are told to create a help sheet, you will only be asked to write instructions for a small number of tasks. However, there will be associated tasks that are required in order for the application to work properly.

### < Example >

- The presentation will need to be opened before the photo can be imported.
- The camera will need to be connected to the computer before the photo can be imported and the photographs found on the computer.
- If the presentation is supposed to run automatically then, when the photo has been imported, it will need to have its animation changed.
- If a new slide has to be created then an instruction for this will be required, including where to put it and a menu slide may need a button adding to it.

The instructions that you have written down should now be used as the basis of writing your instructions.

## Sub-titles

In order to make the instructions easy to follow, you should break them down into smaller sections.

< Example >

- Opening the presentation
- Taking the photograph
- Connecting the camera to the computer
- Creating a new slide
- Importing the photograph into the presentation
- Updating the menu
- Testing the presentation
- Saving the presentation

## Bullets and numbering

Using bullet points and automatic numbering enables the instructions to be broken down into small manageable steps which are easier for the user to follow. Numbers, rather than bullets, should always be used for a sequence of steps because the user can then follow the list and remember where they got to. The instruction guide can also tell the user to repeat some steps (for example, repeat steps 2 to 5 to take another picture).

| Do | Do not |
| --- | --- |
| 1 Press the small button at the top of the camera to turn it on. <br> 2 Point the camera at what you want to take a photograph of. <br> 3 Look through the viewfinder or at the LCD panel to see the image. <br> 4 Adjust the position of the camera until you are ready to take the photograph. <br> 5 Press the big button at the top right of the camera. <br> 6 Repeat steps 2 to 5 to take another picture. | Press the small button at the top of the camera to turn it on and then point the camera at what you want to take a photograph of by looking through the viewfinder to see the image. Adjust the position of the camera until you are ready to take the photograph then press the big button at the top right of the camera. If you want to take another picture then repeat all of the above except turning the camera on. |

## Screenshots/photographs

There is a saying that a picture is worth a thousand words. Screenshots are a picture of the screen that can be used to show the end user what they need to do. Screenshots should always be used within instructions, but it is not always necessary to show screenshots of every single stage.

< Example >

Compare this example using a screenshot with the one below that does not use a screenshot.

**Using a screenshot**

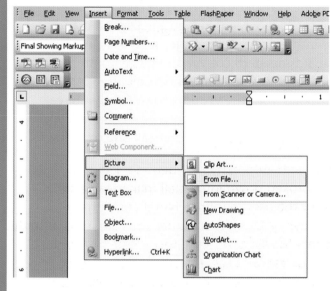

To import a picture, click Insert > Picture > From File...

**Figure 13.5** Inserting a picture

**Not using a screenshot**

To import a picture, you firstly need to click **Insert** on the menu bar. This can be found at the top left of the screen after File, Edit and View. When you have clicked this a menu will appear and you need to click **Picture** which is about half way down. Now another menu will appear to the right and you should click **From File...** which is the second option down.

If you are trying to explain how to use a peripheral, such as a digital camera, then you could include photographs to help. This can save a lot of words trying to describe something.

< Example >

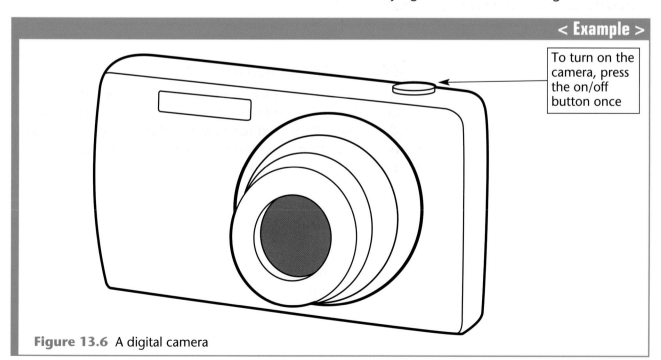

To turn on the camera, press the on/off button once

**Figure 13.6** A digital camera

Whether you are using screenshots or photographs, you should crop your images to only show the area that is required. This will make it easier to see the screenshots/pictures. If you crop them before you import them into the documentation then it will also save disk space. One way of doing this is to take the screenshot by pressing the PrtScr (Print Screen) key on the keyboard and then to paste the image into a painting package, such as Paint. Then select the area that is needed, copy it and paste it into the documentation. There are also some very useful free utilities available to download from the World Wide Web that have specialist functions for taking screenshots. You could ask your school/college technicians if they could install one onto the network for you.

**Do**                                                                 **Do not**

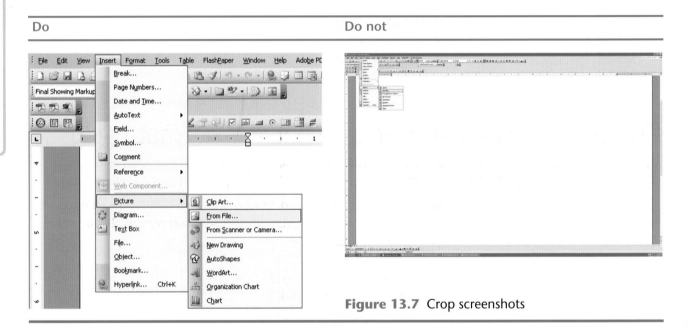

**Figure 13.7** Crop screenshots

## Lines

You will notice that throughout this book, lines have been used to identify areas of photographs or screenshots. Sometimes these have arrowheads. This helps to identify to the user what they should be looking for more easily. This is therefore a good idea within a user guide.

## Opening, saving, testing and printing

Whatever the documentation you are producing, there should always be instructions for:

- opening the document/application
- saving the document.

When providing instructions for opening the document, you must not assume that the user knows how to find the file. Therefore, your instructions should include:

- the full filename
- the location of the file (i.e. which folders to open).

When giving instructions to save a document, you must not assume the user will know how to save the document, therefore it is necessary to tell the user which menu and option to use. If the file needs saving in a different location then you may need to specify the location and explain how to find that location.

Some documentation might involve making changes (such as importing a picture into a presentation). In this case it is necessary to include instructions to test the presentation.

Some documentation might involve printing. If it does, then the instructions for printing may need to include:

- the page range
- the number of copies
- landscape/portrait settings
- the choice of printer.

# Prepare documentation in an electronic format using text, images, sound, animation and video

Electronic documentation can be accessed directly from within an application without the need for paper instructions. It might be accessed by:

- clicking Help on the menu bar
- clicking a 'Help' hyperlink
- clicking a 'Help' button
- pressing a keyboard shortcut like 'F1'.

It would normally be produced using one of the following pieces of software:

- presentation software
- web design software
- specialist help system software
- ordinary application software (by simply creating an extra page called 'help', i.e. a link to another page).

Specialist help system software is not normally available in schools and colleges. Web design software is often used to create web pages that can be used as help pages (this is because web pages can be viewed on any computer). Presentation software can be used to create an online tutorial.

## Contents

Whatever method is used, there should be a contents page for the help system. This would normally be a set of hyperlinks or buttons to each of the pages.

## Hyperlinks/buttons

Hyperlinks and buttons should also be used within each page to:

- go to related topics
- return to the contents page
- exit the help system.

## Screenshots

Screenshots should be used in the same way as they are in ordinary documentation.

## Sound

Sound can be used to read out the help pages. This could either occur automatically or there could be an option to select sound. Sound could also be used directly within an application itself. Small sound icons could be placed on the screen and when the user needs help they could click them. Instructions could even be read out automatically as the user uses an application.

< Example >

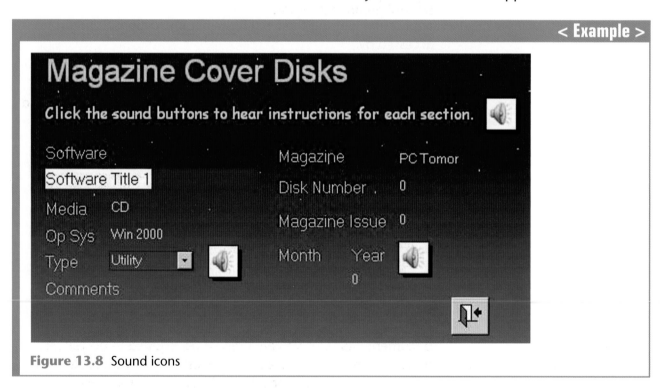

**Figure 13.8** Sound icons

### ▨ Video/animation

One of the most powerful facilities available within online documentation is to use videos or animation. Imagine being able to watch a video of how to take a picture using a digital camera rather than having to look at 2-D photographs. Or imagine being able to watch an animation of the sequence of instructions that need to be followed within a piece of software.

Videos and animations could appear and play automatically or they could be accessed by a button or hyperlink.

# Prepare technical documentation to show how a software solution was developed

Technical documentation is created for the purpose of future maintenance so that the application can be repaired or upgraded.

It should include:

- contents
- an introduction/overview
- the hardware requirements
- the software requirements
- configuration/settings.

The first four are similar to user documentation.

### ▨ Configuration/settings

The person using this documentation (e.g. a technician) will need to know how the application was developed and the configuration/settings used. This will include:

- data structures (field types, relationships, etc.)
- programming code (annotated)
- back-up routines
- validation
- filenames used
- functions and formulae
- macros
- buttons and hyperlinks, including their destinations.

These are just some examples. At AS level, the level of technical documentation that you are likely to be required to do will be much less than all of the above. A question will most likely direct you to the sort of evidence that is required. Alternatively, the documentation will appear to be user documentation but is actually about making changes to the application and is therefore really technical documentation.

This technical documentation will show you how to:

- open the presentation
- change prices of lessons
- take digital photographs of cars and instructors
- include those photographs in the presentation
- add a new screen to the presentation.

# Index

019533

conditional formatting 256–7
designing 214, 220–1
formulae 97, 254–6, 282–3
functions 97, 254–6, 282–3
macros 76–7, 241–3
mathematical modelling 94–5
rows, columns and headings 101,
   253–4
security methods 277
simulations 99
validation of data 238, 240
variables 96
'What if...?' questions 98–9
workbooks/worksheets 100–1
stand-alone computers 174
standard software *see* generic software
standardisation of hardware and
   software 43–5, 175
static vs dynamic information sources
   15–17
sticky keys 57
stock control systems 71–2
storage devices 52–4
story boards 212
string data type 11, 126
styles in documents 77, 86, 136,
   296–7

tables, database 108, 116–18
   normalisation 119–23, 124–5
   notation for structure of 123,
     216–7
   *see also* entities, database
takeovers and standardisation 45
tape drives 53
technical documentation 307–8
telephony 181
teleworking 186–7
templates 74–5, 83, 86–8, 244–5
testing 279
   of software solutions 291–4
   producing a test plan 285–91
   selecting test data 280–5
text 5, 6, 84, 141, 146
text data type 11, 126
text-to-speech systems 56
thumbnail images 142
transcription errors 30
transitions, slide 148–9, 151, 265–6
transposition errors 27, 30
troubleshooting documentation 297
turnaround documents 38–9
type checks 25

user documentation 293–8
user guides, producing 298–303
user IDs 170–1
user interfaces 58
   command-based 59–60
   customising/tailoring 82–3
   designing for an audience 233–6
   forms 60–1, 81–2

menu-driven 61–2
natural language 62
utility programs 58

validation of data 24–8, 31
   customised methods 236–40
   databases 116, 218–20, 237, 238
   testing validation rules 280–1,
     287–8
variables 95, 96
vector graphics 144–5
verification methods 29–31
video 147, 209, 266–7, 274, 307
visually impaired people, devices for
   54–5
voice recognition 62

web browsers, lack of standardisation
   44–5
web design tools 68–70, 262
web pages/websites
   and CD-ROMs, comparing 16–17
   creating and editing 68–70,
     259–60
   design specification 214
   evidence for data types 230
   file structures 261
   hyperlinks 69, 149, 210, 261–2,
     286
   testing 289–90
   validation of forms 237, 240
   *see also* Internet
'What if...?' questions, spreadsheets
   98–9
WIMP (Windows Icons Mouse Pointer)
   interface 58
wizards 73–4, 243–4, 275
word-processing
   formatting attributes 140–1
   mail merge 139–40, 244–52
   packages 66–7
   security methods 276
   templates 74–5, 86–7, 244–5
   *see also* documents
work, effect of ICT on 186–7
workbooks and worksheets 100–1
WYSIWYG (what you *see* is what you
   get) 67